# LEAD LIKE JESUS

## BEGINNING THE JOURNEY

KEN BLANCHARD

PHIL HODGES

LEE ROSS

AVERY WILLIS

NELSON IMPACT™
A Division of Thomas Nelson Publishers
*Since 1798*

www.thomasnelson.com

The authors would like to express appreciation to
Barbara Ross and Kathy Baker for their work on this project.

Design: Lookout Design Group, Inc.

ISBN 1-4041-0122-5

Printed and bound in the United States of America

www.thomasnelson.com

www.jcountryman.com

# P R E F A C E

JESUS OF NAZARETH was and is the
greatest leadership role model of all time. During His
earthly ministry He invested His life into the lives of
His disciples in order to make them "fishers of men."
His skill as a leader is unparalleled in history, and
yet this dimension of His time on earth has been
almost completely overlooked until recent years. The
time He spent developing His disciples translated
into the greatest organization the world has ever
known—His church. What Jesus did to develop His
disciples and how He interacted with them is the
definitive lesson in leadership and is provided for us
in His Word. The leadership legacy that Jesus left is
one of servanthood. As you will learn from this
study, there was no "Plan B." Christian leaders are to
be servant leaders—to *Lead Like Jesus*. This eight-
week study incorporates the leadership principles of
Jesus with practical application of those principles to
your life as a leader.

KEN BLANCHARD is the Chief Spiritual Officer of The Ken Blanchard Companies, a full–service management consulting and training company that he and his wife, Margie, founded in 1979. Ken co–authored *The One Minute Manager*® with Spencer Johnson, and the book has sold more than ten million copies and been translated into more than twenty–five languages. Some of his recent books are: *Raving Fans* and *Gung Ho* (both with Sheldon Bowles), *Leadership by the Book* (with Phil Hodges and Bill Hybels), *Whale Done!* (with Thad Lacinak, Chuck Thompkins, and Jim Ballard), *The Generosity Factor* (with S. Truett Cathy), and *The One Minute Apology* (with Margaret McBride). Ken is one of today's most sought–after authors, speakers, and business consultants, and he is co–founder of the Center for Faithwalk Leadership, a non-profit ministry committed to challenging and equipping people to *Lead Like Jesus*. Ken has degrees from Cornell University, where he also serves as a trustee emeritus and visiting lecturer.

PHIL HODGES currently serves as Vice Chairman of the Center for Faithwalk Leadership which he co–founded with longtime friend Ken Blanchard in 1999. The Center for Faithwalk Leadership is a non-profit organization dedicated to challenging and equipping people to *Lead Like Jesus*. In 1997 Phil concluded a thirty–five year career in

human resources and industrial relations with Xerox Corporation and U.S. Steel to serve as a Consulting Partner with The Ken Blanchard Companies prior to founding the Center. During six years as Chairman of the Elder Council in his local congregation, Phil developed a passion for bringing effective leadership principles into the life of the modern church. He is a graduate of Cornell University and co–author of two books; *Leadership by the Book* with Ken Blanchard and Bill Hybels and *The Servant Leader* with Ken Blanchard. Phil and his wife, Jane Kinnaird Hodges, live in Southern California.

LEE ROSS is the executive director for The Center for Faithwalk Leadership and is responsible for training and developing materials for use in faith–based organizations. Before coming to the center, he was a specialist for the Leadership Development Ministries office of the Georgia Baptist Convention, where he created an ongoing process of leadership development training for the local church and other faith-based organizations. He also is a resource trainer for The Ken Blanchard Companies. Lee has over twenty–six years of experience in the area of training and developing leaders in both faith–based and non–faith–based organizations. He has served local churches in staff positions as well as serving as senior pastor. Lee has a passion to see Christian leaders across the country

use Jesus as their role model for leadership. Lee holds a bachelor of science degree in psychology from Mercer University and a master of theology degree from Southwestern Baptist Theological Seminary.

AVERY WILLIS currently serves as the Senior Vice President of Overseas Operations for the International Mission Board of the Southern Baptist Convention where he oversees the work of 5,600 missionaries in 183 countries. His experience includes serving as a pastor, seminary president, author and developer of innovative educational methodologies. He and his wife, Shirley, served with their five children as missionaries to Indonesia for fourteen years. Avery is perhaps best known as the author of *MasterLife Discipleship Training*, which has been translated into more than 50 languages and *MasterBuilder: Multiplying Leaders*. He has authored or co–authored 16 books in English and Indonesian including *On Mission with God* with Henry Blackaby. Avery has a passion to equip Christians to *Lead Like Jesus* and to reach the peoples of the world without Christ. He has led the International Mission Board to embrace Lead like Jesus and helped develop this study guide so it can be applied worldwide. Avery holds a Bachelor of Arts degree from Oklahoma Baptist University and a Master of Divinity and Doctor of Theology degrees from Southwestern Baptist Theological Seminary.

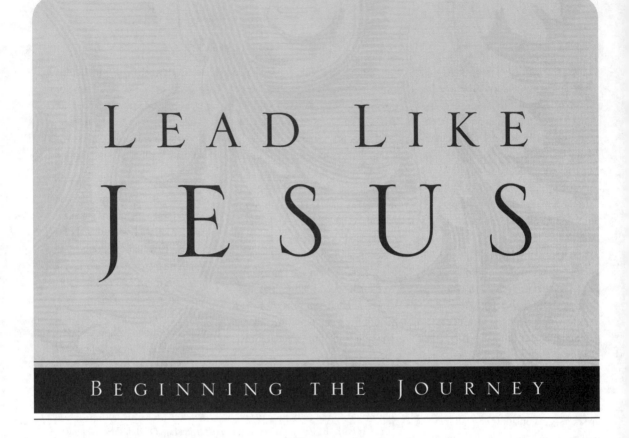

# LEAD LIKE JESUS

## BEGINNING THE JOURNEY

## WEEK ONE

### THE BIG PICTURE:

*Lead Like Jesus*

*"Not so with you. Instead, whoever wants to become*

*great among you must be your servant." —Matthew 20:26*

## 1 DAY

# Whom Are You Following?

A WORD FROM KEN BLANCHARD

*Business and belief. Jesus and your job.*

*Personal and professional. Servant and leader.*

EVEN SEEING THOSE WORDS PAIRED together makes many people uneasy. Our sophisticated culture encourages us to draw lines and keep our spiritual lives separate from our secular lives. Faith is for Sundays or family gatherings only. Right?

I, too, once modeled my life after that tired pattern, and I had a generally good, successful life. I had earned full professor with tenure at age thirty–five at the University of Massachusetts. In 1976–77 my wife Margie and I went on sabbatical leave and then decided to stay in California and start our training and consulting company. Blanchard Training and Development was a quick and early success and began to grow in leaps and bounds. But the Lord was not central in my life. In fact He was on the back burner. Let me explain.

Our first job was at Ohio University in Athens, Ohio, in the late 1960s. That was a time of tremendous concern and unrest about the Vietnam War. When we were at Ohio University, some of the kids down the road at Kent State were killed by the National Guard. During our time in Athens, we befriended a wonderful minister whom we thought was terrific. However, he became a concern to his congregation because he was leading a lot of the student protests. As a result the church fired him in a most un–Christian way. Margie and I said, "If that's what Christianity is all about, you can have it." And we turned our backs on the church. Not just for a short period of time, but for fifteen years. To illustrate how far we drifted, our son, Scott, was age three and our daughter, Debbie, was age two at the time. When they became eighteen, if you had put a gun to their heads and said, "Give me the Lord's Prayer or I'll shoot," unfortunately, you would have had to shoot, because they didn't even know that basic prayer.

It wasn't until the publication of *The One Minute Manager* nationally in 1982 that I began to think about God. That book was so amazingly successful in such a short period of time that even I had trouble taking credit for its success. I began to think somehow it was a "God thing."

Opening my mind to that possibility, the Lord began to send all kinds of people into my life, starting with long–time friend and colleague Phil Hodges. Phil and I had met on the bus going to orientation camp at Cornell University in 1957. He had turned his life over to the Lord a few years before, and ever since he'd been praying for me. With the success of *The One Minute Manager,* Phil called and said, "Ken, let's take a walk on the beach." During our walk he said, "Why do you think this book is so successful? Do you think you're smarter than other people or a better writer?" I said, "No, Phil, I think somehow God is involved."

Phil was delighted with my answer and began to give me things to read. But I was slow to commit. A year or so after that, I got a call from Larry Hughes, the president of our publishing company, William Morrow. Larry posed an intriguing question: "Would you be interested in writing a book with Norman Vincent Peale?" I certainly was familiar with Peale's *Power of Positive Thinking,* but my initial response was, "Is he still alive?" After all, my mom and dad had gone to Peale's church before I was born. Larry's response was, "Not only is he alive, but he is fabulous at age eighty–six."

Meeting and working with Norman Vincent Peale and his wife, Ruth, was a major turning point in my spiritual journey. Right from the beginning Norman said to me, "Ken, the Lord's always had you on His team, you just haven't suited up yet." My journey continued with people coming into my life like Bob Buford, author of *Halftime,* and Bill Hybels, founding pastor of Willow Creek Community Church outside of Chicago. The big difference they made is that they helped me understand the power of grace. As a humanist, I had always questioned the concept of original sin. "Why do we have to start off bad as sinners?" I wondered. "Why not original potentiality? As human beings don't we have the capability to be good or bad, depending on the choices we make?"

When I asked that question of Bob Buford—whom I think God deliberately seated next to me on a plane going to a YPO (Young President's Organization) University in Mexico City—Bob responded with a question of his own. He asked me if I thought I was as good as God. I said, "Obviously not. If there is a God, that's perfection." Bob said, "Well, then why don't we give God 100? We can give ax murderers 5." Mother Teresa was alive then, so Bob said, "Why don't we give her 95? She's a pretty good gal." And then Bob continued, "Ken, you're not too bad. You're trying to help people. Why don't we give you 75? The unique thing about Christianity is that the Lord sent Jesus down to make up the difference between your score and 100." That really hit home with me. I hate labels. When you call somebody a sinner, that really gets their back up. But everybody would admit that they fall short of 100. Seeing my excitement, Bob said, "Ken, before you get too excited, let me give you the whole picture. The ax murderer has the same shot at the ball as Mother Teresa. Grace is a gift from God; it doesn't have anything to do with achievement." That sounded like pretty good deal to me.

Seeing that he had made some progress with me, Bob handed me off at the conference to Bill Hybels, who also was speaking there. Bill continued to open my eyes about grace when he told me that the difference between Christianity and religion is how it's spelled. He said, "Religion is spelled "**D–O**". It has a to–do list of all the things you need to do to get God's grace. The problem is, most people with a "**DO**" religion give up, because they never know when enough is enough and the rules are often changed. On the other hand," Hybels said, "Christianity is spelled '**D–O–N–E.**' The Lord sent Jesus down to make up the difference between us and 100. The only requirement is to believe in Him." With my new spiritual team of

Hodges, Peale, Buford, and Hybels, I finally couldn't deny the power of God's grace and the gift that He offers us. I turned my life over to the Lord.

As my perspective on faith changed by accepting Jesus as my Lord and Savior, so did my views on leadership change. I realized that Christians have more in Jesus than just a great spiritual leader: we have a practical and effective leadership model for all organizations, for all people, for all situations. The more I read the Bible, the more I realized that Jesus did everything I've ever taught or written about over the thirty years on leadership. He is simply the greatest leadership model of all time. As a result, my new mission in life through the Center For FaithWalk Leadership, which Phil Hodges and I co-founded with God, is to challenge and equip people to Lead Like Jesus.

What is leadership? It's an influence process—any time you are trying to influence the thoughts and actions of others toward goal accomplishment in either their personal life or professional life you are engaging in leadership. Given that definition, you can see that Jesus is our role model for leadership wherever we go—not just at work. But you might say, "I'm not a leader—no one reports to me." But our response is . . . "Yes you are. You are a leader in at least two ways. First, God has given you the freedom to choose how you will lead your personal life—in submission to Him or not. Second, because leadership involves influencing others, you are a leader in all areas of your life—at home, at work, at church and in the community. While you are trying to influence others in all of those places, remember that Jesus is the leadership answer—what is the question? That's why I am excited about writing this interactive study with my colleagues Phil Hodges, Lee Ross, and Avery Willis as a way of sharing the *Lead Like Jesus* message with you.

## THE AUTHORS' HOPE FOR THIS STUDY

We want you to experience Jesus in a whole different way—to grow to trust Him as the perfect One to follow as you seek to lead others. He is so clear about how He wants us to lead. He asks us to make a difference in the world we live in by being effective servant leaders.

It is our prayer and desire that this *Lead Like Jesus* study will be the beginning of a new exciting chapter in your personal journey to becoming an effective servant leader. It is designed to guide you in exploring your personal response to Jesus' call to "Follow Me" and put into action the principles of servant leadership.

So, is this a leadership study for business? Yes, Is this a guide to improve personal relationships? Yes. Is this an inspirational guide to a more intimate relationship with God? Yes. Simply put it's a tool to help you to take God out of the spiritual compartment of your private spiritual life and give Him free reign in all your daily actions and relationships, especially your leadership roles. Remember, don't worry if you do not have a formal leadership role in going through this study—*think of your relationships to your spouse, kids, friends, co-workers, and colleagues you interact with every day.*

Don't just approach this study guide as an intellectual exercise, take it to heart. We want you to change not only your knowledge, but also your attitudes, actions and behaviors—your very life! Do you know how long it took Jesus to change the attitudes and behaviors of the disciples related to servant leadership? Three years of daily interactions!

So we have designed this book to impact your daily interactions with others. We want Jesus' leadership to penetrate your knowledge, attitudes, and behavior . . . and eventually your organization's or family's behavior. That is a tall order. So we ask you to complete every learning activity marked with the ✚ sign.

Imagine this setting. You, Jesus, and the four of us are sitting together each morning conversing about His kind of leadership. Just as the Master Teacher did with His disciples we will ask you questions, give you assignments, explain His stories, and help interpret what you are experiencing. So as you respond to our questions the Holy Spirit will take what you are thinking and begin to apply it to your life. The Holy Spirit will be your Coach when you do the assignments in your daily workplace. We will give you feedback after you have written your answers or completed an assignment to help you begin to Lead Like Jesus. We don't promise that you will complete the total transformation in just eight weeks, but we will help you start in the right direction and give you tools that will guide your continuing journey as a leader who Leads Like Jesus.

We suggest the following steps to help you reap the greatest benefits from this study.

1. *Pray for focus and insight* each day as you meet the Lord through this study. Let Him lead you to experience His personal direction in your life through every learning activity and real–life application.

2. *Experience the focus* for each day as you study and then apply it to your life that very day. As you encounter "Aha!" ideas that challenge your leadership behaviors and motives, stop right there. Ask yourself how you can realign your leadership over the next few days. Be specific. Jot your ideas in the margin. Check them the next day to see how you have applied them in your life and the results you have experienced.

3. *In addition to your daily notes* in this book you might want to keep a separate journal of your 'Aha!' ideas, action steps, and plans on how you can apply what you are learning in your day–to–day life and work.

4. *Review your progress* each week and give yourself some praise. You will be surprised at what God will do through your leadership as you apply these biblical principles.

5. *Participate in the group sessions* or get another person to study daily and meet weekly with you. Your group will follow the instructions in the Leader's Guide, which is available from your publisher or bookstore in the *Lead Like Jesus* kit that also includes illustrations on DVDs. The small group experience is indispensable for you to learn to Lead Like Jesus. You cannot learn to lead others like Jesus did unless you are involved with people. If it is impossible to get a small group to study with you, at least get one other person to do the group sessions with you.

We want you to come to trust Jesus as *your* leadership model, so whether you're leading in business, in nonprofit organizations, in your community, in your church, or at home, you will make Jesus smile.

—KEN BLANCHARD, PHIL HODGES,
LEE ROSS, AVERY WILLIS

# How Will You Lead?

Welcome to the adventure of leading like Jesus. It is our prayer that on this day you will invite Jesus into your leadership life to begin to transform you and the quality and effectiveness of your leadership relationships.

✛ *Because leading like Jesus starts with a relationship with the Lord, have you ever bowed your head, admitted to Him that you fall short of 100, and accepted Jesus as your Savior? If not, maybe this is a good time to make that commitment. If you have any questions or concerns about this, ask your pastor or group leader.*

## THE CALL TO SERVANT LEADERSHIP

Jesus' disciples were arguing about who was the greatest.

*Jesus called them together and said, "You know that the rulers of the Gentiles lord it over them, and their high officials exercise authority over them. No so with you. Instead, whoever wants to be great among you must be your servant. And whoever wants to be first among you must be your slave—just as the Son of Man did not come to be served but to serve. And to give His life as a ransom for many." — Matthew 20:25–28*

✛ *Think through what Jesus meant when He said, "not so with you." Write a summary of your conclusions below:*

_____

_____

In His instructions to His first disciples (Matt 20:25–28) on how they were to lead, Jesus sent a clear message to all those who would follow Him that leadership is to be first and foremost an act of service. No Plan B was implied or offered in His words. He placed no restrictions or limitations of time, place, or situation that would allow us to exempt ourselves from His command. For a follower of Jesus, servant leadership isn't just an option; it's a mandate.

✛ *Write in your own words Jesus' Plan A for the kind of leadership He wanted His followers to exhibit.*

_____

_____

Did you write something like: Jesus' leadership Plan A was for them to be first and foremost servant leaders. This meant as leaders they were to serve not be served.

✚ *Based on your experience, why do you think there was no Plan B?*

_____

_____

If you encounter a Plan B to Jesus' mandate to servant leadership you should realize that this alternative did not come from Him.

The truly exciting part of following Jesus is that He never sends you into any situation with a faulty plan or a plan to fail. Because of who He is, when Jesus speaks on leadership He speaks to all of us about what is both right and effective.

> *I am the vine; you are the branches. If a man remains*
> *in Me and I in him, he will bear much fruit; apart from Me you can do nothing.* —John 15:5

A common barrier to embracing Jesus as a leadership role model lies in skepticism about the relevance of His teaching to your specific leadership situations. One way of putting Jesus to the test would be to apply the same criteria to His knowledge, experience, and success that you would to the hiring of a business consultant.

✚ *Would you hire Jesus as a consultant in your business? Why or why not?*

_____

_____

Take a few moments to reflect on the following leadership challenges you might be facing and consider again if you would hire Jesus as your personal leadership consultant based on His earthly experience as a leader.

✚ *Does Jesus have any relevant practical knowledge or experience in dealing with the following types of leadership issues I face? Write "Yes" or "No" beside each situation listed below:*

_____ *Dealing with and accomplishing a mission with imperfect people.*
_____ *The need to establish a clear sense of purpose and direction*
_____ *Recruitment and selection of people to carry on the work*
_____ *Training, development, and delegation issues*
_____ *Constant conflicting demands on time, energy, and resources*
_____ *Fierce competition*
_____ *Turnover, betrayal, and lack of understanding by friends and family*
_____ *Constant scrutiny and challenges of commitment and integrity*
_____ *Temptations of instant gratification, recognition, and misuse of power*
_____ *Effective handling of criticism, rejection, distractions, and opposition*
_____ *Pain and suffering in serving the greatest good*

Chances are you wrote "Yes" to every situation. Why? Because Jesus had experience in every situation you face. The book of Hebrews says of Jesus:

*For we do not have a high priest who is unable to sympathize with our weaknesses, but we have one who has been tempted in every way, just as we are—yet was without sin. Let us then approach the throne of grace with confidence, so that we may receive mercy and find grace to help us in our time of need.— Hebrews 4:15*

*Because He Himself suffered when He was tempted,*
*He is able to help those who are being tempted.—Hebrews 2:18*

✝ *With your answers to the questions and Scriptures above in mind, write how you think Jesus would do your job differently than you do:*

_____

_____

_____

As the following Scriptures suggest, Jesus says He wants to do His work in you and through you.

*Come, follow Me," Jesus said, "and I will make you fishers of men."—Matthew 4:19*

*Come to Me, all you who are weary and burdened, and I will give you rest. Take My yoke upon you and learn from Me, for I am gentle and humble in heart, and you will find rest for your souls.—Matthew 11:28–29*

*I am the vine; you are the branches. If a man remains in Me and I in him, he will bear much fruit; apart from Me you can do nothing. — John 15:5*

*If you remain in Me and My words remain in you, ask whatever you wish, and it will be given you. —John 15:7*

*If you love Me, you will obey what I command. And I will ask the Father, and He will give you another Counselor to be with you forever—the Spirit of truth. The world cannot accept Him, because it neither sees Him nor knows Him. But you know Him, for He lives with you and will be in you. I will not leave you as orphans; I will come to you.—John 14:15–18*

✝ *How can you get in touch with Jesus as your leader? Check the statements that apply to you and your situation.*

\_\_\_\_\_ *1. From the examples in the Bible I can imagine what Jesus would do.*

\_\_\_\_\_ *2. Just do the best I can.*

\_\_\_\_\_ *3. Ask Jesus who lives in me to direct me.*

\_\_\_\_\_ *4. Consult with the Holy Spirit who is my Coach.*

\_\_\_\_\_ *5. Take a vote of those with whom I work.*

\_\_\_\_\_ *6. Check the best business books.*

\_\_\_\_\_ *7. Ask Him to show me in the Bible words of wisdom for my situation.*

\_\_\_\_\_ *8. Talk and pray with a Christian mentor or friend.*

\_\_\_\_\_ *9. Worship the Lord and wait on Him to show me.*

Because there may be some debate on which of these statements are best, plan to bring your answers to the group session this week and share and discuss them with the members of the group. We checked 1, 3, 4, 7, 8, 9 as the best, although others might be acceptable in some cases.

✠ *This is the end of today's study. As you go about your activities today ask yourself these two questions: Whom will I follow? How will I lead? At the end of your day's work, write what Jesus has taught you thus far about being a servant leader:*

_____

_____

_____

_____

# Leading Like Jesus Is a Transformational Journey

As the subtitle of this Group Study Guide suggests—**Beginning the Journey**—learning to Lead Like Jesus is more than an announcement; it is a commitment to lead in a different way. This change will not happen overnight. In fact, as the diagram below shows, we believe leading like Jesus is a transformational journey that begins with personal leadership, then moves to leading others, then leading a team, and finally, leading an organization.

While this Study Guide will emphasize your own personal leadership and your one–on–one leadership with others, we want you to understand the ultimate destination. Jesus set the basic foundation for this leadership journey throughout His ministry. During His time on earth, Jesus poured His life into the training of His disciples in the first three leadership arenas, and during that process, He equipped them to follow His leadership philosophy after He was gone as they moved to the organizational level and attempted to establish the church.

## THE TRANSFORMATIONAL LEADERSHIP MODEL

**Personal Leadership Arena:** Effective leadership starts on the inside. Before you can hope to lead anyone else, you have to know yourself. We call it Personal Leadership because it involves choice. Every leader must answer two critical questions:

*1. Whose are you going to be?*     *2. Who are you going to be?*

The question "Whose are you going to be?" deals with choosing the audience for your life. In other words, whom are you trying to please? Leaders often have an incorrect view of success in today's world. They think success has to do with performance and the opinion of others. You can state it anyway you like, but Scripture teaches us that ultimately we are created to please God. In the Personal Leadership Arena you first have to choose whether or not you will please God!

✠ *Whom are you trying to please most?*
*Check the ONE you are most trying to please.*

\_\_\_\_ Your boss      \_\_\_\_ Your spouse

\_\_\_\_ Your children      \_\_\_\_ Your fellow workers

\_\_\_\_ Your friends      \_\_\_\_ God

\_\_\_\_ Your neighbors      \_\_\_\_ Yourself

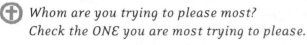

**Personal Leadership** — OUTCOME = PERSPECTIVE — Matt. 3:13–4:11

**One On One Leadership** — OUTCOME = TRUST — Matt. 4:18-22

**Team Leadership** — OUTCOME = TRUST — Matt. 10:5-10

**Organizational Leadership** — OUTCOME = EFFECTIVENESS — Matt. 28:19-20

*Lead Like Jesus*
The Transformational Journey

The question "Who are you going to be?" deals with your life purpose. Why did the Lord put you on earth? What does He want to do through you? Scripture teaches that true success is the fulfillment of the life mission God planned for you. It is all about your relationship with Christ and what level of control you will let Him have in your life. Are you willing to surrender all to Him and live as He would have you live, rather than how you want to live? Jesus made His choice when He surrendered all to His Father and insisted that John baptize Him "to fulfill all righteousness."

✠ *What is your personal commitment level to follow Christ's vision*
*for your life and to subordinate your own desires to Him?*

_____

_____

The natural outcome of deciding to please God as well as turning over control of your life to Him is a change in your **perspective**. If you live a life that is not designed to please God, and give Him control, your perspective will be inward and focused on self or ego. If you live your life to please God, and put Him in charge, your perspective will be outward, and God–given confidence will lead your life.

✠ *What is the difference between living a life designed to please God and give*
*Him the reins and one that is designed to please yourself and keep control*
*in your own hands?*

_____

_____

Early in His ministry Jesus demonstrated His desire to please only the Father and to turn control of

His life over to Him. This was demonstrated dramatically when He went into the wilderness and was tempted by Satan. The events recorded for us in the Gospels show us that during this time Jesus had to decide whose He was and who He was. Would He live by the mission His Father planned for Him or would He give in to the temptations of Satan? Would He use the gifts His Father had given Him for the accomplishment of His Father's purpose or Satan's purpose? In all these situations we read that Jesus chose the will of His Father.

✚ *Have you had a personal life-changing experience when God changed your perspective from your purposes to His? If so, describe the experience and the resulting change in your life.*

_____

_____

_____

*One-on-One Leadership Arena:* Once leaders have life in proper perspective through self-examination, they are able to develop a trusting relationship with others. Without **trust** it will be impossible for any organization to function effectively. Trust between individuals is essential for two people to be able to work together. It is important to note though, that the outcome of trust never will be achieved or maintained if the first arena of development has not been addressed. If a leader has a self-serving perspective on life, people never will move toward him or her. We can turn to Jesus again as our example.

At the beginning of His ministry, after spending time in the wilderness addressing His own personal development and putting His life in perspective, Jesus began the process of calling His disciples. Once they agreed to follow Him, Jesus spent three years building a culture of trust between Himself and these men. This trust between Jesus and His disciples never would have developed if Jesus had not first spent time in the wilderness deciding whom He would follow in life and who He was going to be!

✚ *What is the essential element in one-on-one relationships?*

_____

✚ *In order to be trusted you must first be . . .*

_____

_____

*Team Leadership Arena:* As leaders develop a trusting relationship with people at the one-on-one arena they must be trustworthy. Then, they are ready for team development through empowerment. Effective leaders working at the team, or **community**, level realize that to be good stewards of the energy and efforts of those committed to work with them, they must honor the power of diversity and acknowledge that "none of us is as smart as all of us."

Once again we look to Jesus as a model for this concept. After Jesus spent time personally teaching and modeling the type of leadership He wanted them to adopt, He sent His disciples out (Matthew 10) to minister in teams of two. In doing so Jesus empowered them to act on His behalf to support one another in accomplishing the work they had been trained to do.

Trust is also a key factor in the successful implementation at the team level. Without the outcome of trust developed in the one–on–one relationship, empowerment will never happen. Individuals in the group will never "empower" each other to accomplish an assigned task if they do not trust each other. Failure to empower is one of the key reasons why teams or committees are ineffective.

✝ *How did Jesus as a leader "empower" that first group of disciples to complete the work they had been trained to do?*

_____

_____

✝ *What is the desired outcome of Team Leadership?*

_____

_____

*Organizational Leadership Arena:* Whether a leader can function well in the organizational arena depends on the outcome of perspective, trust and community attained at the first three levels in the life of his or her transformational leadership journey. The outcome of focusing on this level is organizational **effectiveness**.

It is important to note that when Jesus began His ministry on earth, He did not start at the organizational level. He could have come to the existing organizations of the faithful in His day and said, "Okay, gentlemen, I'm here, I'm in charge, and this is the way we will change things!" Instead, Jesus chose to take the approach of a Servant Leader and quietly influence the lives of a small group of men whom He then trusted and empowered to impact the world.

Jesus, by valuing both relationships and results, created the environment for developing an effective organization. In His own life He was aligned with the purpose His Father had for Him. Jesus also clearly identified the purposes for His followers and their organizations when He gave us the Great Commandment and the Great Commission. In reality, Jesus, in His incarnate form, never implemented the organizational level. He equipped His disciples in the first three levels and then sent the Holy Spirit to guide them at the organizational leadership level that we see developing in the book of Acts.

One of the primary mistakes that leaders today make, when called to lead, is spending most of their time and energy trying to improve things at the organizational level before ensuring that they have adequately addressed their own credibility at individual, one–on–one, or team leadership levels.

We hope that this study will make the excitement and power to *Lead Like Jesus* come alive at all levels.

✝ *What is the desired outcome of Organizational Leadership?*

_____

_____

_____

Avery Willis found that to be true as he worked with the International Mission Board of the Southern Baptist Convention. As he reflected on the transformational leadership journey, he realized the importance of moving through the four leadership arenas sequentially. The IMB decided in 1997 that they needed to re–engineer their organization with over 5,000 personnel in 130 countries. They doubled the measurable statistical results in five years, but at the cost of many personal relationships. In reflecting on the change effort five years later, Avery said, "As I studied the *Lead Like Jesus* Transformational Model I had an "aha" moment when I realized that we had started at the wrong place. I saw that we should have addressed Personal Leadership, One–on–One Leadership, and the Team Leadership arenas before addressing Organizational Leadership issues. Now, using the *Lead Like Jesus* Transformational Model, we are having to back up to do that very thing."

✝ *Which dimensions or levels do you think your organization most needs to focus on at this time?*

_____ *Personal Leadership to give perspective.*
_____ *One–to–One Leadership to develop trust.*
_____ *Team Leadership to create community.*
_____ *Organizational Leadership to increase effectiveness.*

✝ *Today talk with some of your fellow workers or family about the Transformational Leadership Model. Explain the four arenas and discuss where your organization needs to focus. Be prepared to write what you discovered tomorrow.*

# The Four Dimensions of Leadership

**4 DAY**

As we begin today's study jot down what you discovered yesterday when you talked with your fellow workers or family. If you did not get a chance to have that discussion with them, then try to do it this week before the small group session. Make notes below when you have talked with them.

✝ *Write what you discovered yesterday when you talked with your fellow workers or family about where you are in the Transformational Leadership Model.*

_____

_____

_____

_____

As we begin to realize that Jesus was the greatest leadership role model for all time, we learn there are four dimensions to His effectiveness:

THE HEART —— *His intentions and motivations of a leader*
THE HEAD —— *His beliefs about leadership and influencing others*
THE HANDS —— *His methods and behaviors of a leader*
THE HABITS —— *His daily disciplines that kept Him focused on His mission*

## THE FOUR DIMENSIONS OF LEADERSHIP

The Heart and the Head are internal domains, while the Hands and the Habits are external. As we explore what it means to *Lead Like Jesus*, we will journey through these internal and external domains. The internal motivations of your *heart* and the leadership point of view of your *head* might be things you keep inside at first, or even disguise if it suits your private purpose. Your external public leadership behavior, or *hands,* and *habits* as experienced by others will determine whether others will follow you or not. When the Heart, Head, Hands, and Habits are aligned, extraordinary levels of loyalty, trust, and productivity will result. When they are out of alignment, frustration, mistrust, and diminished long-term productivity will result. These four dimensions of leadership form the outline for the rest of this study guide.

**1. The Heart.** The heart is your character—why you are leading. To serve or be served? When your heart is wrong you quickly lose your way on the leadership journey. Proverbs 16:23 says, *"A wise man's heart guides his mouth, and his lips promote instruction."* When Jesus talks about the heart He is referring to the center of your spiritual nature and consciousness rather than the physical heart. In a word, when He refers to your heart He is talking about *you*—the essence of who you are. In Weeks Two and Three we will focus on your leadership motivation, attitudes, and character.

✝ *To begin thinking about why you lead—your leadership motivations and intentions—consider this question: Are you a servant leader or a self-serving leader? Why did you answer that way? Write your answer below.*

_____

_____

_____

Your answer to the above question will be discussed in the small group session. It gets at the essence of what it means to Lead Like Jesus.

✝ *EGO can stand for Edging God Out. You often edge God out without thinking. Write some ways you Edge God Out of your life or leadership:*

_____

_____

_____

**2. The Head.** By "head" we mean the beliefs and assumptions you have about leadership. Effective leaders have clear leadership points of view that they are willing to teach to others. Jesus continually taught His disciples about servant leadership. He emphasized that servant leadership begins with clear direction, and ends with effective implementation and goal accomplishment.

We will examine these two vital aspects of leadership in Week Four of our study.

✝ *If you were put on the spot and given three minutes to state clearly your leadership point of view, could you do it? Try to state it out loud in three minutes.*

✝ *How did you do?*

_____

By the time you finish this study we hope you will be able to state a clear leadership point of view modeled by Jesus.

**3. The Hands.** By "hands" we mean your leadership behaviors. The journey to leading like Jesus turns outward when the heart and mind guide your behavior as you interact with those who choose to follow you. Your decision–by–decision behaviors can make or break your long–range effectiveness and your ability to inspire trust. Here is where good intention and right thinking start to bear good fruit. Even the purest leadership motives and clear leadership thinking, when coupled with inept or self–serving behaviors, will bring frustration and inefficiency into any leadership effort. "Doing the right thing" and "doing things right" are equal parts of successful leadership. James 1:22 urges, *"Do not merely listen to the word, and so deceive yourselves. Do what it says."* In Week Five of this study you will use the *Situational Leadership II®* model to learn skills that will help you to mentor and develop those you lead.

✝ *Can you state the basic idea of Situational Leadership II®? You might have studied Situational Leadership II® in another book or seminar, but if not just try to guess the meaning from the name. Write your understanding of Situational Leadership below in your own words.*

_____

_____

Even if you have not had a *Situational Leadership II®* seminar or read about the concept, you might have guessed that Situational Leadership teaches that leaders must adjust their style of leadership to the situation and who they are attempting to influence. In Week Five we study Situational Leadership and how you can utilize the principles in your own situation.

**4. The Habits.** Your habits are how you renew your daily commitment to develop into an effective servant leader. On a daily basis, effective servant leaders recalibrate and renew their commitment to serve rather than be served. In Week Six we will study the five disciplines that should be part of any leader's life who wants to Lead Like Jesus.

SOLITUDE —*Spending time alone with God*

PRAYER —*Speaking with God*

STORING UP GOD'S WORD— *Preparing for the challenges that are yet to come by knowing the Scriptures*

FAITH IN GOD'S UNCONDITIONAL LOVE—*Proceeding with confidence grounded in the love of God*

INVOLVEMENT IN ACCOUNTABILITY RELATIONSHIPS— *Having a small group where vulnerabilities can be shared and support received*

✛ *Underline the habits above that you practice on a daily basis.*

*Proverbs 27:17 As iron sharpens iron, so one man sharpens another.*

Because these are the main points along the way to your developing into a servant leader who leads like Jesus, let's picture them another way that will help you remember them:

✛ *In the illustration below connect each part of the body with one of the four dimensions of leadership by drawing a line between them.*

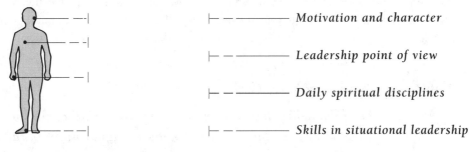

├ – ———— *Motivation and character*

├ – ———— *Leadership point of view*

├ – ———— *Daily spiritual disciplines*

├ – ———— *Skills in situational leadership*

To conclude today's study answer the following questions:

✛ *What do you think happens when the Heart, the Head, the Hands, and the Habits are all aligned?*

_____

_____

✛ *What do you think will happen if they are not all aligned?*

_____

_____

If you need help look back early in today's lesson under the heading "The Four Dimensions of Leadership."

✠ *As you go through your day today, check each of these elements to see if you are staying aligned with Jesus' kind of leadership. Tomorrow we will ask you to describe how well you did.*

# Evaluating Where
# I Am on the Journey

✠ *Describe how well you kept the Heart, Head, Hands, and Habits aligned yesterday.*

_____

_____

As a conclusion to this week's study we want you to evaluate yourself in preparation for the rest of the *Lead Like Jesus* encounter. Write your answers. This will take time for you to think through them, but it will be worth it. You will be given an opportunity to share some of your answers in the small group if you desire.

### 1. My Greatest Personal Leadership Challenge

✠ *Write a brief summary description of the greatest challenge you currently face as a leader or a problem that has kept you up at night in the past. Describe both your internal struggles and those created by specific relationships and situations.*

_____

_____

_____

_____

### 2. My Leadership Reason (Why I lead.)

✠ *My personal reasons for being _____ are: (Fill in your organizational leadership title—such as CEO of Highest Hopes, Inc.—or your most significant personal role of influence on the thinking and behavior of others—Brian's mom, Heather's husband, Dave's friend.)*

_____

_____

_____

_____

**3. My Leadership Results (I lead so that . . . )**

✠ *I measure the results of my leadership and efforts to influence others by: (Write some specific results that you can use as measurements of progress, such as goals or key result areas.)*

_____

_____

_____

_____

**4. My Leadership Relationships (My impact on others)**

✠ *The people who are most directly impacted by my leadership thinking and behavior are: (Fill in individual names and relationship categories, such as my son, my friend, my husband.)*

_____

_____

**5. My Leadership Security**

✠ *What do I rely on to keep me secure as a leader?(Check the items that apply.)*

| | | |
|---|---|---|
| _____ *Keeping Control* | _____ *Relationships* | _____ *Attention to detail* |
| _____ *Policies* | _____ *Favors* | _____ *Energy* |
| _____ *Skill* | _____ *Money* | _____ *Fear* |
| _____ *Performance* | _____ *Knowledge* | _____ *Busyness* |

✠ *Which of these security factors can I trust 100% to keep me safe forever?*

_____

_____

Of course none of these factors will keep you safe forever. Your ultimate security is not found in such behaviors. We will address security in next week's study.

### 6. My Leadership Focus

✚ *Please mark the statement below that best describes how much of your focus is on results and how much is on relationships.*

_____ *I am more focused on results than relationships.*

_____ *I am more focused on relationships than results.*

_____ *I am not focused on either relationships or results.*

_____ *I am focused on both results and relationships.*

Based on your leadership behaviors, which of these statements would the people who work with you check? If their answers about you would be the same, why? If not the same, why not?

_____

_____

✚ *What three things do I do that make it easy for people to follow me?*

1. _____

2. _____

3. _____

✚ *What three things that I do that make it difficult for people to follow me?*

1. _____

2. _____

3. _____

✚ *What three things could your leader or supervisor do that would make it easier to follow him or her?*

1. _____

2. _____

3. _____

We have covered a lot of territory this week. Don't worry about remembering everything. Throughout this study, we will take the time to explore in more depth each aspect of the four dimensions of leadership. Have a great group meeting this week!

# LEAD LIKE JESUS

## BEGINNING THE JOURNEY

# WEEK TWO

### THE HEART — *Transforming Your Motivation and Intentions*

*"May the words of my mouth and the meditation*

*of my heart be pleasing in Your sight,*

*O Lord, my Rock and my Redeemer" —Psalm 19:14*

Everybody today recognizes the need for more effective leaders. Millions of dollars are spent every year to train people in leadership skills, but there still is a perception that we have a shortage of skilled leaders. Why? Because most leadership training tries to change leaders from the outside. Most books and seminars focus on leadership behavior and try to improve leadership style and methods. Yet, in teaching people to Lead Like Jesus, we have found that effective leadership starts on the inside—it is a heart issue. Jesus wanted to give us a "heart attack." If He could get inside of you and make you a loving, caring, honest, and serving person inside, then He knew there was a good chance that you would be that kind of person on the outside. We believe that if you don't get the heart right, then nothing we can do will make you a servant leader. You can learn all the techniques of servant leadership, but you will never Lead Like Jesus until your heart longs to serve rather than be served.

And yet it is not easy to get the heart right when it comes to servant leadership. Why? The reality is that we're all self-serving to some degree because we came into this world with self-serving hearts. Is anything more self-serving than a baby? A baby doesn't come home from the hospital saying, "Can I help around the house?" The *Lead Like Jesus* journey is moving from a self-serving heart to a servant heart. You finally become a mature adult when you realize that life is about what you give rather than what you get. This week we examine what hinders us in moving through this heart journey, and why aligning our heart is a daily battle. Next week we will look at prescriptions for our heart problem.

# Self-Serving Leaders
# vs. *Servant Leaders*

As we talk about the heart issues of leadership, ask yourself again, "Am I a servant leader or a self-serving leader?" Last week we mentioned that is the key character question for leaders. It gets at your intentions or motivations. Why are you leading? Why are you a parent? Why are you a pastor? Why are you a manager? Why are you a volunteer? Are you playing the role to be served or to serve?

Few people would admit that they are self-serving leaders: "Given a choice I'll always make a decision that benefits me." And yet we observe self-serving leaders all the time. We read about them in the paper. These are people who act like the sheep are there for the benefit of the shepherd. If these leaders are working in an organization, all the money, recognition, power, and status move up the hierarchy towards them.

What makes people self–serving? In his classic book *Ordering Your Private World*, Gordon McDonald identifies a helpful distinction; he says there are two types of people in the world: *Driven* people and *Called* people.

**Driven people** think they own everything. They own their relationships, they own their possessions, they own their positions. In fact, they perceive their identity as the sum of those relationships, possessions, and positions. As a result they spend most of their time protecting what they own. We see this in a family, when a parent wants to make sure everyone knows that he is the father or she is the mother and everyone else should cater to their wishes without questioning their authority. And if you mess with any of their toys you're in trouble.

**Called people** believe everything is on loan. They believe their relationships are on loan. The terrorist attacks of September 11, 2001, reminded us that we have no guarantee that we will see those we love tomorrow. We have to keep our "I love you's" up to date.

Called people believe their possessions are on loan. They enjoy them during good times, but when the economy turns downward, they are willing to "downsize" their things. Driven people, on the other hand, think "he who dies with the most toys wins." Their possessions are an important part of who they are.

Called people believe their positions are on loan. For leaders, from whom is their position on loan? Answer: the people the leaders are attempting to influence. Rather than protecting what they own, called leaders believe they need to steward what has been "loaned" to them.

✛ *This week we will give you some tests to determine whether you are more of a self-serving leader or a servant leader. We will look at the first two today.*

TEST 1: FEEDBACK

*Do you welcome and want feedback?* Self–serving leaders spend most of their time protecting their status. If you give them feedback—information on how they are doing as a leader—they usually react negatively. They think your feedback means you don't want them to lead anymore. That is their worst nightmare! The biggest fear self–serving leaders have is losing their positions. Much of their self–image is tied up in their positions.

Because servant leaders believe their positions are on loan, and they're only leading to be helpful, they love feedback. They look at feedback as a gift. When they receive feedback their first response is "Thank you." Then they usually want more information. "Is there anyone else I should talk to?" "Do you have any more thoughts?" Why do they respond so positively? Because they are leading in order to serve, and if you have any suggestions on how to improve their leadership they welcome your insights.

✛ *Are you self-serving and defensive about feedback because you want to hold on to your position, or are you a servant leader who believes your position is a gift on loan for a season? Using the test of feedback, mark an X on the continuum below to indicate where you think you are on the continuum from being a self-serving leader to a servant leader.*

*React Negatively*   1 _____ 2 _____ 3 _____ 4 _____ 5   *Welcome and*
*To Feedback*                                                              *want Feedback*

## TEST 2: SUCCESSION PLANNING

*Are you preparing a successor for when your season of leadership is complete?* In Matthew 25:21 Jesus summed up what we all would like to hear when final judgment is rendered for our efforts to make a difference—"Well done, good and faithful servant." One aspect of a job well done as a servant leader is how you prepare others to carry on after your season of leadership is completed. Perhaps you haven't thought of your leadership position as a *season* of leadership. But if you reflect on your experience you probably can see that you have had several seasons of leadership as you have been promoted from one position to another or volunteered for different projects in your community. In the family your succession–planning efforts are around preparing your kids to effectively manage their own lives. After all, the important thing as a parent is not what happens when you are there with your kids, but what happens when you are not around! Are you preparing them to stand on their own feet? Remember . . . all your leadership positions are on loan to you.

✠ *Check all the ways that you are preparing others to succeed you in your present season of leadership:*

_____ Modeling what they are to do.

_____ Consciously teaching them to do your job after you are gone.

_____ Talking to them about assuming your position.

_____ Sharing your "trade secrets" so they will be successful.

_____ Delegating work to them and then giving them helpful feedback.

_____ Giving them special projects to develop them as leaders.

_____ Recommending them to superiors.

_____ Developing a succession plan and keeping a file on possible successors.

_____ Constantly helping them move from dependence to independence.

Your personal succession–planning efforts and attempts to help "people stand on their own" speak volumes about your motives as a leader. Thinking that you own your position can prevent you from preparing others to succeed you. If you are driven and involved in promoting and protecting yourself, you are apt to spend little time in training and developing other leaders around you. Just as avoiding or discouraging honest feedback on a day–to–day basis is a mark of a self–serving leader, so is failure to develop someone to take your place.

Servant leaders, who consider their positions as being on loan and as an act of service, look beyond their own season of leadership and prepare the next generation of leaders. In the use of His time and efforts on earth, Jesus modeled sacrificial passion for ensuring that His followers were equipped to carry on the movement. He lived His legacy in intimate relationship with those He empowered by His words and example. Leighton Ford in *Transforming Leadership* observes: "Long before modern managers, Jesus was busy preparing people for the future. He wasn't aiming to pick a crown prince, but to create a successor generation. When the time came for Him to leave, He did not put in place a crash program of leadership development—the curriculum had been taught for three years in a living classroom."

*Jesus said, "I no longer call you servants, because a servant does not know his master's business. Instead I call you friends, for everything that I learned from My Father I have made known to you" (John 15:15).* Jesus modeled the true servant leader by investing most of His time training and equipping the disciples for leadership when His earthly ministry was over. Jesus said, *"I tell you the truth, anyone who has faith in me will do what I have been doing. He will do even greater things than these, because I am going to the Father" (John 14:12–13).*

✝ *How are you doing in preparing others to take your place or to be able to manage themselves? Do you consider them a threat or an investment in the future? Are you willing to share with those who will come after you the secrets of your job and provide opportunities for them to learn and grow? If not, why not? A few minutes of brutal honesty regarding your motives as a leader are worth years of self-deception. Write how you are training your successor(s) or developing those around you to be peak performers.*

_____

_____

_____

Today as you go about your business, give yourself the first two tests of a servant leader:

*1. Welcoming and wanting* _____.
We said that a servant leader welcomed feedback. We think feedback is the "breakfast of champions."

*2.* _____ *when your season of leadership is past.*

We contend that servant leaders constantly try to develop the leadership capabilities of the people around them by succession planning.

## How Do We Edge God Out?

Yesterday you were given the first two tests of servant leadership:

*Welcoming and wanting* _____ .

_____ *when your season of leadership is past.*

Today we want to help you check yourself on the third test of servant leadership:

## TEST 3: CONTROL

*Do you let God be the Leader and you be the servant?* The term *leader* or *leaders* is mentioned only six times in the King James Version of the Bible, while the term *servant* or *servants* is mentioned more than 900 times. That very fact underlines the truth that forms our third test: **God is not looking for leaders but for servants who will let Him be the Leader.** When God came to Abraham, God had the plan and Abraham was to carry it out according to God's promise. When God came to Moses, God provided the leadership for the shy, withdrawing man. When God came to David, it was not to ask him to lead but to serve Him, whether with harp, slingshot, or sword. When God was the Leader and these men were the servants, things worked out well and according to God's plan. Whenever we become the leader and try to make God the servant, things never work out. Why? Because we <u>E</u>dge <u>G</u>od <u>O</u>ut. If we want life to work out, then we have to recognize that it is all about God, not us.

The diagram below illustrates a self–serving leader. It will serve as a roadmap for the rest of this week's study. You will be able to use it to diagnose the extent to which you are a self–serving or servant leader.

✚ *See how much you can understand about your heart from studying the diagram. Later, we will analyze what it says together.*

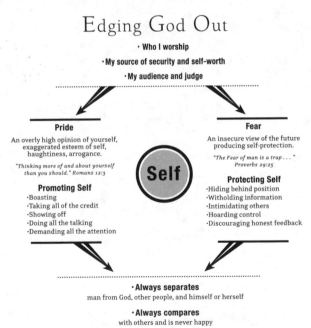

### Edging God Out

· Who I worship

· My source of security and self-worth

· My audience and judge

**Pride**

An overly high opinion of yourself, exaggerated esteem of self, haughtiness, arrogance.

*"Thinking more of and about yourself than you should." Romans 12:3*

**Promoting Self**
·Boasting
·Taking all of the credit
·Showing off
·Doing all the talking
·Demanding all the attention

**Self**

**Fear**

An insecure view of the future producing self-protection.

*"The Fear of man is a trap . . ." Proverbs 29:25*

**Protecting Self**
·Hiding behind position
·Witholding information
·Intimidating others
·Hoarding control
·Discouraging honest feedback

· **Always separates**
man from God, other people, and himself or herself

· **Always compares**
with others and is never happy

· **Always distorts**
the truth into false sense of security or fear

*What's Your Leadership EGO?* In 1923, pioneer psychoanalyst Sigmund Freud defined the ego as the conscious part of a person's psyche, the part that controls thought and behavior and interprets external reality. In short, he said ego is self–awareness. Freud's ego theory has long since fused with pop culture, and we're now used to hearing people talk about "ego trips," "bruised egos," and "egomaniacs." But in this study, when we talk about ego, we're not talking about a psychological term; we're talking about major heart issues. Here are two simple ways to define the EGO difference of self–serving and servant leaders.

*For Self–Serving Leaders:*
EGO — EDGING GOD OUT

— O R —

*For Servant Leaders:*
EGO — EXALTING GOD ONLY

It doesn't get much simpler than that.

✚ *Now we'd like for you to look at a case study early in the ministry of Jesus. Read the Scripture and take note of the servant leader behaviors that you see Jesus model.*

*Then Jesus came from Galilee to the Jordan to be baptized by John.*
*But John tried to deter Him, saying, "I need to be baptized by You, and do You come to me?"*
*Jesus replied, "Let it be so now; it is proper for us to do this to fulfill all righteousness." Then John consented.*
*As soon as Jesus was baptized, He went up out of the water. At that moment heaven was opened, and He saw the*
*Spirit of God descending like a dove and lighting on Him. And a voice from heaven said, "This is my Son,*
*whom I love; with Him I am well pleased." — Matthew 3:13–17*

✝ *Write the behaviors of Jesus in His interaction with John the Baptist that showed He was a servant leader.*

_____

_____

Jesus demonstrated two very significant attributes of servant leadership in His interaction with His cousin, John the Baptist. He validated and affirmed John in his ministry, and He submitted Himself to the same type of surrender by doing the right thing before He would require it of others. Servant leaders never ask anyone to do something they wouldn't be willing to do themselves.

Look at the EGO diagram. At the top are three ways we edge God out.

✝ *Today we will focus on learning these three ways:*

**1. You edge God out when you put something else in God's place as the object of your worship.**

Whenever anything becomes more important to you than God, you are in effect bowing to it, adoring it, or giving yourself to it. That idol becomes your answer to the question "whose are you?" In short, you worship it. It may be an object such as money, a house, a car, or a business. It may be a desire for power, recognition, or appreciation. It may be a habit that becomes more important than God to you, such as, running, watching TV or movies, eating, or sleeping.

✝ *Circle any of the things in the paragraph above that at times become more important to you than worshiping God.*

Now let's look at whom you worship in terms of your leadership when you face a difficult decision.

✝ *Check anything that you ever put in God's place as the object of your worship when you're making a leadership decision:*

_____ *The boss's opinion*    _____ *The money involved*    _____ *Potential promotion*
_____ *Fellow workers*    _____ *Fear of failure*

Power, recognition, appreciation, money—whatever it is, it's not worth it if it takes the place of your worship of God. *"For we who worship God in the spirit . . . put no confidence in human effort. Instead, we boast about what Christ Jesus has done for us"* (Philippians 3:3, NLT).

**2. You edge God out when you rely on other sources for your security and sufficiency.**

One of the greatest temptations is to rely on yourself instead of God—until you are at your wit's end. When you trust in something other than the unconditional love of God—other than in His care for you—you edge God out. When you put your security in other things—it can be your intellect, your position, your business contacts, anything—you're counting on the temporal instead of the eternal. *"Trust in the LORD with all your heart. And lean not your own understanding; in all your ways acknowledge Him, and He will make your paths straight"* (Proverbs 3:5–6).

✚ *Sometimes you rely on other things or other people to get you out of trouble. Check any of the items below that you have ever relied on as your security instead of God:*

____ *Wealth*          ____ *Intellect*          ____ *Business contacts*

____ *Education*       ____ *Experience*         ____ *Money*

____ *Position*

✚ *Now circle any of the above items that you currently are relying on.*

Anything that you count on instead of God is temporal rather than eternal. Your security is in the unconditional love of God and in His care for you. *"Cast all your anxiety on Him because He cares for you"* (1 Peter 5:7).

**3. You edge God out when you put others in His place as your major audience.**

If your self–worth or security is based on what others think, then you don't have any security. In Robert S. McGee's *The Search for Significance*, we learn that if the devil could get you to buy into a formula for self–worth, it would be:

Your self–worth = your performance + the opinion of others.

If you constantly base your self–worth on your performance or the opinions of others, you're always going to be chasing an elusive, frustrating fantasy. All the world is a stage and God is the audience of One. *"Whatever you do, work at it with all your heart, as working for the Lord, not for men"* (Colossians 3:23).

Not only is God the Audience you are to please, He is the Judge of all the earth. He determines your destiny. How many businessmen or even church leaders thought they were getting away with devious deals only to discover that God makes known from the housetops the secrets that were whispered in the closet! Your character is revealed when no one is watching. (Except be sure that God is always watching!) He must be your audience of One . . . the One you honor above all.

✚ *Name a few people in the news, or even people you know, who got caught while playing to the wrong audience.*

_____

_____

✛ *Complete the statements below about ways we Edge God Out.*

1. When you put something else in God's place as the object of your _____ .
2. When you rely on other _____ for your security and sufficiency.
3. When you put others in God's place as your major _____ and _____ .

Jesus was tempted to edge God out immediately after John baptized Him.

✛ *Read in your Bible the story of Jesus' temptations in Matthew 4:1-11 and meditate on why they were temptations to Jesus to become a self-serving leader:*

It is easy to concentrate too much on the physical hardships of Jesus' fasting experience in the wilderness and miss the profound spiritual conditioning for servant leadership that took place.

When tempted by three of the most universal and powerful temptations a leader can face—instant gratification, recognition and applause, and improper use and lust for power—Jesus was at His spiritual best.

In every season of leadership you enter, you will be faced with the same temptations. The quality of your service will be a direct result of your spiritual preparation.

✛ *Write examples of how you have faced these three heart temptations to become a self-serving leader:*

1. Instant gratification of self _____

_____

2. Recognition and applause of others _____

_____

3. Improper use and lust for power _____

_____


Notice that Jesus used the Word of God He had stored in His heart and mind to confront and defeat the devil. This should give you a clue why we are asking that you memorize a key verse each week of this study!

✛ *Write your memory verses and references for the first two weeks:*

_____

_____

_____

_____

_____

To successfully combat the temptation to be self–serving, every day you must surrender your motives and actions to Christ as your guide and role model for how you will lead. God has given us His promise:

*"No temptation has seized you except what is common to man. And God is faithful;*
*He will not let you be tempted beyond what you can bear. But when you are tempted,*
*He will also provide a way out so that you can stand up under it" (1 Corinthians 10:13).*

✟ **Today, what do you think will be your greatest temptation to Edge God Out and act like a self-serving leader? How will you deal with it? Write how you think you will respond below.**

_____

_____

✟ **Tomorrow, we will ask you to describe any encounter you experienced today when you were tempted to be a self-serving leader and how you handled the situation.**

# Pride Edges God Out

✟ **Yesterday I asked you to be ready to share how you handled a temptation to Edge God Out and be a self-serving leader. Write any temptation encounter that you experienced and how you handled it.**

_____

_____

_____

Look again at the EGO diagram in Day Two of this week. You edge God out by putting Self in His place. Pride and fear are evidences that Self wants to replace God.

## INCREASE YOUR HEART—AWARENESS

You have been given three tests to see how much of a servant leader you are in these first three tests.

✟ **Complete the missing words in the first three tests:**

1. *The first test is welcoming and accepting* _____ .

2. *The second test is* _____ *when your season of leadership is past.*

3. *The third test is letting God be the* _____ *and you be the* _____ .

Today we want to help you check yourself on the fourth test of servant leadership.

## TEST 4 — REACT OR RESPOND

**When you are treated like a servant, do you respond like a servant?**

Self–serving leaders react to things that happen to them. They are almost a stimulus–response machine. If you say or do something that hooks their pride or fear, they react.

Servant leaders, on the other hand, respond to things that happen to them. Their response is led by their intentions and motivations to serve.

⊕ *What have you ever said (or wanted to say) when someone asked you to do something that you felt was below you? Check the reaction you have given or thought about giving when you were asked to be a servant.*

____ Why did you ask me to do that?

____ Why don't you do it yourself?

____ I have more important things to do.

____ Anybody could do that!

____ I don't have time to do things like that.

Self–serving leaders don't like it if they are bossed around, taken for granted, or treated as inferior. However, if you are a servant you aren't offended when someone treats you like one. You are always ready to respond as a servant.

⊕ *Pride is an overly high opinion of your self. Add the core letter in the word P R _ D E. What does that tell you about how self and pride are related?*

_____

_____

How would you describe pride? Here are some ways:

1. Pride is when you are engaged in a discussion and you said or felt, "The righter you sound, the madder I get."
2. Pride is when you start to promote yourself by taking too much credit, doing all the talking, demanding attention, being boastful, or showing off.
3. Pride is when you start to act out of fear as you seek to protect yourself regardless of the truth.
4. Pride is when the origin of an idea is more important than the idea itself. During negotiations and times of change, if you can put an idea out there for a while without its author, then you can work with it and see what happens. But if you get tied into who said it, then the idea often becomes a poorly chosen battleground.
5. Pride is when you feel something boiling up within you without realizing that you are harboring a hurt, a slight, or another situation that is on your mind.

⊕ *You might have identified with some of those expressions of pride. But look at the company pride keeps according to Proverbs 6:16-19.*

"There are six things the LORD hates, seven that are detestable to Him:

*haughty eyes* [The King James Version translates "haughty eyes" as "a proud look."]

*a lying tongue*

*hands that shed innocent blood*

*a heart that devises wicked schemes*

*feet that are quick to rush into evil*

*a false witness who pours out lies*

*and a man who stirs up dissension among brothers."*

When you make decisions out of pride you need to ask, "Do I really want to make a decision based on that?" You can be sure that pride–based decisions won't give you the best long–term results. You might get a mile or so down the road, but such decisions won't see you through the entire trip.

# The Demon of Fear

Before we discover the fifth test of a servant leader, let's review the first four tests:

✚ *Review the four tests of a servant leader by completing the statements below:*

1. *The first test is welcoming and accepting* _____ .

2. *The second test is* _____ *when your season of leadership is past.*

3. *The third test is letting God be the* _____ *and you be the* _____ .

4. *The fourth test is when you are treated like a servant you should respond like a* _____ .

✚ *Yesterday you were asked to remember and review the four tests for a servant leader and review them during the day. Make a note below on how this affected your thinking and behavior during the day. Be prepared to talk about this in your small group.*

_____

_____

_____

Today we want to help you check yourself on the fifth test of servant leadership:

## TEST 5: FEAR

***Do you lead out of your own fear or create fear in those you lead?*** The spiritual contest between fearing God and fearing man is nothing new or any less intense today than when it was played out in lives of the heroes the Bible. Heroes who performed monumental acts of courage also fell victim to the temptations of fear.

✝ *Supply the names of Biblical heroes who succumbed to fear. (You may look up their names using the Bible references if necessary.)*

_____ *when he lied about his relationship with his wife Sarai, for fear of his own life. (Genesis 12:10–17)*

_____ *when he pleaded with God to send someone else to talk to Pharaoh about releasing the Jews because he felt inadequate as a public speaker. (Exodus 4:10–17)*

_____ *when he tried to cover up his infidelity with Bathsheba by having her husband killed. (2 Samuel 11:1–18)*

_____ *when he denied knowing Jesus at the time of His arrest. (Matthew 26:69–75)*

Like Abraham, Moses, David, and Peter we often fail to trust God as a secure and sufficient supply of unconditional love and safety! Fear makes it easy for us to edge God out as the focus of our worship, as our source of security and self–worth, and as our audience and judge. But when you start to edge God out in your daily decision–making, things start to happen that are not consistent with being a servant leader.

***Naming The Demon Of Fear and Avoiding the Trap of Toxic Fear.*** We have been given the capacity of fear as part of God's design for our protection and participation with Him in a relationship of unconditional love. When the capacity to fear is directed toward protecting unreliable sources of love and security, it draws us away from God and into a dangerous trap.

We're most likely to be fearful when we are heavily dependent on sources of security and measurements of self–worth that are temporary and always at risk.

In the previous group session we identified that we have an ego problem—addicted to self, fear, and pride. An addiction is an ever–increasing desire for something that has an ever–decreasing ability to satisfy. The total focus of addictive behavior is to maintain a secure source of supply. So what makes us addicted to self? The answer lies in our addictive dependence on unreliable, always–at–risk sources of security and self–worth. Poorly grounded foundations of self–esteem and security inject lethal levels of toxic fear and self–protection into the mainstream of our relationships. When we are addicted to self our fear can become toxic and poison our lives and the lives of people around us. This is especially true when we fear that the fuel source of our addictions is at risk.

✚ *Evaluate your levels of fear and reliance on inadequate sources of security or self-worth. In answering each question feel free to be hard on yourself. However, the questionnaire is for your own awareness and you do not need to share it with others.*

## QUESTIONNAIRE

1. Which of the following do you rely on as a source of your sense of security and self-worth in your relationships? Circle the number that best indicates your level of dependence on that element. One is the lowest and five is the highest

| 1 2 3 4 5 | Applause | 1 2 3 4 5 | Performance |
| 1 2 3 4 5 | Money | 1 2 3 4 5 | Knowledge & intellect |
| 1 2 3 4 5 | Position & power | 1 2 3 4 5 | Health & fitness |
| 1 2 3 4 5 | Style & fashion | 1 2 3 4 5 | Physical appearance |
| 1 2 3 4 5 | Sex | 1 2 3 4 5 | Relationships |
| 1 2 3 4 5 | Mystery | 1 2 3 4 5 | Busyness |
| 1 2 3 4 5 | Credentials | 1 2 3 4 5 | Heritage & history |

2. Which of the following fears tend to negatively impact your relationships? As you examine your heart, remember that others are many times much more aware of your fears than you we are. Check any that apply:

| _____ Fear of rejection | _____ Fear of job loss | _____ Fear of loss of control |
| _____ Fear of inadequacy | _____ Fear of competition | _____ Fear of the future |
| _____ Fear of failure | _____ Fear of success | _____ Fear of disclosure |
| _____ Fear of change | _____ Fear of exclusion | _____ Fear of obsolescence |
| _____ Fear of loneliness | _____ Fear of criticism | _____ Fear of intimacy |
| _____ Fear of retaliation | | |

3. How do you deal with the following situations? Place an X below to indicate how you react to each. Be honest with yourself.

| | OUT OF CONFIDENCE | OUT OF FEAR |
| --- | --- | --- |
| Imperfect people and relationships | _____ | _____ |
| Fallible organizations and institutions | _____ | _____ |
| Material assets | _____ | _____ |
| Obsolescent skills, information, knowledge | _____ | _____ |
| Luck and good intentions | _____ | _____ |
| Past successes and future actions | _____ | _____ |

The questionnaire above is for your own personal use, and you do not need to share it with anyone else unless you want to talk about it. However, if you feel free sharing some of the things you have discovered with a trusted friend or your small group you will learn even more. Now we will look at a fear that is not often recognized.

✠ *Here are some common examples of toxic fear. If you know of anyone who matches one of these case studies, write their initials beside the addictive behavior of toxic fear.*

_____ *hides feelings of inadequacy and low self–esteem in perpetual purposeful activity or feels trapped and victimized by a call for help from a neglected spouse or by a forced period of inactivity due to illness.*

_____ *chooses to be overworked and keep other people dependent on him/her for information rather than risk loss of his/her source of power and security.*

_____ *goes into an emotional and relational tailspin at the first sign of illness or aging in himself/herself or in someone with whom he/she identifies.*

_____ *a people pleaser, broods over a two percent negative rating on feedback form or an overheard piece of unfavorable gossip.*

_____ *an applause–addicted person, drives himself/herself into nervous exhaustion and compromise trying to look better than he/she is and behave better than he/she feels.*

_____ *the teenage relationship junkie, abandons his/her own values in order to protect his/her supply of peer acceptance by doing bad things with bad people rather than face being alone.*

As you consider others who live out their fears, you also might identify some of your own behaviors that are motivated by fear. Fear can cause you to rely on the wrong sources for security and self-worth. The questionnaire you took also may help you identify potential false sources of security and potential toxic fears. Now we will examine a fear that often is not recognized.

## THE FEAR OF INTIMACY

One of the greatest EGO factors leaders have is the fear of intimacy or vulnerability—that ability to admit that you don't know all the answers, that you may need help, that if you let people in, then your leadership might be questioned.

When we lose intimacy with God's unconditional love, we fear intimacy with others. One of the greatest EGO factors that self–serving leaders driven by pride and fear have is the fear of intimacy with others. Like the Wizard behind the curtain in Oz, they create scary false fronts and barriers between themselves and their people rather than admit that they don't know all the answers or that they might need help. They fear that if they are vulnerable with people, their leadership might he questioned. The isolation that results from fear of intimacy leaves the leader separated from the realities of what is going on and from the good ideas others can offer. When fear enters into a relationship or an organization it quickly acts like a virus. And when that fear enters through the heart and actions of a leader it is particularly nasty and hard to cure.

If you're not careful, you can become addicted to using fear as an easy method of manipulation and control to produce short–term results. It might be easier to realize how this can happen if you consider people who used fear to motivate you. It could be a parent, a teacher, a boss, even a spouse. But never assume that you don't use fear to motivate others to do your bidding.

✝ *Ask yourself the following questions and answer them as if your fellow workers or family were going to grade them:*

1. *Am I leading out of internal fears that cause me to act as if I am more sure of myself than I really am?*
_____ *Yes* _____ *No* _____ *Sometimes*

2. *What do I do to cover up my fears?*

_____

_____

3. *Am I leading by using fear to cause others to do what I say?* _____ *Yes* _____ *No* _____ *Sometimes*

4. *How do I use fear to get people to do what I say?*

_____

_____

5. *Do I cause fear in others by the way I lead?* _____ *Yes* _____ *No* _____ *Sometimes*

6. *What do I do that causes fear in others?* _____

_____

Next week we will look at how to solve some of the problems of Edging God Out by Exalting God Only. For now I am going to ask you to use your sanctified imagination to picture a world without fear as a driving force. Read the following questions and take time to think through each situation and try to describe how you think things might be different. You might share your insights in your group session.

✝ *On a personal level, just suppose you were able to free yourself from the fear of what other people could or might do to you. Jot some notes on how you think freeing yourself from fear would impact your personal relationships.*

_____

_____

_____

✝ *Just suppose fear was replaced by trust and respect as a motivating force in your organization. Describe what you think would happen to you and your fellow workers' productivity, sense of self-worth, and attitude about spending a major portion of your life at work.*

_____

_____

✠ *Just suppose the barriers of mutual distrust and self-protection came down and you discovered that you don't have to hoard anything anymore. There is enough for everyone. Write what society would look like if we truly lived as if "In God We Trust."*

_____

_____

_____

✠ *Just suppose you bowed your head and bent your knee to an all-sufficient Savior and surrendered your fears to His care. Write how you think the world would look if the Golden Rule replaced the Toxic Rule of "Fear thy neighbor," which steals the joy from our lives that God designed us to enjoy to His Glory.*

_____

_____

✠ *Now that you understand more about how fear impacts you and those you lead, what will you do differently today?*

_____

_____

*"For God hath not given us the spirit of fear; but of power, and of love, and of a sound mind" (2 Timothy 1:7, NKJV).*

**5 DAY**

## Becoming a *Servant Leader*

This week we have examined five tests of a servant leader. They are principles for leading like Jesus.

✠ *Evaluate your progress in applying the tests of a servant leader who leads like Jesus in your daily decisions by marking a number on a scale from 1 to 5. Use the scale of 1-rarely; 2-once in a while; 3-often; 4-frequently; 5-consistently.*

1 | 2 | 3 | 4 | 5     *I seek and encourage feedback on my leadership.*
1 | 2 | 3 | 4 | 5     *I am developing successors for my job.*
1 | 2 | 3 | 4 | 5     *I let God be the Leader and I am the servant.*
1 | 2 | 3 | 4 | 5     *I respond as a servant when treated like one.*
1 | 2 | 3 | 4 | 5     *I do not operate out of fear or cause fear in those I lead.*

Look back at the Edging God Out diagram on Day Two of this week. Notice at the bottom the three results of our addictions to self, pride, and fear—separation, comparison, and distortion.

## SEPARATION

Self, pride, and fear always separate and isolate man from God, man from man, and man from himself. If we are not careful as leaders we will build our own private isolation booths.

✝ *Prayerfully examine the three isolation booths below that you can create for yourself. Write T (True) for behaviors you practice that isolate you and F (False) for the behaviors that are not a problem for you.*

*1. Separation from God*

___ *Too ashamed about my failure to talk to God*

___ *Too arrogant to think I need to pray*

___ *Too afraid of the answer to ask God the question*

___ *Too full of my own agenda to wait for God*

*2. Separation from Other People*

___ *Too pride–filled to say "I need help" or "I am sorry"*

___ *Too fearful of criticism to take a stand*

___ *Too fearful of rejection to say "No" when "No" is the right answer*

___ *Too fearful of losing control to share information or power*

___ *Too convinced of my own opinion to consider conflicting information*

___ *Too focused on accomplishing my agenda to see the needs and dreams of others*

___ *Too starved for recognition to express joy for the success of others*

*3. Separation from Yourself*

___ *Too busy fixing problems and others to look at the mess inside*

___ *Too much making excuses and too little repenting*

___ *Too much sensitivity to the opinion of others to listen to my own heart*

___ *Too much seeking external causes for internal problems*

___ *Too little time spent on taking care of my basic needs for rest, recreation, and reflection*

___ *Too afraid of failure to take a chance*

## COMPARISON

The second negative impact of addiction to self, pride, and fear is that they result in unhealthy horizontal comparisons. Instead of measuring success in terms of how well you are following God's plan for your life, you constantly are tempted to look to the right and left to see how you compare to others around you.

Seeking to learn from others and aspiring to emulate good role models are signs of a healthy state of humility of mind and heart. However, the EGO issues and toxic impact of envy, jealousy, or self–esteem have been polluting human relationships ever since Cain slew Abel.

**An Antidote for Unhealthy Comparisons.** The best antidote for the temptation to compare yourself with others is a healthy respect and trust for who God made you to be. When you exalt God only you begin to see that He has made you a significant person and has created you for His purposes.

One antidote for unhealthy comparison is developing a keen understanding of the standards God has for measuring the success of His followers. Learn to see what God values and major on those characteristics.

✠ *Read Matthew 5:3-11 in the margin and write the number of the verse next to the values that listed below:*

_____ *Those who seek His will*            _____ *Mercy*

_____ *Humility*                           _____ *Peace making*

_____ *Those who acknowledge their dependence on Him*    _____ *Purity of purpose*

_____ *Perseverance under pressure*           _____ *The bereaved*

*³Blessed are the poor in spirit, for theirs is the kingdom of heaven.*

*⁴Blessed are those who mourn, for they will be comforted.*

*⁵Blessed are the meek, for they will inherit the earth.*

*⁶Blessed are those who hunger and thirst for righteousness, for they will be filled.*

*⁷Blessed are the merciful, for they will be shown mercy.*

*⁸Blessed are the pure in heart, for they will see God.*

*⁹Blessed are the peacemakers, for they will be called sons of God.*

*¹⁰Blessed are those who are persecuted because of righteousness, for theirs is the kingdom of heaven.*

*¹¹Blessed are you when people insult you, persecute you and falsely say all kinds of evil against you because of Me.*

Notice none of the things mentioned in the Beatitudes call for you to do or be anything other than obedient to the Lord in your own circumstances. Did you write the verses in the blanks in this order: 6, 3, 5, 10–11, 7, 9, 8, 4? A second antidote is to meditate on Scriptures that teach us not to compare ourselves with others.

✠ *Read the following Scripture and meditate on it. You might want to memorize it if this toxin is a particular problem for you.*

*Let not the wise man boast of his wisdom or the strong man boast of his strength or the rich man boast of his riches, but let him who boasts boast of this: That he understands and knows Me, that I am the Lord, who exercises kindness, justice and righteousness on earth, for in these I delight. (Jeremiah 9:23–24)*

## DISTORTION

The third impact of addiction to self, pride, and fear is deception and distortion of the truth. The root cause of toxic fear is a life view built on a lie. The nature of this lie tells us "we are not safe playing it God's way" and "we are going to miss out on something really good." It is **F**alse **E**vidence **A**ppearing **R**eal—FEAR. When pride and fear isolate you from everyone else, including God, your view of reality will become increasingly misguided and your decisions more prone to error.

✠ *Read and meditate on Proverbs 3:5-6: "Trust in the Lord with all your heart and lean not on your own understanding; in all your ways acknowledge Him and He will make your paths straight."*

One of the major antidotes to Edging God Out of our lives is accepting God's love for our lives. Before we end this week, let's take some time to examine God's love for us and to begin to realize how important His love is if we are to be servant leaders.

God is love. If you want to understand the love of God look at Jesus. Jesus "*. . . is the radiance of God's glory and the exact representation of His being, sustaining all things by His powerful word*" (Hebrews 1:3). Jesus demonstrated the love of God to a watching world. The love of God, incarnated in Christ, is wrapped up in one verse. You would expect me to quote John 3:16, which is God's love verse to the world. But do you know the *other* John 3:16? "*This is how we know what love is: Jesus Christ laid down His life for us. And we ought to lay down our lives for our brothers*" (1 John 3:16). This verse explains God's love for us through Jesus' sacrifice and our love for others as we lay down our lives for them. So *1 John 3:16 fulfills John 3:16 in our lives.*

Today we want to see how Jesus modeled the quality of love so that we can love as He did. We'll look at it from three perspectives: ***Unconditional Love      Unlimited Love      Unending Love.***

## UNCONDITIONAL LOVE

> *Your life is never the same once you comprehend the unconditional love of God for you*
> *that was demonstrated in Jesus. For example, to apply it to this week's study on fear,*
> *"There is no fear in love. But perfect love drives out fear" (1 John 4:18).*

Jesus loved unconditionally. No condition was beyond His love. He loved sinners—prostitutes, thieves, cheats, betrayers, murderers, enemies, unfaithful disciples—everybody!

✠ *In contrast to Jesus we often put conditions on our love. Examine the list below and check those situations in which you tend to tend not to love unconditionally.*

_____ *I would love you but you are not the same color I am.*

_____ *I would love you but you but you don't speak the same language I do.*

_____ *I would love you but you don't have the same values I do.*

_____ *I would love you but you don't talk like I do.*

_____ *I would love you but you have AIDS.*

_____ *I would love you but you just cheated me.*

_____ *I would love you but I can't relate to homeless people.*

_____ *I would love you but you are a terrorist.*

_____ *I would love you but you just hurt me.*

✠ *Now answer these questions "by circling "yes" or "no":*

*Does Jesus love them?*        **Yes ∣ No**

*Does God love them?*        **Yes ∣ No**

*Should you love them?*        **Yes ∣ No**

*What are you going to do about it?* _____

_____

Of course that is a hard question. You might say, "Although I should love unconditionally, I just can't!" That may be true if you have to love them on your own. Go back to 1 John 3:16 above and add to it 1 John 4:11–12: *"Dear friends, since God so loved us, we also ought to love one another. No one has ever seen God; but if we love one another, God lives in us and His love is made complete in us."*

✝ *Read the following three times the disciples struggled with this question. Then visualize a person you need to love unconditionally and circle the response you will apply to your situation:*

*1. You could make the response* the disciples did when rejected by Samaritan villagers: *And He sent messengers on ahead, who went into a Samaritan village to get things ready for Him; but the people there did not welcome Him, because He was heading for Jerusalem. When the disciples James and John saw this, they asked, "Lord, do you want us to* **call fire down from heaven to destroy them***?" But Jesus turned and rebuked them, and they went to another village.* (Luke 9:52–56)

*2. You could react* like the disciples did when Jesus told them they should accept whatever their wives did and that except for marital unfaithfulness should not divorce: *The disciples said to him, "If this is the situation between a husband and wife,* **it is better not to marry"** (Matthew 19:10). You could just say, "It is better not to be a disciple if I have to love that person unconditionally."

*3. You could make the response* the disciples did in a different situation when Jesus taught about forgiveness: *"So watch yourselves. If your brother sins, rebuke him, and if he repents, forgive him. If he sins against you seven times in a day, and seven times comes back to you and says, 'I repent,' forgive him." The apostles said to the Lord,* **"Increase our faith!"** (Luke 17:3–5)

We cannot love unconditionally like Jesus does unless He is living in us and loving people through us. Sometimes I have had to say, "Lord, I just can't love that person, but I will allow You to love them through me. Just show me what You want to do to show Your love to them and I will do it."

## UNLIMITED LOVE

Unlimited love goes beyond unconditional love because it has the element of loving regardless of how long and how difficult the situation persists. Again Jesus is our example.

✝ *Read the situations below where Jesus showed unlimited love.*

> *Jesus loves us regardless of our sins and no matter how many times we fail.*
> *Jesus loves us no matter how many times we reject Him or are disobedient.*
> *Jesus loves us no matter how far we run from Him.*
> *Jesus loves us no matter how long we delay our coming to Him or dependence on Him.*
> *Jesus loves us no matter what we do to Him and says, "Father, forgive them for they know not what they do."*

✛ *Write any situations you face that God needs to give you unlimited love like Jesus and through Jesus. Then stop and ask God to extend His love to you and through you.*

_____

_____

_____

## UNFAILING LOVE

Unlike our human love, God's love is unfailing.

✛ *Look at the situations below in which Jesus' love did not fail.*
Jesus' love did not fail for the dying thief on the cross, and He stopped dying long enough to save him.
Jesus' love did not fail for His disciples when they ran away, denied Him, or betrayed Him.
Jesus' love did not fail for His mother when He was dying on the cross and He told John to care for her.
Jesus' love has never failed you.

✛ *Now look at the situations below in which your love may fail and you feel like making one of the statements below. Check any that you are feeling now.*

_____ I'll love you until you hurt me.

_____ I'll love you until you leave me.

_____ I'll love you until you shut me out.

_____ I'll love you until you scatter malicious gossip about me.

_____ I'll love you until you lie about me.

_____ I'll love you until you quit loving me.

_____ I'll love you until I can't take it anymore.

_____ I'll love you until you are beyond hope.

_____ I'll love you until I feel like I have to give up.

If we are to be like Jesus in loving without conditions, without limits, and without end we must allow Him to give us His kind of love.

✛ *Read 1 Corinthians 13 and put your own personal pronouns in it. Then stop and pray that God will put this kind of love in your heart and that as a servant leader you will be able to love like Jesus does.*

That is all for this week. Have a great group session.

# LEAD LIKE JESUS

## BEGINNING THE JOURNEY

# WEEK THREE

### THE HEART — *Exalting God Only*

*"He must increase, but I must decrease."* —John 3:30 KJV

## Altaring Your Leadership Ego?

Medicine lives by a wise saying "Prescription without diagnosis is malpractice." In last week's study we devoted our attention to diagnosing the causes and effects of the heart conditions of pride and fear and the negative impact of the Self on our attempts to Lead Like Jesus. We came to understand that when we Edge God Out of the center of our lives we become vulnerable to the addictive nature of self–centered motivations. This week we are going look at how we as leaders can move from a self–centered heart that has Edged God Out to a God–centered heart that Exalts God Only. The "Altaring" in the title for today's study is not a misspelling, but refers to offering your ego on God's altar. That's the destination for the journey this week.

In Week Two's small group session we discovered in the EGO's Anonymous activity that we are not alone in dealing with these challenges. Was the EGO's Anonymous activity a shock to you? For most of us it is difficult to admit that we are addicted to self through pride and fear. It is so hard to say, "I have an ego problem because . . ." Your first reaction might have been, "Well, I know that I do have an ego, but it is not so out of control that I would admit to having an ego problem."

Examine your inner thoughts and evaluate how much your ego dominates you. What is your first thought when a change is introduced? Isn't it, "How will it affect me?" What is your first response when someone criticizes you? Don't you begin to defend yourself? What is your first response when you fail? Don't you think "What will people think of me?" Our whole lives revolve around self and everything is interpreted in light of how it affects self. So go ahead and admit it—your ego is in control. You have an ego problem!

✝ What was your reaction to the EGO's Anonymous activity in the last group session? Do you agree you have an ego problem?

_____

_____

_____

Good, we are glad you admitted you have an ego problem. Once an addict of any kind is ready to own the problem and seek help, there is the chance of recovery. However, even then recovery is better described as remission; it's not permanent. Addicts must admit that they are addicts and will always be in recovery.

✝ *So will you admit that you have an ego problem and will always be in recovery? Read the first three of the Twelve Steps for EGO's Anonymous. Respond by circling "Yes" or "No".*

*Step 1.* I admit that on more than one occasion I have allowed my ego needs and drive for earthly success to negatively impact my role as a leader and that my leadership has not been the servant leader-ship that Jesus modeled.     **Yes | No**

**Step 2.** I've come to believe that God can transform my leadership motives, thoughts, and actions to the servant leadership that Jesus modeled.     **Yes | No**

**Step 3.** I've made a decision to turn my leadership efforts to God and to become an apprentice of Jesus and the servant leadership He modeled.     **Yes | No**

Leading like Jesus is more than an effort to adopt a certain discrete set of behavioral principles, atti-tudes, and thought processes. It is a challenging journey in daily surrender of your motivations to the guidance of the Holy Spirit. It means laying your pride and fears on the altar and letting them be trans-formed. We have used the words, "heart attack" in the twelve steps to describe what needs to happen to make us servant leaders. The words "heart attack" almost always signal a life changing experience—although usually negative. It usually indicates an undesirable crisis. However, in seeking to *Lead Like Jesus*, "heart attack" accurately describes the prerequisite cost. We really need a heart transplant.

✝ *Before you can Exalt God Only you have to Edge Self Out. Read Luke 9:57-62 below and Jesus' requirements to follow Him. Circle the answers to the ques-tions that most nearly indicate your response at this time: Yes, No or Not Yet:*

> *As they were walking along the road, a man said to Him, "I will follow You*
> *wherever You go." Jesus replied, "Foxes have holes and birds of the air have nests,*
> *but the Son of Man has no place to lay His head."*

**Anywhere: Are you willing to follow Jesus anywhere He leads?**     *Yes | No | Not Yet*

> *He said to another man, "Follow Me." But the man replied,*
> *"Lord, first let me go and bury my father." Jesus said to him, "Let the dead bury*
> *their own dead, but you go and proclaim the kingdom of God."*

**Anytime: Are you willing to change your schedule at any time if it hinders you from following Jesus as your leader?**     *Yes | No | Not Yet*

> *Still another said, "I will follow You, Lord; but first let me go back and say goodbye to my family."*
> *Jesus replied, "No one who puts his hand to the plow and looks back is fit for service in the kingdom of God."*

**Anyone: Are you willing for Jesus to be your priority over any person?**     *Yes | No | Not Yet*

## TAKING THE FIRST STEP: SURRENDER

The power of leading like Jesus can be poured only into a surrendered heart and can flow only out of a surrendered heart. There is no shortcut around Self that will allow you to *Lead Like Jesus*. Norman Vincent Peale, a dear friend and mentor to Ken Blanchard, once told him, "The toughest test of self-esteem is to bend your knee, bow your head, and admit you can't make it on your own—you need God in your life." Without surrendering your leadership to the work of the Holy Spirit you will never *Lead*

*Like Jesus.* To tell you anything less would be like selling you a medicine without the active ingredient. It just won't work.

✝ *Maybe your initial reaction to the word "surrender" is to resist the concept. Look at the usual meanings of surrender below and check any that you are feeling now.*

_____ *Surrender means I am acknowledging that I can't win a battle that was important to me.*

_____ *Surrender means that I will be under another's control from now on.*

_____ *Surrender sends up emotional flares, indicating a loss of my freedom and my self-esteem.*

_____ *Surrender means I will have lost to someone bigger or better than I am.*

_____ *Surrender is scary when applied to the way I lead my life, handle my relationships, do my work, and deal with my secret thoughts and fears.*

_____ *Surrender sounds like the giving up of myself.*

_____ *To ask me to surrender voluntarily, when other options still seem to be available, is not fair.*

You may feel that the arguments have to be exceptionally convincing for you to believe that surrender is in your best interest. You want to maintain some level of control just in case things don't work out as you planned. You may feel that you want to back off for a while.

✝ *Here are some back-off strategies that Self would like to propose as alternatives to total surrender. Read them and check the one that best signifies what you are willing to do right now. If you are willing to totally surrender to God, then congratulate yourself.*

_____ *Partial surrender*          _____ *Delayed surrender*

_____ *Conditional surrender*      _____ *Total surrender*

You might be asking, "Why does God want total surrender?" He has good reasons for asking for total surrender.

✝ *Consider these possible reasons He asks for total surrender, and then pray a prayer of surrender:*

• Because He has already paid a terrible price to give me peace in His presence.
• Because He knows me so well and how easily I can be tempted to look for loopholes and reasons to justify retaking control.
• Because He knows that the only way He can bless me in the work He has set before me is in response to my choice of total surrender.
• Because I am only vaguely aware of all the consequences of taking a first step of faith.

*Be assured that you can trust God not to go back on His word. He says, "God, who has called you into fellowship with His Son Jesus Christ our Lord, is faithful" (1 Corinthians 1:9).*

In an interview not long before his death, Bill Bright, founder of Campus Crusade for Christ, told of his surrender as a young man. He said:

*One Sunday afternoon, God led my wife and I to sign a contract—literally to write out a contract of total surrender of our lives to the Lord Jesus Christ—to become His slave. [The Apostle] Paul refers to himself in Romans 1:1 "a slave of Jesus Christ." We felt the most important thing we could do was to become as slaves of Jesus—signing a contract to that effect, laid everything we owned or ever would own on the altar. We've been slaves now for fifty some years, and I must tell you it's the most liberating thing that's ever happened to me.*

✠ *Are you willing to surrender your leadership efforts to the guidance of the Holy Spirit? Choose one of the following options:*

**If your answer is "Yes" then complete the following statement:**

I _____ acknowledge that I cannot now or ever will be able to *Lead Like Jesus* without the guidance of the Holy Spirit and as of this date _____ will stop trying to do it on my own and invite the Holy Spirit to guide me from now on.

_____
(Signed)

**If your answer is "No" or "I'm not sure" or "I don't think I can follow through on a commitment to do so," then complete the following statement;**

I _____ acknowledge that there are some barriers right now that prevent me from surrendering my efforts to *Lead Like Jesus* under the guidance of the Holy Spirit. They include: (Check the appropriate ones.)

_____ Not knowing how
_____ Fear of what will happen if I do
_____ Lack of confidence in my own level of commitment
_____ Lack of confidence that leading like Jesus will work in my situation
_____ Other _____

Even in the face of these barriers I offer a heartfelt prayer on this date _____ that God will help me overcome my doubts and concerns so I can fulfill my desire to *Lead Like Jesus*.

_____
(Signed)

✠ *Several times today review "The EGO's Anonymous 12-Step Process" that was given you in the small group session.*

# How To Be God-Centered

We have been looking in a mirror much of our study to understand our self–serving hearts. But a mirror has no power to change you; it only reveals you. Can you imagine a person whose beard is all lathered up trying to clean his face with a mirror? It is not enough to know that we Edge God Out by our addiction to self. The key is to turn our focus to the One who can change our hearts. The only way to become a servant leader is to worship God in spirit and in truth. When we worship Him our hearts are changed and we begin to reflect Him. *"And all of us have had that veil removed so that we can be mirrors that brightly reflect the glory of the Lord. And as the Spirit of the Lord works within us, we become more and more like Him and reflect His glory even more"* (2 Corinthians 3:18, NLT).

✚ *Study the chart below on Exalting God Only. It will be the heart of our study this week and point us to a life of servant leadership.*

## WORSHIP GOD ONLY

If we are to *Lead Like Jesus* then we need to worship like Jesus. He is our model. Today we will look at what Jesus did in worship and what He taught about worship.

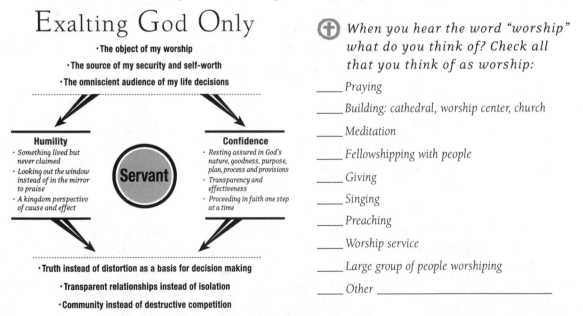

## Exalting God Only

- The object of my worship
- The source of my security and self-worth
- The omniscient audience of my life decisions

**Humility**
- Something lived but never claimed
- Looking out the window instead of in the mirror to praise
- A kingdom perspective of cause and effect

**Servant**

**Confidence**
- Resting assured in God's nature, goodness, purpose, plan, process and provisions
- Transparency and effectiveness
- Proceeding in faith one step at a time

- Truth instead of distortion as a basis for decision making
- Transparent relationships instead of isolation
- Community instead of destructive competition

✚ *When you hear the word "worship" what do you think of? Check all that you think of as worship:*

\_\_\_\_ *Praying*

\_\_\_\_ *Building: cathedral, worship center, church*

\_\_\_\_ *Meditation*

\_\_\_\_ *Fellowshipping with people*

\_\_\_\_ *Giving*

\_\_\_\_ *Singing*

\_\_\_\_ *Preaching*

\_\_\_\_ *Worship service*

\_\_\_\_ *Large group of people worshiping*

\_\_\_\_ *Other* _____

All of the above can be elements of worship. What we really hoped you would do is to write "God" in the "Other" space. Worship is all about God. In the Bible worship is always pictured as a human response to God's revelation of Himself. The English word *worship* comes from the Anglo–Saxon word *weorthscipe* or worth–ship. It means to bow down and adore the One who is worthy. Worship is both individual and corporate. Individual worship is the foundation of corporate worship.

Jesus spoke directly about worship three times, and those instances will form the basis of our study today.

Satan's temptations of Jesus were all attempts to get Jesus to focus on Himself and serve Himself. Read again the third temptation of Jesus.

> Next the Devil took Him to the peak of a very high mountain and showed Him the nations of the world and all their glory. "I will give it all to you," he said, "if You will only kneel down and worship me." "Get out of here, Satan," Jesus told him. "For the Scriptures say, 'You must worship the Lord your God; serve only Him.' "Then the Devil went away, and angels came and cared for Jesus" (Matthew 4:8–11, NLT).

Jesus knew that He had come to earth to be inaugurated as Lord of the earth. The question was how. Satan tempted Him to take the "easy" road of just falling down and worshiping him instead of giving His life on the cross as a sacrifice for sin. Satan offers the same thing to you in a different form. Have you sensed Satan offering you any of the following?

✝ *Check any of the following that have even briefly been a temptation for you to Edge God Out.*

| | |
|---|---|
| _____ The job you have always wanted | _____ Wealth |
| _____ Acclaim or fame | _____ Things that give status |
| _____ Influence over people | _____ A degree or title |
| _____ A person you loved | _____ Respect |

Jesus answered the temptation with Scripture. The Word of God is our source of strength when we are tempted. Jesus went back to the first four commandments that all relate to the worship of God.

✝ *Read in your Bible the first four commandments (Exodus 20:3-8). Take a few moments and think of as many modern applications as possible for each one. Then stop and worship God as He commands.*

Satan comes to us to tempt our selfish hearts with promises of the world—promises of wealth, fame, pleasure, or significance. If we are self–serving we are ripe pickings. We must answer as Jesus did. *"You must worship the Lord your God; serve only Him."* Only as we worship God are we able to break the cycle of serving self. How do you break that cycle of being centered on self? As Jesus did—worship God only.

## WORSHIP GOD WITH YOUR WHOLE HEART

> When a lawyer asked Jesus what the greatest commandment was Jesus replied: "The most important one" answered Jesus, "is this: 'Hear, O Israel, the Lord our God, the Lord is one. Love the Lord your God with all your heart and with all your soul and with all your mind and with all your strength'." —Mark 12:29–31

Worship is a heart issue. All the forms and kinds of worship are empty if your heart isn't in it. In the Bible people worshiped when they saw God or some evidence of God's presence, power, or worth. So worship starts with God and ends with God. We respond to His initiative. Worship means to bow down or to serve. Worship is an act of reverence and has the root idea of trembling or fear.

Jesus' second use of the word "worship" was in relation to people who went through the forms of worship in a public setting without engaging their hearts in response to God's revelation. By public worship we mean the ordered response of the believing community to the revelation of Almighty God, who alone is worthy of our devotion, praise, prayers, and thanksgiving. Because it is a shared public response it is even more open to misuse.

✝ *Think back on the most recent corporate worship experience you had and try to remember how many times your mind wandered to your work, home, relationships, responsibilities. Jesus quoted Isaiah concerning inappropriate corporate worship. Read what Jesus said and ask Him to evaluate how He sees your personal worship in the corporate worship setting. Write what you sense He is saying to you about it.*

*You hypocrites! Isaiah was right when he prophesied about you: "'These people honor Me with their lips, but their hearts are far from Me. They worship Me in vain; their teachings are but rules taught by men.'" Jesus called the crowd to Him and said, "Listen and understand. What goes into a man's mouth does not make him 'unclean,' but what comes out of his mouth, that is what makes him 'unclean'." —Matthew 15:7–11*

_____

_____

_____

✝ *Jesus' third mention of worship was to the woman at the well. Read their conversation in John 4:19-26 and think about what the heart of worship is.*

*"Sir," the woman said, "I can see that You are a prophet. Our fathers worshiped on this mountain, but you Jews claim that the place where we must worship is in Jerusalem." Jesus declared, "Believe Me, woman, a time is coming when you will worship the Father neither on this mountain nor in Jerusalem. You Samaritans worship what you do not know; we worship what we do know, for salvation is from the Jews. Yet a time is coming and has now come when the true worshippers will worship the Father in spirit and truth, for they are the kind of worshippers the Father seeks. God is spirit, and His worshippers must worship in spirit and in truth." The woman said, "I know that Messiah" (called Christ) "is coming. When He comes, He will explain everything to us." Then Jesus declared, "I who speak to you am He."*

✝ *Respond to the following: God is seeking people to worship Him but on His terms—in spirit and truth. By "spirit" He means with all your heart. By "truth" He means according to His revelation of Himself in His Word. Rate yourself on your worship of Him by circling the appropriate number using 5 as the best:*

|  |  |  |  |  |  |
|---|---|---|---|---|---|
| **In Spirit** | 1 | 2 | 3 | 4 | 5 |
| **In Truth** | 1 | 2 | 3 | 4 | 5 |

## DEPEND ON GOD COMPLETELY

To Exalt God Only we must worship Him above all, rely on Him as the source of our self–esteem and security, and honor Him as omniscient audience for our decisions. Jesus is the supreme example of this second emphasis of depending on God, the Father, as His source for everything—including self–esteem and security.

✚ *Read the following Scriptures and answer the questions:*

*Jesus said to them, "My Father is always at His work to this very day, and I, too, am working." — John 5:17*

**1. Who took the initiative in what Jesus did?** _____

Jesus gave them this answer: *"I tell you the truth, the Son can do nothing by Himself; He can do only what He sees His Father doing, because whatever the Father does the Son also does. For the Father loves the Son and shows Him all He does. Yes, to your amazement He will show Him even greater things than these . . . By Myself I can do nothing; I judge only as I hear, and My judgment is just, for I seek not to please Myself but Him who sent Me." — John 5:19–20, 30*

**2. Who was the source of His vision, direction, power, and work?** _____

*"The words I say to you are not just My own. Rather, it is the Father, living in Me, who is doing His work. Believe Me when I say that I am in the Father and the Father is in Me; or at least believe on the evidence of the miracles themselves. I tell you the truth, anyone who has faith in Me will do what I have been doing. He will do even greater things than these, because I am going to the Father. And I will do whatever you ask in My name, so that the Son may bring glory to the Father. You may ask Me for anything in My name, and I will do it." — John 14:10–14*

**3. Who provided the words and did the works that Jesus did?** _____

Jesus did not take the initiative in anything. He watched what the Father did . . . and did it. He said what He heard the Father say . . . and repeated it. How often do you take the initiative instead of asking God's guidance? How many of your words are God's words?

**4. What is your source of direction, power, and work?** _____

**5. Will you make God your source to fulfill all your need? Will you rely on Him?** _____

In Week 6 we will talk about the Habits that help you daily to worship God and rely on Him.

## EXALT GOD AS YOUR ONLY AUDIENCE AND JUDGE

True worship means that your eyes are on God and not on others. He is our audience of One; everyone else is in the cast. Jesus was scathing in His judgment of the Scribes and Pharisees, whom He called hypocrites because they did their good deeds to be seen by men.

✚ *Read what Jesus said and underline the four things these hypocrites did to be seen by people.*

*"Everything they do is done for men to see: They make their phylacteries wide and the tassels on their garments long; they love the place of honor at banquets and the most important seats in the synagogues, they love to be greeted in the marketplaces and to have men call them 'Rabbi'." —Matthew 23:5–7*

Don't do acts of worship for people. Instead, Jesus said acts of worship were to be done in secret for

Him to see rather than for you to make it a show before people.

✝ *Read Matthew 6:1-8, 16-18 and write specific ways you will worship God as your audience instead of performing for other people.*

1. Giving _____

2. Praying _____

3. Fasting _____

[1]*"Be careful not to do your 'acts of righteousness' before men, to be seen by them. If you do, you will have no reward from your Father in heaven.*

[2]*"So when you give to the needy, do not announce it with trumpets, as the hypocrites do in the synagogues and on the streets, to be honored by men. I tell you the truth, they have received their reward in full.* [3]*But when you give to the needy, do not let your left hand know what your right hand is doing,* [4]*so that your giving may be in secret. Then your Father, who sees what is done in secret, will reward you.*

[5]*"And when you pray, do not be like the hypocrites, for they love to pray standing in the synagogues and on the street corners to be seen by men. I tell you the truth,* they have received their reward in full. [6]*But when you pray, go into your room, close the door and pray to your Father, who is unseen. Then your Father, who sees what is done in secret, will reward you.* [7]*And when you pray, do not keep on babbling like pagans, for they think they will be heard because of their many words.* [8]*Do not be like them, for your Father knows what you need before you ask Him. . . .* [16]*"When you fast, do not look somber as the hypocrites do, for they disfigure their faces to show men they are fasting. I tell you the truth, they have received their reward in full.* [17]*But when you fast, put oil on your head and wash your face,* [18]*so that it will not be obvious to men that you are fasting, but only to your Father, who is unseen; and your Father, who sees what is done in secret, will reward you."*

## BE AWARE THAT GOD IS WATCHING YOU

Our tendency is be aware only of people who watch us. When we recognize that God is our Audience and Judge it affects everything we do. All of life becomes a worship experience if you are always aware of His presence and doing everything to His glory.

✝ *Read Psalm 139:1-12 and meditate on the God who watches you. Think about how you are to live since you are always in His presence.*

*O Lord, You have searched me and You know me.*

*You know when I sit and when I rise; You perceive my thoughts from afar.*

*You discern my going out and my lying down;*

*You are familiar with all my ways.*

*Before a word is on my tongue You know it completely, O Lord.*

*You hem me in—behind and before; You have laid your hand upon me.*

*Such knowledge is too wonderful for me, too lofty for me to attain.*

*Where can I go from Your Spirit? Where can I flee from Your presence?*

*If I go up to the heavens, You are there; if I make my bed in the depths, You are there.*

*If I rise on the wings of the dawn, if I settle on the far side of the sea,*

*even there Your hand will guide me, Your right hand will hold me fast.*

*If I say, "Surely the darkness will hide me and the light become night around me," even the darkness will not be dark to You;*

*the night will shine like the day, for darkness is as light to You.*

✝ *Did you stop and meditate and ask God to make you aware of His presence and prominence in your life? If not, do so now.*

## GIVE GOD THE CREDIT AND THE GLORY

Leaders get a lot of credit for things they had little to do with. Of course, they also get blamed for things with which they had nothing to do. Mature leaders give God the credit for what He does and the glory for Who He is. We need to give Him the credit and the glory in our hearts as well. Many are effusive in their praise of God to others, but in their hearts they reserve a throne for Self.

✝ *Read Revelation 5:6-14 and take a few minutes to worship.*

✝ *Read again the first three steps in EGO's Anonymous and make them a prayer.*

**Step 1.** I admit that on more than one occasion I have allowed my ego needs and drive for earthly success to negatively impact my role as a leader and that my leadership has not been the servant leadership that Jesus modeled.

**Step 2.** I've come to believe that God can transform my leadership motives, thoughts, and actions to the servant leadership that Jesus modeled.

**Step 3.** I've made a decision to turn my leadership efforts to God and to become an apprentice of Jesus and the servant leadership He modeled.

# Becoming a *Servant Leader*

## HOW TO BE A SERVANT

The best way to Exalt God Only is to be His servant. We hope you have a desire to be one, but how do you become a servant? Again, Jesus is our example.

✝ *Read Philippians 2:3-8 below and write in your own words after each section a positive action that you can take today to have the servant attitude of Christ.*

*Do nothing out of selfish ambition or vain conceit, but in humility consider others better than yourselves. (vs. 3)*

_____

_____

_____

_____

*Each of you should look not only to your own interests, but also to the interests of others. (vs. 4)*

_____

_____

_____

_____

*Your attitude should be the same as that of Christ Jesus: Who, being in very nature God, did not consider equality with God something to be grasped, but made Himself nothing, taking the very nature of a servant, being made in human likeness. And being found in appearance as a man, He humbled Himself and became obedient to death—even death on a cross! (vs. 5–8)*

_____

_____

_____

_____

A servant has no rights—only the privilege to serve. Jesus made this clear in His parable of a servant in Luke 17:7–10 below.

✚ *Read the verses below and match the verses with the rights the servant gave up by drawing a line between the ones that match.*

**1. The right to self–aggrandizement**

> 7"Suppose one of you had a servant plowing or looking after the sheep. Would he say to the servant when he comes in from the field, 'Come along now and sit down to eat'?

**2. The right to self–pity**

> 8 Would he not rather say, 'Prepare my supper, get yourself ready and wait on me while I eat and drink; after that you may eat and drink'?

**3. The right to self–gratification**

> 9 Would he thank the servant because he did what he was told to do? 10 So you also, when you have done everything you were told to do, should say, 'We are unworthy servants; we have only done our duty'."

Jesus' point is clear. The servant gave up the right to self–pity when he was not invited to eat although he had been working in the fields all day. He gave up the right to self–gratification when he had to prepare the master's meal instead of eating himself. The servant gave up the right to self–aggrandizement when finished, because Jesus said he had only done his duty and was an unprofitable servant. This seems harsh to us today, but it was the norm for a servant in that era and was accepted by Jesus' hearers. The rights of our Master are absolute, and when we voluntarily become His servants we give up our rights. We are following Jesus' example of surrendering His rights as God to become a man and to die for our sins.

Avery Willis relates how God impressed these servant roles on him while he was serving as the president of the Indonesian Baptist Theological Seminary. Here is the story:

"One morning during my quiet time I was reading through Matthew's gospel when I got to Chapter 23. I almost skipped it because I knew it was about the scribes, Pharisees, and hypocrites, and I didn't think it applied to me. I seemed to hear the Lord say, "No, don't skip it. Camp here a while. I want to talk to you."

### ✛ Read Matthew 23:1-15 (KJV) and Avery's responses in this dialogue:

³All therefore whatsoever they bid you observe, that observe and do; but do not ye after their works: for they say, and do not.

"Okay, Lord, I understand that the teachers were teaching what was right but that they weren't practicing it. I will be sure to practice what I preach."

⁴For they bind heavy burdens and grievous to be borne, and lay them on men's shoulders; but they themselves will not move them with one of their fingers.

"Oh, I see. If I require others to do what I am not willing to do, then I am just laying heavy burdens on them that I am not willing to carry myself. Okay, I commit to practice what I teach and not teach what I am not willing to practice."

⁵But all their works they do for to be seen of men: they make broad their phylacteries, and enlarge the borders of their garments, [6]And love the uppermost rooms at feasts, and the chief seats in the synagogues, [7] And greetings in the markets, and to be called of men, Rabbi, Rabbi.

"I agree that You are not pleased when I do things for people to see, seek to be recognized as a leader at ceremonies, or when I love to be greeted with titles."

⁸But be not ye called Rabbi: for one is your Master, even Christ; and all ye are brethren.

"What is a Rabbi today? A professor (which I am), or a doctor (which I am)! You mean that I am not supposed to let people call me those titles? Those titles are important to get people to listen to me when I teach. How can I get people to follow me without the credentials?"

⁹And call no man your father upon the earth: for one is your Father, which is in heaven.

"But Lord, I have tried for several years to train people to call me 'bapak' [Or, father, in Indonesian] because here everyone goes by family titles, and that is better than 'tuan' which they only use for foreigners. Of course, I like the respect that fathers receive in this culture. Fathers expect people to listen to them and to follow them because they have more experience than others. I guess that is strike two! I missed on both of these two commands."

¹⁰Neither be ye called masters: for one is your Master, even Christ.

"What is a master in this society? It's a leader. But, Lord, I have been elected as the leader. If I can't use 'professor' or 'doctor' that show I know more than the students, and I can't use 'father' to show that I have more experience than they do, or if I can't use 'leader' to show my leadership role, how can I get people to follow me?"

¹¹The greatest among you will be your servant. [12] For whoever exalts himself will be humbled, and whoever humbles himself will be exalted.

"Oh, Lord Jesus, now I see it. You were the greatest but You became a servant. Because You were a servant the disciples were willing to follow, serve, and even die for You. Make me a servant. I'll get people to call me by my first name; I'll not use my position or role to get people to follow me. I'll follow You and then Your true disciples will follow me."

¹⁵Woe unto you, scribes and Pharisees, hypocrites! for ye compass sea and land to make one proselyte, and when he is made, ye make him twofold more the child of hell than yourselves.

"Wow, now I understand why. If people follow others because they have a title, or more experience, or a position, then the followers will become proselytes, not disciples. And proselytes are sterile. People will follow them but they won't reproduce, because they are looking for the same things they have—titles, positions, or power. They follow only for what they can get from the leader instead of following because of what the leader is."

"Then I remembered what happened when we made radical changes in the seminary. We had phased out the campus program partly because the students were not willing to go to the rural areas to plant churches where the harvest was. The students, teachers, and pastors were upset. We missionaries also had made some sacrificial changes in our lifestyles such as selling some of the large houses we lived in and beginning to ride bicycles like the Indonesian pastors rode. When they finally got to the place where we could talk openly with them about their reactions they said, 'We didn't want you to sell your houses or ride bicycles instead of cars. We just want what you've got!' Did you catch it? They wanted what we *had* rather than what we *were*.

"A couple of weeks after reading Matthew 23 I took our family on a vacation on the south coast of Java. We had rented a bungalow with two bedrooms with twin beds in them. We have five children so it was obvious that some of us would need to sleep on the floor. We knew that and had brought sleeping bags. The question was, 'Who is going to sleep on the floor?' The two youngest children, ages five and six, obviously would. I took the three teenagers to the other room and said, 'Kids, there are three of you and only two twin beds. You decide who sleeps on the floor and when.' I walked out and left them to work it out. I came back by the room a few minutes later and you can't imagine the argument that was going on about who was to sleep on the floor. Just as I passed the door the senior in high school said, 'Well, seniority ought to count for something!' Each of them had an excuse for their not sleeping on the floor. I didn't stop them from debating. I just walked down the beach scratching my head and asking myself, 'What makes my children like that?' Then it dawned on me that I had taught by my example exactly the opposite of being a servant. I had reasoned that everyone knew that parents ought to get a bed!

"That night at dinner I said to the teenagers, 'Sherrie, tonight you sleep in the room with Mom; I'm going to sleep on the floor.' Their attitude totally changed and they said, 'Oh, no, Dad. We've got it all worked out.' That is how Jesus taught me to be a servant."

✚ *Reflect on Matthew 23 and Avery's experience and answer the following questions:*

1. *What is God saying to you about being His servant?*

_____

_____

_____

2. *What will you do today to apply these teachings to your life?*

_____

_____

Avery learned from that experience the importance of becoming a servant leader. He has carried the tract printed below in his Bible ever since to remind himself that he is a servant who has given up his rights.

✠ *Read the tract printed below that Avery keeps in his Bible and ask God to make you His servant.*

*If God has called you to be really like Jesus He will draw you into a life of crucifixion, and humility, and put upon you such demands of obedience that you will not be able to follow other people, or measure yourself by other Christians, and in many ways He will seem to let other good people do things which He will not let you do.*

*Other Christians and ministers who seem very religious and useful may push themselves, pull wires, and work schemes to carry out their plans, but you cannot do it; and if you attempt it, you will meet with such failure and rebuke from the Lord as to make you sorely penitent.*

*Others may boast of themselves, of their work, of their success, of their writings, but the Holy Spirit will not allow you to do any such thing, and if you begin it, He will lead you into some deep mortification that will make you despise yourself and all your good works.*

*Others may be allowed to succeed in making money, or may have a legacy left to them, but it is likely God will keep you poor, because He wants you to have something far better then gold, namely, a helpless dependence on Him, that He may have the privilege of supplying your needs day by day out of an unseen treasury.*

*The Lord may let others be honored and put forward, and keep you hidden in obscurity, because He wants you to produce some choice, fragrant fruit for His coming glory, which can only be produced in the shade. He may let others be great, but keep you small. He may let others do a work for Him and get the credit of it, but He will make you work and toil on without knowing how much you are doing; and then to make your work still more precious He may let others get the credit for the work which you have done, and thus make your reward ten times greater when Jesus comes.*

*The Holy Spirit will put a strict watch over you, and with a jealous love, and will rebuke you for little words and feelings, or for wasting your time which other Christians never seem distressed over.*

*So make up your mind that God is an infinite Sovereign, and has the right to do as He pleases with His own. He may not explain to you a thousand things which puzzle your reason in His dealings with you, but if you absolutely sell yourself to be His love slave, He will wrap you up in a jealous love, and bestow upon you many blessings which come only to those who are in the inner circle.*

*Settle the "I" forever. Remember, that you are to deal directly with the Holy Spirit, and that He is to have the privilege of tying your tongue or chaining your hand, or closing your eyes, in ways that He does not seem to use with others. Now when you are so possessed with the living God that you are in your secret heart, pleased and delighted over this peculiar, personal, private, jealous guardianship and management of the Holy Spirit over your life, you will have found the vestibule of heaven.*

(G. D. Watson in Living Words. Good News Tract Society, Chicago)

✠ *Read the first six steps of EGO's Anonymous below and reaffirm them in your heart. Be prepared to acknowledge them as your commitment in the group study session.*

*Step 1.* I admit that on more than one occasion I have allowed my ego needs and drive for earthly success to negatively impact my role as a leader and that my leadership has not been the servant leadership that Jesus modeled.

*Step 2.* I've come to believe that God can transform my leadership motives, thoughts, and actions to the servant leadership that Jesus modeled.

*Step 3.* I've made a decision to turn my leadership efforts over to God and to become an apprentice of Jesus and the servant leadership He modeled.

*Step 4.* I've made a searching and fearless inventory of my leadership motives, thoughts, and behaviors that are inconsistent with servant leadership.

*Step 5.* I've admitted to God, to myself, and to at least one other person the exact nature of my leadership gaps—when I behave in ways that do not make Jesus proud.

*Step 6.* I am entirely ready to have God remove all character defects that have created gaps in my leadership.

# How To Develop Humility

One of the basics of effective leadership is clarifying what good results will look like. Without a clear vision and understanding of where we are headed it's easy to get sidetracked or stop short of our final destination. This holds true for our journey to understand the heart condition of <u>E</u>xalting <u>G</u>od <u>O</u>nly.

Two key heart characteristics that grow out of becoming a servant are humility and God–grounded confidence. Today we will consider how to develop humility.

## HUMILITY IS A HEART ATTITUDE
### *Two Definitions of Humility*

"People of humility don't think less of themselves, they just think about themselves less."
— Ken Blanchard and Norman Vincent Peale, *The Power of Ethical Management*

"People with humility don't deny their power, they just recognize that it passes through them not from them." — Fred Smith, *You and Your Network*

As a leadership trait, humility is a heart attitude that reflects a keen understanding of your limitations as a leader to accomplish something on your own. It gives credit to forces other than your own brilliance or effort when a victory is won or an obstacle overcome. According to Jim Collins in his book *Good To Great*, a leader with a humble heart looks out the window to find and applaud the true causes for success and in the mirror to find and accept responsibility for failure.

Leading like Jesus requires humbly receiving and honoring the non–negotiable boundaries He has set for accomplishing true and lasting results. Jesus said, *"I am the vine; you are the branches. If a man remains in me and I in Him, he will bear much fruit; apart from me you can do nothing"* (John 15:5).

There is a difference in putting on the appearance of humility before men and being truly humble in the presence and purposes of God. True humility is being brutally honest about yourself. It is seeing yourself as God sees you. You are not to be piously humble about what He has given you or arrogantly proud of what you have or have done.

## HUMILITY IS TO BE ADMIRED IN OTHERS BUT NEVER CLAIMED FOR ONESELF

There is a story of a minister in Chicago at the turn of the nineteenth century who was having a great personal struggle with an addiction to pride. In attempt to cure himself, he decided to undertake the most humiliating experience he could devise. So he made up two sandwich board signs that read. 'I am the most wretched of prideful sinners and am worthy of your scorn" and wore them on his back and in front for entire day on a busy street corner in the middle of town. All day people mocked him, laughed at his foolishness, and totally humiliated him. When he went home that night the minister felt totally degraded and exhausted. After a hot bath, a simple meal, he went to bed. Just as he was drifting off to sleep he thought to himself. "That was a truly humiliating experience, but well worth it as the price of overcoming my pride" and as his final waking thought he said to himself, "I bet there isn't another minister in all of Chicago who would have willingly suffered the way I did today."

One of the first leadership lessons Ken Blanchard ever learned was taught to him by his dad when he came home after school all excited about having just been elected president of his seventh grade class. His dad had commanded a squadron of Landing Craft Infantry (LCI's) in some of the fiercest battles in the South Pacific during World War II during which over seventy percent of his men were either killed or wounded. When Ken told his dad the great news he replied, "Son, it is great that you have this new position, but don't ever use it as a way of getting others to do what you want. The best use of power is not to have to use it at all. People follow great leaders because they respect them, not because they have power."

Ken's mom was also a wise teacher in the meaning of what a healthy self–esteem should look like. She told him on more than one occasion, usually with the wagging of the bent forefinger, "Never treat anybody as if you are better than they are, but also never let anybody make you think they are better than you." Jesus demonstrated true confidence and humility in all He did. He supremely trusted His Father and represented Him fully, but He always gave the credit for His words and His works to the Father.

## HUMILITY WAS A LEADERSHIP QUALITY OF JESUS

The humility Jesus demonstrated did not arise from the lack of self–esteem, love, power, or ability. His humility came from the fact that He knew who He was, where He came from, where He was going, and who was backing Him. In fact, that is the point—knowing all this He humbled Himself and became a servant. For over three years He had taught servant leadership to His disciples, but they never could quite grasp it. Then at the end of His earthly ministry He demonstrated humility in a way that would touch their hearts and burn a picture of true humility into their minds.

✟ *Read John 13:1-17 printed in sections below and answer the questions about Jesus' humility.*

> *It was just before the Passover Feast. Jesus knew that the time had come for Him to leave this world and go to the Father. Having loved His own who were in the world, He now showed them the full extent of His love.*
> *The evening meal was being served, and the devil had already prompted Judas Iscariot, son of Simon, to betray Jesus. Jesus knew that the Father had put all things under His power, and that He had come from God and was returning to God; (John 13:1–3)*

✠ *Often we think humility comes from having a poor self-image, or at least it comes out of weakness and poverty. What did Jesus understand about Himself and His Father?*

1. *Jesus knew that* _____

2. *Jesus knew that* _____

3. *Jesus knew that* _____

4. *Jesus knew that* _____

Check your answers with the Scriptures above.

✠ *In contrast to what Jesus knew, Peter was not sure of much even though he tried to sound and act like he did. Read John 13:4-11 below. What did Peter NOT understand?*

*So He got up from the meal, took off His outer clothing, and wrapped a towel around His waist.*

*After that, He poured water into a basin and began to wash His disciples' feet, drying them with the towel that was wrapped around Him.*

*He came to Simon Peter, who said to Him, "Lord, are You going to wash my feet?"*

*Jesus replied, "You do not realize now what I am doing, but later you will understand."*

*"No," said Peter, "You shall never wash my feet."*

*Jesus answered, "Unless I wash you, you have no part with Me."*

*"Then, Lord," Simon Peter replied, "not just my feet but my hands and my head as well!"*

*Jesus answered, "A person who has had a bath needs only to wash his feet; his whole body is clean. And you are clean, though not every one of you." For He knew who was going to betray Him, and that was why He said not every one was clean. (John 13: 4–11)*

✠ *Check all the answers that apply about what Peter did NOT understand:*

_____ *Where Jesus came from*         _____ *What Jesus was doing*

_____ *Jesus' relationship with the Father*    _____ *Why Jesus was washing his feet*

_____ *Who Jesus was*

At the very least we would say that Peter did not understand what Jesus was doing and why Jesus was washing his feet.

✠ *Read the rest of the passage. What was Jesus teaching the disciples?*

*When He had finished washing their feet, He put on His clothes and returned to His place. "Do you understand what I have done for you?" He asked them. "You call Me 'Teacher' and 'Lord,' and rightly so, for that is what I am. Now that I, your Lord and Teacher, have washed your feet, you also should wash one another's feet. I have set you an example that you should do as I have done for you. I tell you the truth, no servant is greater than his master, nor is a messenger greater than the one who sent him. Now that you know these things, you will be blessed if you do them. (John 13: 12–17)*

✚ *Write "T" for True and "F" for False in front of the statements that show what Jesus was intentionally teaching the disciples:*

_____ *1. Because He was their Master and Lord, He was a servant.*

_____ *2. A good host washes the guests' feet.*

_____ *3. He expected them to follow His example.*

_____ *4. Cleanliness is next to godliness.*

_____ *5. That you need to wash others' feet only once.*

_____ *6. The servant is not greater than his master, nor the messenger greater than the one who sent him, the master is greater and shows it by being a servant.*

_____ *7. That one will be blessed if he is a servant.*

✚ *Jesus was intentionally teaching the principles listed one, three, six, and seven above. Have you ever washed someone's feet to demonstrate your humility and servant heart? Write one way you can serve someone today as a demonstration of your servant heart and humility.*

_____

_____

✚ *Today apply the way you just stated that you can serve someone as a demonstration of your servant heart and humility. Tomorrow come back and write what you did and the reaction of the people you served. Be sure to complete this activity before the group study session.*

What I did to show a servant heart and humility. _____

_____

_____

_____

The reaction of the people I attempted to serve. _____

_____

_____

_____

How I was blessed by serving those people. _____

_____

_____

_____

✠ *Read the next two steps of EGO's Anonymous and commit to doing them.*

**Step 7.** I humbly ask God to remove my shortcomings and to strengthen me against the temptations of recognition, power, greed and fear.

**Step 8.** I've made a list of people whom I may have harmed by my ego-driven leadership, and I am willing to make amends to them all.

✠ *My list of people whom I may have harmed by my ego-driven leadership:*

_____

_____

_____

_____

# Developing God-Grounded Confidence

Your degree of effectiveness in leading like Jesus will be proportional to the quality and level of your trust in God's promises and your obedience to His instructions. If your trust is weak or selective, so will be your ability to implement the sometimes counter-intuitive actions that Jesus calls you to do as a leader. If you trust in God to honor His promises, then you will be able to wait for Him even when all the indicators seem to point in the opposite direction.

## HOW DO YOU TRUST?

In researching the word "trust," Phil Hodges found descriptions of a variety of legal trusts in a law dictionary. They can be very revealing and challenging when applied to how you trust God.

✠ *Read the following descriptions of legal trusts and how Phil applies them to our trust in God. Can you think of situations when your trust in God has taken on one of these forms? Circle any that describe how you have trusted God.*

**Illusory Trust** — *It takes the form of a trust but has no real substance.*
You know all the Bible verses relating to trust and readily share them with others. You can even repeat them to yourself, but when the temptations of impatience or fear of earthly consequences bubble up you resume control and run on your own.

| | | |
|---|---|---|
| **Dry Trust** | — | *Never called on to perform its legal function.* |
| | | You are so addicted to your own efforts and ego that you rarely, if ever, call on God. |
| **Revocable Trust** | — | *The right to revoke the trust is always available.* |
| | | Commitment is only temporary and when you feel that your agenda is no longer being promoted, you revoke it. |
| **Limited Trust** | — | *Only covers a specific time period.* |
| | | During times of crisis you pull the emergency cord and seek to get extra help until it's over. Then it's back to business as usual with yourself in charge. |
| **Partial Trust** | — | *Only covers specific situations.* |
| | | You trust God for spiritual guidance, big–ticket items, and only where you feel you don't have expertise. |

*The Scripture says, "Trust in the Lord with all your heart and lean not on your own understanding; acknowledge Him in all your ways and He will keep your paths straight" (Proverbs 3:5–6).*

## ARE YOU TRUSTING GOD ENOUGH?

A young couple was asked to go to dinner with the president of the man's company and his wife. Walking down the street towards the restaurant, the president stopped suddenly on the sidewalk and bent over and picked up a penny. He stood quietly for about fifteen seconds and then moved on towards the restaurant. The couple noticed what the president did and wondered why he seemed to covet a penny.

Later in the meal, after the young couple felt comfortable with the president and his wife, they asked him about his behavior.

The president smiled and said: "Every time I see a coin on the ground I stop and pick it up and find the statement on it, 'In God We Trust.' Then I spend a few moments asking myself if I am trusting God enough. It is a great reminder to me that trusting Him is so important for us all."

✚ *Are you trusting God enough in your life? Will you make a commitment now to fully trust God and His promises?* _____

## EXAMPLES OF TRUST IN ACTION

Bill Bright, the Campus Crusade for Christ founder, taught a powerful lesson in God–grounded confidence. At the very beginning of his ministry, Bill and his wife, Vonette, made the decision that they would give God the glory for whatever they accomplished in His name. They also decided that if they gave God all the glory it would be fair to give Him all the problems as well. For over fifty years Bill and Vonette praised and trusted God, and He blessed their ministry with unparalleled results.

Putting your trust in God into action creates trustworthiness and becomes the foundation of trusting relationships and confident leadership.

Immediately after the tragic events of September 11, 2001, The Ken Blanchard Companies, experienced a 1.5 million dollar loss in expected revenue due to the wholesale cancellation of training contracts as the fear of flying gripped the nation. All the key financial indicators and conventional wisdom told Ken and his family they should lay off thirty to forty people to compensate for the losses. They had a choice to panic and go against their two top values of relationships and ethics or find other ways to meet the challenge.

They decided to follow the example of Bill and Vonette Bright. The Blanchard family chose to trust and remain trustworthy. By opening their books to the entire company and inviting them to help meet the challenge in creative ways, they were able to keep everyone working and eventually returned to profitability. As Ken explains it, "God's promises, contained in Proverbs 3:5 [quoted above] was a crucial factor in the leadership choice we made."

The story of Shadrach, Meshach, and Abednego in Daniel 3 is a perfect example of God–Grounded Confidence. When faced with the alternative of Edging God Out as the sole object of their worship or facing a horrible death by fire they responded by Exalting God Only. They said to the King "... *we do not need to defend ourselves before you in this matter. If we are thrown into the fiery furnace, the God that we serve is able to save us from your hand, O King. But even if He does not, we want you to know O King that we will not serve your gods or worship the image of gold you have set up*" (Daniel 3:16–18).

✚ *Describe a time when you trusted God and His promises and He blessed you.*

_____

_____

_____

## THE RESULTS OF EXALTING GOD ONLY

Leading like Jesus requires developing a perspective and standard for moment by moment decision–making based on the way God sees things. God revealed Himself to us through the life and teachings of Jesus. He showed us how we can fulfill His purpose for our lives and glorify Him in the process. Such trust and obedience bring positive results in our lives. Reexamine the EGO diagram on Day 2 of this week. The results of Exalting God Only are:

### TRUTH INSTEAD OF DISTORTION AS A BASIS FOR DECISION—MAKING.

*Transparent relationships instead of isolation.*
*Community instead of destructive competition.*

The first step in developing a Lead Like Jesus perspective is to understand and honor your Christian leadership "blood lines." Through Jesus you have inherited certain specific rights, privileges, gifts, and obligations that are irrevocable as a member of God's family. *"God's gifts and His call are irrevocable"* (Romans 11:29). The degree to which you honor and apply them to your leadership choices will go a long way in determining if you will Lead Like Jesus.

Take a look at some of the elements of your Christian leadership heritage. Any successful attempt to Lead Like Jesus starts with knowing whose you are and who you are. It means acknowledging who God is and how you are related to Him through Jesus. It requires surrendering the use of the rights, privileges, and gifts you have received to accomplish the work God has set before you.

✝ *Consider the following statements and check the answer that most closely describes the level of impact each perspective currently has on your leadership decisions.*

1. I have been personally called and have accepted the invitation to enter into a special intimate relationship with Jesus Christ as my Savior, my Lord, my Teacher, and my Friend.
   *Low Impact* _____    *Moderate Impact* _____    *Strong Impact* _____

2. As a follower of Jesus I enjoy great privilege in personal access to His wisdom and provisions for living in harmony with God's plan and purpose for me.
   *Low Impact* _____    *Moderate Impact* _____    *Strong Impact* _____

3. I am the object of God's affection and through the blood of Jesus enjoy an inexhaustible supply of unconditional love, acceptance, and eternal value that is not at risk or dependent on my performance or the opinion of others.
   *Low Impact* _____    *Moderate Impact* _____    *Strong Impact* _____

4. I am a steward of time, talent, treasures, and opportunities to influence others that God has provided to fulfill His mission through my life and the lives of others.
   *Low Impact* _____    *Moderate Impact* _____    *Strong Impact* _____

5. I will be called to give account for the quality of my stewardship over my leadership choices and opportunities.
   *Low Impact* _____    *Moderate Impact* _____    *Strong Impact* _____

6. Every person I seek to lead is made in God's image and is precious in His sight.
   *Low Impact* _____    *Moderate Impact* _____    *Strong Impact* _____

7. My influence with others results in helping them accomplish the mission God has set before them.
   *Low Impact* _____    *Moderate Impact* _____    *Strong Impact* _____

8. The success of my leadership is not a matter of the scope of my influence or its impact, but whether it reflects surrender and obedience to what God wants me to do in His name.
   *Low Impact* _____    *Moderate Impact* _____    *Strong Impact* _____

✝ *In light of your responses, which truths do you see as crucial to begin believing and living by? Circle the numbers of the ones you need the Holy Spirit to transform for you to be able to Lead Like Jesus.*

✠ *Review the three results of Exalting God only and write the first one below.*

1. _____

2. *Transparent relationships instead of isolation.*

3. *Community instead of destructive competition*

### TRANSPARENT RELATIONSHIPS INSTEAD OF ISOLATION

Leaders operating out of pride and fear construct their own personal isolation booths and make it increasingly difficult for anyone to get through to them. Isolation and a fear of intimacy continue to thwart their efforts to become effective servant leaders in the image of Christ. The antidote for these barriers lies primarily in developing a surrendered relationship with Jesus and participating in truth–telling accountability relationships with people. Acting consistently out of a sense of humility and God–grounded confidence results in improved communications and improved information flow. Leaders who can acknowledge they don't know it all, and who demonstrate a willingness to listen and learn, multiply their own effectiveness.

When leaders are cut off, either by choice or by circumstance, from timely feedback and the insights of others, they often fall prey to managing their reputations instead of serving the best interests of their followers. Falling into an image–protecting mentality is easy for leaders who feel cornered by their own expectations and the expectations of others. Generals too far behind the lines, CEOs with too many informational gatekeepers, pastors desperately trying to conceal the stress of living up to unrealistic images of perfection—*all* shut out sources of information and help. They block transparent relationships and are prone to act out of their distorted views of reality.

The price of relational information is intimacy. It takes courage and ego control to have a willingness to ask questions and share information that might reveal your own shortcomings and vulnerability. Expressing your own needs and being willing to deal positively with the shortcomings of others places you in the position of being a true servant leader. Developing true trust and unconditional love allows people into your life.

The price for gaining confidence and humility is intimacy with God. Every day you need to surrender your pride and your fears to His guidance and sufficiency through preemptive prayer, solitude, and Bible study. These disciplines are as essential to your spiritual life as brushing your teeth and showering are to your physical and social well being.

Transparent relationships are based on good stewardship. Good stewardship can be defined as the wise care and active use of another's property for purposes set forth by the owner. Leading like Jesus entails honoring God by being accountable for developing, protecting, guiding, and providing for those He has put within your sphere of influence.

Imagine that a generous friend has invited you to make use of his lakeside cottage for your summer vacation. In his invitation he has made it clear that you should feel free to eat his food, sleep in the beds, and use his fishing equipment and anything else that would increase your enjoyment of your visit. Good stewardship entails making use of all that has been provided for the purposes the owner had in mind. As a good steward you would care for what you had been given to use (but not to own) and then return it in as good or better shape than when you received it. Intimate relationships with God and people depend on your being a good steward of the leadership that God and others have entrusted to you. God has provided for you the time, talent, treasures, and opportunities to lead others for His purposes and others' good. Self–serving leaders, on the other hand, satisfy their own ego needs for security and earthly success by exercising rights of ownership over people they don't own. They act as if the sheep are there for the benefit of the shepherd. Their actions isolate them from transparent relationships with those they seek to lead.

✠ *Review the three results of Exalting God only and write the first two below.*

1. _____

2. _____

*3. Community instead of destructive competition*

## COMMUNITY INSTEAD OF DESTRUCTIVE COMPETITION

Jesus modeled for us the essence of an effective servant leader as He developed community instead of fostering competition. He ate with, walked with, and talked with a wide variety of people of differing ages, genders, positions, levels of sophistication, and spiritual discernment. It was not just for their benefit, but for His as well. In His personal contact with the crowds He gathered information about what they were thinking. Jesus was not acting as a pollster seeking public approval, but rather He acted as a servant leader testing their level of understanding and determining the best way to meet their needs. Jesus created community by His commitment to truth, His unconditional love, and His transparent relationships.

✠ *Write the three key words from the statements about the results of Exalting God Only.*

1. _____

2. _____

3. _____

## INVITING GOD IN —

***Putting into Practice the Lead Like Jesus Twelve Step Program.*** The EGO barriers to having a servant heart only can be overcome when we come to the end of ourselves and invite God in to transform us through the power of the Holy Spirit. The process must always begin with surrender, proceed in trust, and involve stepping out in faith. Treating pride and fear as addictions provides a basis for understanding what it will take to overcome their daily impact on your leadership choices. Leadership is the accumulation of the day to day choices you make either to serve self or to serve God by serving others. Inviting God into the process outlined in the twelve steps, in the community of others in recovery from ego addiction, will guide you on the path from Edging God out to Exalting God Only.

✝ *Use the card for EGO's Anonymous to review all twelve steps for ego addiction. Apply the last four in your life today and be ready to report the results in the small group session.*

**Step 9.** I've made direct amends to such people whenever possible unless doing so would injure them or others.

**Step 10.** I continue to take personal inventory regarding my leadership role, and when I am wrong, I promptly admit it.

**Step 11.** By engaging in the disciplines of solitude, prayer, study of the Scriptures, and faith in God's unconditional love for me, I seek to align my servant leadership effort with what Jesus modeled, and to constantly seek ways to be a servant first and a leader second with the people I encounter in my leadership responsibilities.

**Step 12.** Having had a "heart attack" regarding the principles of servant leadership, I have tried to carry this message to other leaders and to practice them in all my relationships.

# LEAD LIKE JESUS

# WEEK FOUR

THE HEAD — *Leadership*

*Assumptions and Methods*

*"Do not conform any longer to the pattern of this world,*

*but be transformed by the renewing of your mind. Then you will*

*be able to test and approve what God's will is—His good,*

*pleasing and perfect will." —Romans 12:2*

## Whom Are You Following?
## Leadership Vision

The journey toward being a servant leader and leading like Jesus starts in your Heart with the surrender of your motivations and intent to serve God by serving others. It must travel through another internal domain, that of the Head, where your beliefs and perspective on leadership are stored.

✝ *In the space below summarize your basic leadership point of view.*

_____

_____

_____

Today we are going to discuss some new ways of looking at leadership and what it involves to lead. Every great leader has a specific leadership point of view that defines how they see their role and their relationships to those they seek to influence. In particular, we want you to first understand the servant leadership point of view modeled and taught by Jesus, and then we want you to learn what changes are required to align your own thinking about leadership with His.

When we talk about servant leadership, most people think that means the "inmates are running the prison" or the leader is trying to please everyone. Is that what Jesus meant by servant leadership?

✝ *Answer the following questions about servant leadership as Jesus modeled it.*

Did Jesus try to please everyone?          _____ **Yes** _____ **No**

When He washed the feet of the disciples and sent them out as His ambassadors, was He commissioning them to help people do anything they wanted?          _____ **Yes** _____ **No**

Of course the answer to both questions is "No." He was completely focused on pleasing His Father as His audience of One. That meant the preaching of the gospel and the salvation of mankind. And He sent His disciples out to help people understand the Good News and live according to the vision and the values of God's Kingdom, not just do whatever they wanted. Jesus made it very clear that what He was asking His followers to do in His name would not please everyone. He told them up front that they would be subject to all kinds of resistance and persecution for telling people what they did not want to hear. But in the midst of all that was swirling around Him, He stopped to bless the children, heal the blind men, call sinners to repentance, and help the downtrodden and oppressed. One of the ways Jesus pleased His Father was the caring way He treated people.

In your own season of leadership, you are called to the deal with the same reality. Following Jesus and leading as He led will mean you're serving a higher purpose and being held accountable at a higher level in a way that will not be universally understood or applauded. But at the same time you will do as He did and focus on people, because that was one aspect of the purpose the Father had in mind when He sent His Son to serve, not to be served.

## THE TWO ROLES OF LEADERSHIP

People who think servant leadership is all about "the inmates running the prison" or "trying to please everyone" don't understand that there are two parts of leadership that Jesus clearly exemplified:

1. A visionary role—doing the right thing with a focus on results
2. An implementation role—doing things right with a focus on people

Some people think leadership is all about the visionary role while management is about implementation. When such a distinction is made, management always seems to get a second class status when compared to leadership. We prefer *not* to distinguish between the two, and as a result, the visionary and implementation roles will both be thought of as leadership roles during this study. These two roles of leadership are directly related to how you view results and people.

✛ *Think of a situation in which you have been trying to accomplish a specific goal by working with other people. Evaluate your personal emphasis on results and people in this leadership effort. Place an X on the line below to indicate to what degree results or people are getting the greater emphasis.*

Results _____ People
          1   2   3   4   5   6   7   8   9   10

The "tyranny of the or" suggests that you have to chose between results and people. And yet, Jesus had a "both/and" philosophy. In fact, the most important concept in the Head section is learning to consider the growth and development of people as an end goal that's as important as achieving results. You don't have to sacrifice one for the other. Jesus did exactly what His Father called Him to do *and* also focused on the development of the people around Him.

The key is both/and.

## YOUR LEADERSHIP POINT OF VIEW

Have you ever thought about your leadership point of view? How do you view the role of leader, and what do you think are a leader's responsibilities? How are you to act as a leader, and how are you to effectively relate to the people with whom you work? Effective leaders have a clear leadership point of view and are willing to teach others.[1]

✝ *Take a few minutes and re-write your leadership point of view—what you think the role of a leader is and what are the most important things a leader should do.*

_____

_____

Let's now look at what it means to Lead Like Jesus in terms of the two leadership roles: vision and implementation.

✝ *Evaluate the two lists below that describe the vision and implementation roles of leadership. Underline one key word or phrase in each statement that focuses on the essence of the concept.*

### VISIONARY:

*Setting the vision with an eternal perspective.*
*Painting a compelling picture of the future.*
*Defining and modeling the operating values, structure, and behavior norms.*

### IMPLEMENTATION:

*Serving the ongoing needs of those involved in doing the work.*
*Creating the follower environment that inspires commitment to the vision.*
*Elevating the growth and development of people from a "means" goal to an "end" goal of equal importance to the product or service mission of the organization.*
*Developing a level of intimacy with the needs and aspirations of the people—to know them instead of just knowing about them.*

In the rest of the week's study we will show why *purpose, picture of the future, values, serving, follower environment, growth and development of people,* and *intimacy* are important to one of the leadership roles. You might have chosen other words or phrases that also are essential to the two concepts. It all adds up to understanding the difference between leadership "success" and "effectiveness." *Success* can involve accomplishing short–term goals to the long–range detriment of those engaged in creating the success. *Effectiveness* on the other hand accomplishes the long–range growth and development of those involved in producing the desired end as well as the result itself. Leading like Jesus means we major on long–range effectiveness instead of short–term success.

[1] Noel M. Tichy, *The Leadership Engine* (New York: Harper Business, 2002)

✝ *Write how you would evaluate the focus of your leadership point of view in terms of "success" and "effectiveness" as it was described above.*

_____

_____

**Leading at a higher level will require three things:**
1. *Effective leadership depends on whom you follow.*
2. *Sustainable servant leadership behaviors will only emerge as an expression of a committed and convicted heart.*
3. *As with all comprehensive theories of leadership, in leading like Jesus, the doing is the hard part.*

✝ *Think about your leadership point of view today, and commit to follow Jesus as your leadership role model and practice servant leadership.*

# Developing Your Own Vision

*No organization will rise above the passion of its leader.*
Servant leadership begins with a clear and compelling vision of the future that excites passion in the leader and commitment in those who follow.

## THE LEADERSHIP VISION

Effective leadership begins with a clear vision, whether you are talking about your personal life or the life of an organization. In practical terms a compelling vision has three parts.[2] To engage the hearts and minds of others you must be able to communicate three things:

**Your Purpose**
*What business are you in? Where are you going and why?*

**Your Picture of the Future:**
*What will your future look like if you are accomplishing your purpose? What will be accomplished if you succeed?*

**Your Values:**
*What do you stand for? On what principles will you make your ongoing decisions?*

---
[2] Ken Blanchard and Jesse Stoner, *Full Steam Ahead: The Power of Visioning* (Berrett–Koehler, San Francisco, 2003)

*A compelling vision tells you who you are, where you are going, and what will guide your journey.*

Let's first begin our discussion of vision by looking at how it relates to our personal lives as leaders.

## CLARIFYING YOUR PERSONAL VISION

Before seeking to influence the thinking and behavior of others as Jesus did, it is important to have a sense of your own personal vision. Who are you? What business are you in? Where are you going? How do you picture the future for yourself? What will guide your journey? What are your personal values? In helping you develop your own personal vision, we will use the personal vision that Ken Blanchard developed for himself.

## WRITING YOUR OWN PURPOSE/MISSION STATEMENT

A life purpose/mission is a statement that tells you who are and what your purpose on earth is. Richard Bolles, in his best–selling book *What Color is Your Parachute?*, suggests that there are three parts of writing a personal mission statement.[3] The first two are goals that you and all the rest of humanity should aspire to, while the third is unique to yourself.

The first part of any mission statement is to get to know God better in your life. Bolles says you cannot talk about your "calling" unless you first talk about the "Caller."

The second part of a personal mission statement is to make the world a better place for having been here. If you ask people whether they want to make the world a better place, they all smile and say "yes." Then when you ask them how they are going to do it, they get blank looks on their faces. The way to make the world a better place is through your moment to moment decisions as you interact with others. Someone yells at you as you are leaving the house in the morning—choice point: you can yell, too, or you can go back into the house, hug the person who yelled at you, and give them a good wish for the day. You get cut off on the way to work—choice point: you can chase them down the road and try to get even or you can pray for them. You make the world a better place by the moment to moment decisions you make as you interact with others.

The third and final aspect of a mission statement is unique to you. What is it you do, that when you do it, you lose track of time? That is probably why you are here on earth. The Lord did not put you here to fight yourself. To help you develop your own unique mission statement answer the following questions.

✛ *List some personal characteristics you feel good about. These will be nouns.*

Examples:

| | | | |
|---|---|---|---|
| *energy* | *charm/wit* | *sense of humor* | *good looks* |
| *physical* | *strength* | *enthusiasm* | *patience* |
| *servant* | *artistic* | *abilities* | *happiness* |
| *creativity* | *people* | *skills* | *listen* |

_____

_____

[3] Richard Nelson Boles, *What Color is Your Parachute?* ( Berkeley, CA: Ten Speed Press, 1983).

✝ *List ways you successfully interact with people. These will be verbs.*

Examples:

| | | |
|---|---|---|
| teach | study | manage |
| produce | lead | motivate |
| educate | love | plan |
| encourage | help | act |
| stimulate | inspire | sell |
| speak | care | build |
| convince | write | organize |

_____

_____

✝ *Write a description of your perfect world.*

Example: *"My perfect world is a place where all people know God, through a personal relationship with Jesus Christ and live according to the mission God has for their life."*

_____

_____

_____

_____

✝ *Combine two of your nouns, two of your verbs and your definition of your perfect world and write a first draft of your life mission statement.*

The nouns Ken picked were *"teacher"* and *"example."* The verbs were *"help"* and *"motivate."* His picture of the world is *"everyone would have the presence of God in their lives."*

As a result, Ken's mission statement is *"To be a loving teacher and example of simple truths that helps myself and others awaken presence of God in our lives."*

_____

_____

_____

_____

_____

_____

YOUR PERSONAL PICTURE OF THE FUTURE.

Your picture of the future suggests what your life would look like if you were living "on purpose" all the time. The way that Ken developed his picture of the future was by writing his own obituary. That might sound morbid, but it is actually a very helpful process. Ken became interested in writing his own obituary when he read about Alfred Nobel. His brother died and Alfred went to get his local paper in Stockholm, Sweden, to read what they said about his brother. Unfortunately, the newspaper mixed up Alfred and his brother, and he had the rare opportunity to read his own obituary over coffee. Some of you might remember that Nobel was involved in the invention of dynamite. What do you think the emphasis of his obituary was? Destruction and devastation. Talk about "destruction and devastation," that is how Alfred Nobel felt! He could not believe that he would be remembered by destruction. In his despair, family and friends gathered around him. They said to Alfred, "What is the opposite of destruction?" He said, "Peace." As a result he redesigned his life so that he would be remembered for peace and not for destruction. That decision launched the Nobel Peace Prize.

*The following is Ken's obituary:* "Ken was a loving teacher, an example of simple truths, whose books and speeches on leadership and management helped himself and others to awaken the presence of God in their lives. He was a caring child of God, spouse, father, grandfather, father–in–law, brother–in–law, godfather, uncle, cousin, friend, and colleague who strove to find a balance between success and significance. He had a spiritual peace about him that permitted him to say "no" in a loving manner to people and projects that got him off purpose. He was a person of high energy who was able to see the positive in any event. No matter what happened, he could find a learning or a message in it. Ken Blanchard was someone who could trust God's unconditional love and believed "he was the beloved". He valued integrity, walked his talk, and was a mean and lean 185–pound golfing machine. He will be missed because wherever he went, he made the world a better place for his having been there."

As you can tell, not everything in your obituary has to be true! Ken is not quite a "185– pound mean and lean golfing machine"! Your obituary is your "*preferred* picture" of the future.

✚ *In the space provided below, over the next few days, why don't you attempt to write your own obituary and then be ready to share it at your next group meeting? Listening to each other's obituaries could give you some new ideas about who you want to be in the world.*

_____

_____

_____

_____

_____

_____

_____

## YOUR PERSONAL VALUES

Your values are what you stand for. They drive your behavior. In developing your personal values remember three things:

1. Don't have too many values. Three to five are the most that you can handle if you expect your values to guide your behavior.
2. Prioritize your values. Life is about value conflicts. Sometimes you have to choose between your values. As a result, they need to be rank–ordered.
3. Your values have to have behavioral indicators. How will you know when you are living according to a value?

### What follows are Ken's personal values.

1. I value *Spiritual Peace* and I know I am living by this value when . . .
   I realize that I am a child of God and He loves me no matter what I do.
   I am grateful for my blessings.
   I pray and feel God's unconditional love.

2. I value *Integrity* and I know I am living by this value when . . .
   I am honest with myself or others.
   I walk my talk.

3. I value *Love* and I know I am living by this value when . . .
   I feel loving toward myself and others.
   I am compassionate.
   I feel love in my heart.
   I feel the love of others.
   I look for the love in others.

4. I value *Intelligence* and I know I am living by this value when . . .
   I do effective evaluation before I act or agree to do something.
   I spend ten minutes to organize my day and ten minutes evaluating my day.
   I spend two or three hours to organize my week/month.
   I learn to say "I choose not to . . ."
   I see the impact of a "yes."

5. I value *Joy* and I know I am living by this value when . . .
   I let my playful child express itself.
   I wake up feeling grateful for my blessings, the beauty around me, and the people in my life.
   I smile and am happy and laugh and kid.

✝ *After you have edited and refined your mission statement and your obituary, begin to identify and define your values in the spaces below.*

*I value:* _____

And know that I am living by that value when:

_____

_____

_____

*I value:* _____

And know that I am living by that value when:

_____

_____

_____

*I value:* _____

And know that I am living by that value when:

_____

_____

_____

*I value:* _____

And know that I am living by that value when:

_____

_____

_____

Bring your life mission statement, picture of the future, and operating values to your next study group. We recognize that for many of you this will be your first attempt at developing a personal vision. Our hope is that by the end of this group study you will have the three elements of a compelling vision well thought out.

Tomorrow we continue our discussion of a compelling vision but move from the personal perspective of vision to the organizational perspective of a vision. Please note that if your primary leadership role is in the home, your family is still an "organization" and much of what will be discussed can and will apply to your home.

# Developing a Compelling
# Vision for Your Organization

*"Whatever you do, work at it with all your heart, as working for the Lord, not for men, since you know that you will receive an inheritance from the Lord as a reward. It is the Lord you are serving."*
—Colossians 3:23–24

For many of us, learning to Lead Like Jesus involves working inside a larger organization where we are not in the position to define the overall purpose, picture of the future, and values. Even in such circumstances we have a responsibility to meet the needs of those in our care in a way that is compatible with the servant leader mandate we have from the One we follow, Jesus.

Avery Willis tells the Baptist missionaries he works with that if they fall out of bed at 2:30 A.M. he expects them to be able to recite the vision of the mission board before they hit the floor. If your people don't know where you are taking them and why, they can't be successful in implementation. If they don't understand the preferred picture of the future to which you aspire, they can't consciously contribute to it or shape it. If they don't see you living out the values you want them to use in their daily decisions they cannot make the right choices.

✚ *Write A for agree and D for disagree in front of the following statements:*

\_\_\_\_ In an organization without a vision, activity is expected but progress is optional.
\_\_\_\_ Without a sense of purpose a life is spent but not invested.
\_\_\_\_ A river without banks is just a large puddle.
\_\_\_\_ If you accomplish your mission it doesn't matter what happens to the people.

Does the organization you work with have statements of its purpose, picture of the future and values? One of the reasons organizations are bureaucratic is because no one knows what the organization does, where it's going, or what should guide its journey.

✚ *Write your organization's purpose, picture of the future and values. You may choose your business, your church, your family, or your group as your organization.*

What is your organizational purpose/mission? _____

_____

What is your organizational view of the future that can excite your people?

_____

_____

_____

What operating values can your customers/clients depend on to guide your organization?

_____

_____

## YOUR ORGANIZATIONAL PURPOSE

What business are you in as an organization? What are you trying to accomplish? What is your mission statement? Jesus called His disciples, not to just become fishermen, but to a greater purpose—to become "fishers of men" (Matthew 4:19).

An effective mission statement should express a higher purpose for the greatest good that gives meaning to the efforts of each individual involved in your organization. If everyone does not understand your purpose or is not excited and passionate about it, your organization will begin to lose its way.

Ken Blanchard's father was a naval officer who retired early as a captain. When Ken asked why he left the service early, he replied, "I hate to admit it, but I like the wartime Navy a lot better than the peacetime one. Not that I like the fight, but in wartime we knew why we were there and what our purpose was. We knew what we were trying to accomplish. The problem with the peacetime Navy is that since nobody knows what we are supposed to be doing, too many leaders think their full–time job is making other people feel unimportant." That's what happens when you run an organization without a clear purpose.

## CREATING A CLEAR PURPOSE

When Walt Disney started his theme parks, he knew how to excite people, He said, "We are in the happiness business—we make magic!" That clear purpose drives everything the cast members (employees) do with their guests (customers).

Even if an organization states its mission, if that statement does not support a higher purpose, it will not motivate people. For instance, a congregation said they wanted to be a 24–hour–a–day church. The idea was that they had a nice facility and they wanted to keep the rooms busy. But attendance went down because the mission wasn't something people there got excited about. Your purpose needs to inspire people. It needs to get them into the act of forgetfulness about themselves.

At another church, the purpose is more inspiring to the congregation. At the beginning of every assembly, the minister says, "We believe that a close encounter with Jesus of Nazareth can transform lives. We're in the business of making Jesus smile." Backing up that statement are clear operating and theological values. Attendance has gone up. It's a place where a community comes together with the main purpose of making Jesus smile.

A clear purpose sets the direction for where you're going. Without a clear direction, leadership doesn't matter. In _Alice in Wonderland,_ Alice came to a fork in the road. Alice asked the Cheshire cat which way she should go. He asked where she was going. She said she didn't know, and the cat responded, "then it doesn't matter which way you go."

At the Center for Faithwalk Leadership, founded in 1999, we experimented with several different purpose statements in the first three years we were in operation. While they were helpful in explaining our general purpose—to help leaders move from success to significance by adopting the concepts of servant leadership—they weren't very inspiring. It wasn't until 2002, with much prayer and the help of some wonderful people at the Brandtrust organization, that we honed in on what we were all about. When we finalized our current purpose statement: *To challenge and equip people to Lead Like Jesus,* the impact was immediate and powerful. We got excited, our staff got excited, our National Board got excited, our customers got excited, and I think God was pleased, too. We have experienced a new sense of freedom and energy from knowing where we are headed and why. On a practical level, our purpose statement has become a powerful tool for helping us decide whether we are being tempted to stray into other missions or being provided with a new opportunity to do the work that God has given us to do.

If your organization does not have a purpose/mission statement or if it is not stated well, why don't you try to restate it? Laurie Beth Jones says a mission statement has three elements.[4]

A mission statement should be no more than a sentence long.

It should be easily understood by a twelve–year–old.

It should be able to be recited from memory at gunpoint.

✚ *Write or rewrite your organization's purpose/mission statement below using these criteria.*

_____

_____

_____

✚ *Now go try it out on a twelve-year-old and adjust it accordingly. Bring it to the study group meeting this week so you can discuss it along with others.*

## YOUR ORGANIZATIONAL PICTURE OF THE FUTURE

The second element of a compelling vision is your picture of the future. The question is, "What will the future look like if things are running as planned?" Jesus outlined this for His disciples when He charged them, "*Therefore, go and make disciples of all nations, baptizing them in the name of the Father and of the Son and of the Holy Spirit, and teaching them to obey everything I have commanded you. And surely I am with you always, to the very end of the age*" (Matthew 28:19–20). That was His picture of the future. At the Center for FaithWalk Leadership, our picture of the future is, *we want to establish the Lead Like Jesus movement everywhere, so someday everyone knows someone who truly leads like Jesus.* To accomplish that we envision the following:

1. Jesus adopted as the role model for all leaders.
2. All Christian churches are being led by Jesus–like leaders.
3. Every Christian being taught how to Lead Like Jesus.
4. Non–Christians are being drawn to Jesus by the practicality and the positive affect of Christians leading like Jesus.

---

[4] Laurie Beth Jones, *The Path: Creating Your Own Mission Statement for Work and Life.* (New York: Hyperion Press,1996), p3

Your picture of the future is what you would like to have happening if you are living according to your purpose and your values and everything is going well. What is your picture of the future? Are you clear about that? What does a good job look like? What will the future look like if things are running as planned? Providing vivid answers to these questions is important both to your people and to the organization.

The view of the future is what keeps people going when times are rough. It will prevent the organization from stopping short or arriving at the wrong destination. In your view of the future it is important to distinguish between "goals" and "vision." A "goal" is a specific event that once achieved becomes a piece of history to be superceded by a new goal. A "vision" or "view of the future" is an ongoing, evolving, hopeful look into the future that stirs the hearts and minds of people who know they will never see its end or limit. President John F. Kennedy challenged the American people with the *goal* to put a man on the moon by the end of the decade. When the moon landing was accomplished NASA lost its purpose until it established a new goal. Dr. Martin Luther King, Jr. challenged America to a *vision* in his "I have a dream" speech. He painted a verbal picture of a spiritually transformed nation, and more than forty years after his assassination Dr. King's vision continues to stir passion and commitment. Walt Disney's picture of the future for his theme parks was that guests would have the same smile on their face leaving one of their parks as they had six, eight, or ten hours earlier when they arrived. Being in the happiness business, that made sense.

Throughout His ministry Jesus spoke of what His Kingdom looked like. He continually talked about the kingdom—its values, teachings, parables, miracles and final fulfillment. He gave the disciples a clear picture of the future, and they committed themselves to it.

✠ *What is the picture of the future of your organization? Suppose that three years from now, word has gotten out about your organization. Your organization is walking its talk. People are calling and desiring to schedule a "best practices" visit. What will they see and what will people say? Write in your own words what you will say as you describe what has happened to fulfill your view of the future. Include the satisfaction of the people who work in your organization as well as the tasks being accomplished.*

_____

_____

_____

_____

_____

_____

_____

Tomorrow we will examine the third part of compelling vision for your organization—your values.

# The Role of Values in *Leading Like Jesus*

## YOUR ORGANIZATIONAL VALUES

The third element of a compelling vision is values—what will govern how you behave in your organization. "Values" are the non–negotiable principles that define character in a leader or an organization. Fewer than ten percent of organizations around the world have clear, written values. But values are important because they drive people's behavior while they work on your purpose and picture of the future.

Most companies that do have stated values either have too many values or they're not ranked in order. Research shows that if you really want to impact behavior you can't emphasize more than three or four values because people can't focus on more than that. Why is it important to state and prioritize your values? Because life is about value conflicts. When these conflicts arise, people need to know what values they should focus on. Walt Disney seemed to sense both of these things when he prioritized and rank–ordered his organization's operating values.

✚ *The four values Disney established for his Theme Parks are listed below. Write the priority you think he put them in from 1 to 4.*

_____ Courtesy      _____ The Show      _____ Efficiency      _____ Safety

Most people, when they think about Disney, put courtesy as the number one value, followed by efficiency because they think that making money would be next in importance. Then they usually put safety third and the show forth. Actually, safety is the first priority. "Ahead of courtesy?" you ask. Yes. Walt Disney knew intuitively that he must put safety ahead of courtesy, the show, and efficiency, because if guests left the park on a stretcher, they would not have the same smile on their faces leaving the park as they had when entering the park. When you reflect back on the fact that they are in the happiness business, it makes sense. Therefore if a cast member heard a scream while being courteous to a guest, they would excuse themselves immediately and focus on the number one value—safety.

The fact that your values must be rank–ordered is important because life is all about value choices. Unless a leader defines what takes priority, it will be left up to individuals to create their own orders of value priority, and that may lead away from fulfilling the desired purpose and picture of the future. As we develop our own value priorities it is important to know and understand what Jesus set before us as His non–negotiable priorities.

*When the Pharisees sought to test Jesus with the question, "Teacher what is the greatest commandment in the Law?" Jesus replied, "'Love the Lord your God with all your heart and with all your soul and with all your mind.' This is the first and greatest commandment. And the second is like it: 'Love your neighbor as yourself.' All the Law and the Prophets hang on these two commandments" (Matthew 29:37–40).*

Jesus rank–ordered the values;
1. Love God with all your heart, soul, and mind.
2. Love your neighbor as yourself.

What's your rallying call? What are your values? What do you stand for? What are the non–negotiables of your organization? How would you describe them in behavioral terms?

✚ *Write the key values of your organization as you understand them to be?*
*Rank them in order of importance.*

_____

_____

_____

_____

Does your organization have four or fewer ranked values? Were you able to write them? Most people cannot. Even if the organization has them, usually they are not rank–ordered or communicated adequately to the employees. True success in servant leadership depends on how clearly values are defined, ordered, and lived by the leader. Jesus lived His values of love of God and love of His neighbor all the way to the cross. "*No greater love has any man than to lay down his life for his friends*" (John 15:13).

Values even if they are rank–ordered will not drive the accomplishment of a purpose or picture of the future unless they are translated into behaviors. Clarifying how values are lived out in behavioral terms allows for accountability and measurement of progress. If your organization has stated values, or if you personally have stated your values, it would be a good exercise to write how you will know that you are living by those values.

✚ *Write several measurable behaviors that will demonstrate you are living by*
*your organization's values. Before you write them look at the example shown.*

_____

_____

_____

_____

_____

Be prepared to share your rank–ordered values in your study group session.

At The Center for FaithWalk Leadership our values priorities and the behaviors they signal there are as follows:

### Honor God in everything we do.

*We will know we are living by this value when we . . .*

Give God all the credit.

Relinquish all problems to His care.

Seek His face through:

Worshiping together.

Studying together.

Praying together.

Love one another as He loves us by:

Being a loving truth–teller.

Honoring each other's commitment.

Encouraging each other's health and well–being.

Proceed by boldly living the message.

### Build relationships based on trust and respect

*We will know we are living by this value when we . . .*

Trust each other.

Seek each other's counsel and involvement in decision making.

Support one another on goal accomplishment.

Engage in unfiltered conflict around ideas.

Commit to decisions and plans of action.

Hold each other accountable for those plans.

Focus on achievement of collective results.

Practice openness and vulnerability.

Use mistakes as opportunities to learn rather than punish.

### Maintain integrity and excellence in programs and services

*We will know we are living by this value when we . . .*

Filter every action through our purpose statement.

Use the Bible, with reference, as our primary source of guidance in the development of all materials and services.

Engage the best thinkers and practitioners of Jesus–like leadership in the work of The Center.

Seek and honor feedback from all stakeholders for continuous improvement.

Speak the truth and deal honestly in all our relationships.

### Practice sound stewardship

*We will know we are living by this value when we . . .*

Share financial statements with all stakeholders.

Budget and expand resources wisely based on our purpose and commitment to stakeholders.

Respond gratefully to our contributors.

Ensure our alliances and funding sources are committed and compatible with our purpose.

Implement sound financial and auditing practices.

Maintain a balance between serving customers and financial responsibility.

Implement effective use of time, talent, and resources.

## MAKING TOUGH VALUE CHOICES

Many of us will be or are already working in organizations and institutions that have established, even by default, a set of operating values. It is a reality of life that conflicts between organizational values and personal values will occur. What do you do when the values of the organization do not align with your own? You may realize this over time as you experience ongoing gaps between formal statements of policy and purpose and what is acted out on a day to day basis. You are faced with a choice to rationalize and justify compromising your values, to seek to be an active influence for change in the organization, or to leave.

Leading like Jesus does not include letting the organization change your values. The core of the temptation to compromise on your own values is likely to stem from EGO issues—particularly toxic fears, such as fear of rejection, fear of failure, fear of poverty, fear of ridicule, fear of confrontation, or fear of lost position. Jesus dealt with this dynamic of choice when He spoke of the impossibility of serving two masters at the same time. *"No servant can serve two masters. Either he will hate the one and love the other, or he will be devoted to the one and despise the other. You cannot serve both God and Money"* (Luke 16:13). He posed the ultimate challenge to compromise by spelling out the long–range price when He said, *"What good is it for a man to gain the whole world, and yet lose or forfeit his very self?"* (Luke 9:25) He also told us that we can trust in His promise never to leave us alone or outside the range of His care and concern for us.

Leading like Jesus does include the possibility of making a choice either to be an agent of change or to seek a more compatible environment. The appropriate response for your circumstance will depend on what God has in mind for you.

Phil Hodges recounts the following story from his own experience of having to decide whether to stay or leave an organization where he was experiencing a major values conflict with his boss.

AS THE SENIOR HUMAN RESOURCES MANAGER for a large manufacturing operation I had become increasingly troubled by the atmosphere of fear and dishonesty that was being generated by my boss who headed up the operation. Although he never treated me personally in a disrespectful manner, he regularly beat up on people who either brought him unfavorable news or didn't perform at his level of expectation.

Regrettably, his personal insecurities and unhealthy perfectionism worked their way into the soul of the organization, creating fear and a look–good–at–any–price mentality. Morale and ethics were at an all time low. During this same period I had the opportunity to take advantage of an early retirement package that would have resulted in my leaving the company several years earlier than I had planned. Because of the frustration and embarrassment I felt regarding the state of human resources in our organization, I decided to leave. I went through all the preliminary steps of signing the

necessary paperwork, and I pursued some interesting new career opportunities in teaching and consulting. Despite all of this, I was not at peace about whether to stay or leave. I had often prayed on the subject, but had received no immediate answer. On the Friday morning of the last day for turning in my retirement papers, I still was waiting on the Lord when I began my morning run around the neighborhood. I determined that I would not go back into the house until God showed me what He wanted me to do. I finished my regular two–mile route and found myself at my front door still without an answer. So I started running a series of two–hundred–yard laps in the street in front of my house while the neighbors were driving off to work. During the second lap I started to think of some Scriptures, mostly about Paul and his perseverance under trial, which eventually led me to believe that I should stay rather than leave my job. When I went to work and let the filing deadline pass, I had a great sense of peace about staying put, although the situation did not look promising.

The following Tuesday morning my boss returned from a business trip to headquarters, walked into my office, closed the door, and proceeded to tell me he had been removed from his job, effective immediately. When he told me who his replacement was to be, I called some friends back East to find out something about him. The word I got back was all positive. "An HR man's dream." "Highly ethical." "Poised professional." And "a very devout Christian." God is Good!

Over the next three years I was blessed to participate in a remarkable turnaround in the ethical and value environment of an organization, based primarily on the leadership of a true servant leader. The things I learned have been invaluable as a basis to helping others learn to Lead Like Jesus.

For me, the decision to stay and be part of the change was the result of trying to be open to what God had planned. What your experience will be I don't know. But I can encourage you to "Wait upon the Lord." What do you stand for? How do you want people to behave?

Life is all about choices. Choices are made based on your values, whether you admit it or not. You are a monument to the choices you have made over the course of your life. If you want to change your life, embrace the values of Christ, the servant leader.

✝ *Stop and pray. Ask God to show you your values and the ones He wants you to have. Ask Him to help you make the right choices based on your values.*

## Leading People

The traditional pyramidal hierarchy is effective for the first role of leadership—the visionary role. People look to the leader for vision and direction. While the leader should involve experienced people in shaping direction, the ultimate responsibility remains with the leader and cannot be delegated to others. In the diagram below the leader is responsible and the followers are responsive. This pyramid illustrates the concepts we've been discussing so far this week.

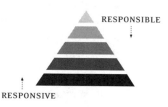

### IMPLEMENTING A CLEAR VISION

But now the pyramid must be turned upside down for the second role of leadership—the implementation of the vision. The people who have the primary contact with the public must be on top and the leader on the bottom supporting them. The implementation phase looks like this:

The implementation role of leaders—living according to the vision and direction—is where most leaders and organizations get into trouble. The traditional hierarchical pyramid is kept alive and well so that all the energy is moving away from the customers, up the hierarchies, because people feel they must please their bosses, leaving the customers neglected at the bottom of the hierarchy. This happens in a lot of organizations. In this environment, self–serving leaders assume "the sheep are there for the benefit of the shepherd." Jesus was talking against this kind of authoritarian hierarchy when He said, *"not so with you"* (Matthew 20:26).

If you don't turn the pyramid upside down, you have a duck pond. When there is a conflict between what the customers want and the boss wants, the boss wins. You have people quaking like ducks. [*Quack, quack*] "It's our policy." [*Quack, quack*] "I just work here." [*Quack, quack*] "Would you like me to get my supervisor?" [*Quack, quack*] Of course, as a Lead Like Jesus leader you don't want that. You want the pyramid turned upside down so the people closest to the customers can soar like eagles. Servant leadership really applies to your behavior in implementation, because now your job is to be responsive to your people and serve and help to be *responsive and responsible* and live according to the vision, accomplish the goals, and take care of the customers.

To do this, you have to get your ego out of the way. When Jesus washed the feet of the disciples, He was transitioning His focus from the visionary/direction part of leadership to the implementation role. As He did that, He was turning the pyramid upside down. He was not implying that they should go out and help people do anything they wanted. The vision was clear. He got it from the top of the hierarchy—His Father. As "fishers of men" they were to "go make disciples of all nations . . ." focusing first on loving God and then on loving their neighbors. But when it came to implementing this vision, Jesus wanted the disciples to be servant leaders. He said the least shall be the greatest, the last shall be first, and the one who would be great would be the servant. In this scenario you have the people closest to the customer—the object of your business—with all the power and all the capabilities to make decisions and to solve the problems. Now the people can soar like eagles rather than quack like ducks.

Horst Schulze helped create The Ritz Carlton—one of the great service organizations in this country. He so believed in turning the pyramid upside down that every frontline associate under his leadership had a $2,000 discretionary fund that they could use to solve customer problems without consulting anybody. That's really putting power with the people! Horst played a major role in setting the vision, but after everyone was clear that they wanted to be the number one service company in the world, he turned the pyramid upside down and became the head cheerleader, supporter, and encourager. In the process, he loved to collect "eagle" stories. One of Ken Blanchard's favorites is the following:

An executive staying in one of the Ritz properties in Atlanta was scheduled to fly to Honolulu to give a major speech to his international company the next afternoon. He was a little disorganized leaving and left his computer in the room. It had all the displays and information that he needed for his talk. Discovering the computer's absence on the way to the airport, he panicked and tried to change his reservation, but had no luck. He called back to the Ritz, told them where they would find his computer, and insisted that housekeeping overnight the computer to Hawaii with a guaranteed early delivery the next day. The following morning Horst was wandering through the Atlanta hotel and got to housekeeping. He said, "Where's Mary today?" He was informed that she was in Hawaii. "Hawaii?" he asked. "What is she doing in Hawaii?" Her co-workers explained that one of the guests had left his computer in his room and needed it for a speech that day, and Mary didn't trust the shipping service anymore.

Did the Ritz Carlton make any money on that deal? No, but what did they make? They made a Raving Fan customer. You might think that Mary wanted a little vacation in Hawaii, but she flew back on the very next flight. What do you think was waiting for her? Flowers and a letter of commendation! That's an incredible example of turning the pyramid upside down and servant leadership in practice.

✝ *Answer the following questions in your own words.*

**What are the advantages of turning the pyramid upside down at the time of implementation?**

_____

_____

**What keeps your organization from turning the pyramid upside down at time of implementation?**

_____

_____

**What will happen in your organization if you make the development of people an equal priority with accomplishing the vision?**

_____

_____

## SERVING THE VISION

Jesus was precise about the vision for His ministry. He was clear about the final exam. Once your vision is clear, and the final exam is set up, then you as the leader are to initiate day to day coaching. You prepare people to be able to pass the final exam, to live according to the vision. Leadership is not about power. It's not about control. It is about helping people live according to the vision. It's the vision—the purpose, picture of the future, and values—that everyone should serve.

Jesus said, *"The Son of Man did not come to be served, but to serve"* (Matthew 20:28). What did He come to serve? He came to serve the vision He had been given by His Father. He came as a teacher, as a leader, as a trainer to prepare people to go out and help other people live according to that vision. To do so, He served the people.

Ken Blanchard once followed Chuck Colson, founder of Prison Fellowship, on the platform at a conference. Colson pointed out during his speech, "All the kings and queens I have known in history sent their people out to die for them. I only know one King who decided to die for His people." That's the ultimate in servant leadership

As servant leaders, we are not asked to die for our people, but Jesus does say, *"Not so with you"* (Matthew 20:26) in terms of traditional hierarchical leadership. Servant leadership that He wants us to practice starts with a vision and ends with a servant heart that helps people live according to that vision.

## LEADING PEOPLE LIKE JESUS DID

When we put the Heart and the Head together in a Lead Like Jesus perspective, people come to the forefront and Self takes a backseat. How do you serve people in a way that reflects the Lead Like Jesus point of view? Jesus' prayer on the last night of His ministry (found in John 17) gives us some guidelines. Jesus knew His people intimately, He respected them profoundly, and He equipped them to be competent and confident leaders.

✝ *Read John 17:6-8 below and answer the question, "How did Jesus equip others by sharing information and being sure they understood the situation?"*

*"I have revealed You to those whom You gave me out of the world. They were Yours; You gave them to Me and they have obeyed Your word. Now they know that everything You have given Me comes from You. For I gave them the words You gave Me and they accepted them. They knew with certainty that I came from You and they believed You sent Me."*

_____

_____

_____

## EQUIPPING OTHERS BY SHARING VITAL INFORMATION AND INSURING UNDERSTANDING OF THE SITUATION

In today's world, almost everyone can access the same information as the leader can with few key strokes. The issue now is one of willingness to share information rather than logistics of sharing it. Practicing open communication and keeping people informed serves the implementation of the vision by building trust and commitment. Ego–driven leaders who are afraid of losing control or who are insecure in their positions tend to hoard information rather than share it. Following someone in the dark is a perilous experience and does not encourage followers to take initiative.

✚ *Read John 17:12 below and answer the question, "How did Jesus protect and equip His future leaders?*

*"While I was with them, I protected them and kept them safe by that name You gave Me."*

_____

_____

## PROVIDING PROTECTION AND COACHING FUTURE LEADERS

Jesus continued to support and interact with the disciples as they grew in competence and commitment. He provided a safe harbor where they could grow in understanding as they practiced right behavior and as their competence and commitment were developed, although imperfectly. He stayed with His followers until it was time for them to go out on their own, and even then He followed up with them.

✚ *Read John 17:11 and John 16:7 below and answer the question, "How did Jesus facilitate growth and the development of His followers by relinquishing control?*

*"I will remain in the world no longer, but they are still in the world and I am coming to You" (John 17:11). "Now I am going to the One who sent Me . . . It is for your good that I am going away. Unless I go away, the Counselor will not come to you but if I go, I will send Him to you" (John 16:7)*

_____

_____

## RELINQUISHING CONTROL TO FACILITATE GROWTH AND DEVELOPMENT

Knowing when to delegate is the fine art of servant leadership. Premature delegation isn't empowerment; it is abdication of responsibility. Continuing to micromanage once you have delegated prevents experimentation and growth. Jesus knew none of His disciples could step to the front as leaders like He intended for them to do (as portrayed in Acts) as long as He was with them. He often warned them that He would be crucified and that they would take up His mission. Only when He left them were they able to do it. However, He did not leave them alone. He promised, " . . . *surely I am with you always, to the very end of the age*" (Matthew 28:20).

✝ *Read John 17:13-18 below and answer the question, "How did Jesus make provision for the future well being of His followers?*

*"I am coming to You now, but I say these things while I am still in the world, so that they may have the full measure of My joy within them. I have given them Your word and the world has hated them, for they are not of the world any more than I am of the world. My prayer is not that You take them out of the world but that You protect them from the evil one. They are not of the world, even as I am not of it. Sanctify them by the truth; Your word is truth. As you sent Me into the world, I have sent them into the world. For them I sanctify myself, that they too may be truly sanctified."*

_____

_____

_____

## MAKING PROVISIONS FOR THE FUTURE WELL—BEING OF THOSE WORKING ON THE VISION

Jesus' prayer shows His deep concern for the future of His disciples. He provided them the full measure of His joy within them. He gave them the Father's Word. He prayed for their protection. He asked the Father to sanctify them as He was. He sent them into the world. He gave them everything they needed, although it was not everything they wanted at the beginning. He promised them, *"no one who has left home or wife or brothers or parents or children for the sake of the kingdom of God will fail to receive many times as much in this age and, in the age to come, eternal life"* (Luke 18:28–30).

As a leader you must do all you can to ensure the future well–being of those who are working with you. There is no higher calling for a leader whose followers have entrusted their days, years, and lives to his care than to lay down his life for them.

In summary, remember that servant leadership, as it relates to *The Head* (*Leadership Assumptions and Methods*) involves seven things. Check the statements you intend to practice.

1. Set the purpose or vision. \_\_\_\_

2. Communicate a compelling picture of the future. \_\_\_\_

3. Define and model the operating values, structure, and behavior that you want from people. \_\_\_\_

4. Create an environment of empowerment. \_\_\_\_

5. Move to the bottom of the pyramid to support those who are now responsible to serve. \_\_\_\_

6. Show respect for everyone. \_\_\_\_

7. Place the development of people on a par with the accomplishment of the vision. \_\_\_\_

*Jesus did all of these things. He was really clear with people about why He came, what the good news was, and what He wanted people to do. Then He modeled implementing servant leadership with everyone He met. "Go and do likewise" (Luke 10:37).*

# LEAD LIKE JESUS

## BEGINNING THE JOURNEY

## WEEK FIVE

### THE HANDS — *Changing Your Leadership Behavior*

*"Come follow Me," Jesus said,*

*"and I will make you fishers of men." –Matthew 4:19*

CHANGING THE WAY YOU LEAD Leading like Jesus is more than theory. Leading like Jesus is about changing the way you lead others. It means that as a leader you make a commitment to actually change your behavior to be more like Jesus. It means that you start asking the question: "What would Jesus do?" before you act as a leader. This week you will evaluate your actions as a leader and how you need to vary your leadership style based on the need of the person or persons you are leading. You will see from the Scriptures how Jesus varied His leadership style so that He could meet the needs of the disciples.

## Jesus: A Situational Leader

In the Week Four studies you learned that leading like Jesus means investing your life in the lives of the people you are leading. Today we want you to look closer at your own behavior as a leader. Modeling the correct behavior is crucial for a servant leader. As Avery Willis tells the leaders of *MasterLife Discipleship Training,* "You cannot teach what you are not practicing, any more than you can come back from where you have never been!" You must align your leadership behaviors to be like Jesus if you are going to become the leader God wants you to be.

The way you serve the vision as a *Lead Like Jesus* leader is by developing people so that they can work on that vision even when you're not around. The ultimate sign of whether you are an effective servant leader is not what happens when you are there, but what happens when you are not there. That was the power of Jesus' leadership—the leaders (the disciples) He trained to be fishers of men went on to change the world when He was no longer with them in bodily form. If you model your values and invest your time in developing others, you can leave a legacy of servant leadership behind when your own season of leadership is finished.

Jesus used a variety of leadership styles as He transformed and trained His disciples in the task of becoming fishers of men. A helpful framework for studying and applying the principles of leadership that Jesus modeled can be found in the concepts of *Situational Leadership II®*[5]. It appears to be a useful tool for not only describing what Jesus did to develop His disciples, but what He would do if He was working with people in your leadership assignments.

---

[5]*Ken Blanchard developed Situational Leadership with Paul Hersey in the late 1960's. It was in the early 1980s that Blanchard and the Founding Associates of The Ken Blanchard Companies created a new generation of the theory called *Situational Leadership II®*. The best description of this thinking can be found in Kenneth Blanchard, Patricia Zigarmi, and Dra Zigarmi's *Leadership and the One Minute Manager* (New York: William Morrow, 1985).

KEN BLANCHARD TELLS US WHY:

"The average leadership theory lasts in the marketplace five to seven years and then a new leadership approach comes into vogue. Not so with Situational Leadership. Paul Hersey and I started developing the concept in 1967 and yet today, over 35 years later, it is used worldwide more than at any other time. In searching for the answer, I found it in the Bible after I turned myself over to the Lord. In reading Matthew, Mark, Luke and John and interacting with knowledgeable believers, I realized that *Situational Leadership II®* describes exactly the way Jesus developed His disciples to carry on after He was gone. In other words, *Situational Leadership II®* is based on truth—Jesus' truth."

As a result we want to share *Situational Leadership II®* with you as you consider taking your good servant leadership intentions from your Heart, and your servant leadership point of view from your Head, and begin to extend your Hands to others and *Lead Like Jesus* in your daily interactions.

Before sharing *Situational Leadership II®* let us make some final comments about what leadership is and what it is not. As we said leadership is an *influence* process. Any time you attempt to influence the activities or behaviors of people to accomplish goals in a given situation you are engaging in leadership.

As Paul Hersey and Ken Blanchard have been saying for a long time:

"It is important to note that this definition makes no mention of any particular type of organization. In any situation in which someone is trying to influence the behavior of another individual or group, leadership is occurring. Thus, everyone attempts leadership at one time or another, whether activities are centered on a business, educational institution, hospital, political organization, or family. It should also be remembered that when this definition mentions 'leader' and 'follower,' one should not assume that we are talking only about a hierarchal relationship such as is suggested by a manager and a direct report. Any time an individual is attempting to influence the behavior of someone else, that individual is the potential leader, and the person subject to the influence is the potential follower, whether that person is the boss, a colleague (associate), direct report, a friend, a relative, or a group."[6]

The concept behind *Situational Leadership II®* is quite easy. First of all, there is no single "best" leadership style; it all depends on the situation. Secondly, the leadership style you use (as indicated by the amount of direction and support you provide) with someone should vary depending on the goal or task that person is working on and their development level (the amount of *competence*—or their knowledge, skill and experience—and *commitment*—or their motivation and confidence) on that goal or task. In other words, effective leadership involves matching the appropriate leadership style to the individual's developmental level. If all this sounds more complicated than we suggest, don't worry, we will make it all clear as we apply it the rest of the week and show you how Jesus varied His leadership style as He helped His disciples become "fishers of men." By the end of the week, you should be able to teach others all about *Situational Leadership II®* and how they can apply it in their leadership relationships.

---

[6]Kenneth H. Blanchard, Dewey E. Johnson, *Management of Organizational Behavior,* 8th Edition (Upper Saddle River, N.J.: Prentice-Hall, Inc., 2001) p. 79

## BELIEFS AND VALUES ABOUT PEOPLE

In sharing *Situational Leadership II®* with you, we are making some basic assumptions about people. Everything we teach you about *Situational Leadership II®* is based on three assumptions about people.

*1. People can and want to develop.*
*2. Leadership is a partnership.*
*3. People value involvement and communication.*

In order to become an effective situational leader, you have to learn three basic skills:

**1. Diagnosis**—*assessing developmental needs*
**2. Flexibility**—*using a variety of leadership styles comfortably*
**3. Partnering for Performance**—*working with others to reach agreements on what the leader and the individual need from each other*

✚ *Which of the three skills listed above relate primarily to the following roles? Write the number of the skill in front of the roles.*

_____ *The Leader*    _____ *The Follower*    _____ *Both the Leader and the Follower*

Were you able to determine that (1) Diagnosis relates more to the developmental needs of the Follower, (2) Flexibility relates to the leadership style of the Leader and (3) Partnering for Performance involves both roles? Diagnosis is a cognitive head skill, Flexibility is a behavioral hands skill, while Partnering for Performance integrates the Head and the Hands with the Heart and the Habits. All three are skills that you, as a leader, need at home, at work, or in the community to help others to accomplish the right goals, in the right way, for the right reasons, so they can continue to develop as people. On Day Two this week we will study diagnosis of the development level of the people you are serving. On Day Three we will study the flexibility of your leadership style. On Day Four we will introduce the Partnering for Performance process that takes all you have learned about leading like Jesus and applies it to your role as a leader in the real world context of helping someone to perform well. That's exactly what Jesus wanted to do. He wanted His disciples to win—to become fishers of men—so they could impact the lives of others.

The final thing we want to do today is begin teaching you the first skill—Diagnosis—by introducing you to the development levels related to a particular person performing any specific task or goal.

The following chart shows the four developmental levels a person may experience related to any task or goal. The chart moves from right to left as the person develops. For example, now you are probably at a D1 development level (Enthusiastic Beginner) in terms of becoming a situational leader. However, we anticipate if you do all of the assignments this week and partici-pate in your study group discussion, by the end of the week, you would have moved to a D4 level (Peak Performer or Self–Reliant Achiever).

| D4 | D3 | D2 | D1 |
|---|---|---|---|
| **Peak Performer** | **Capable but Cautious Performer** | **Disillusioned Learner** | **Enthusiastic Beginner** |
| High Competence | Moderate to High Competence | Low to Some Competence | Low Competence |
| High Commitment | Variable Commitment | Low Commitment | High Commitment |

**DEVELOPED** ◄------------------------------------------------ **DEVELOPING**

✝ *The levels of development may be self-evident. Try to identify the descriptions below with the respective levels mentioned above by circling D1, D2, D3, or D4 in front of the proper description.*

**D1 D2 D3 D4** At this level of development you have been assigned a new task and you are excited about it. You have a high commitment but a low level of competence, because you have never done this task before.

**D1 D2 D3 D4** At this level you have become a peak performer and are highly competent and highly committed to perform a particular task or goal without help from others.

**D1 D2 D3 D4** At this level of development you have acquired a moderate to high level of competence but may have lost some of your enthusiasm or confidence. Even though you are developing you are cautious in performing the task on you own.

**D1 D2 D3 D4** You have begun the task and your competence level has increased somewhat but your commitment is beginning to fall due to a failure during the learning process or a realization that the task is harder than you thought. You can't do it really well.

Were you able to identify the order of the descriptions as D1, D4, D3, and D2? If not, don't worry. We will spend a lot of time tomorrow diagnosing people's level of development.

✝ *To begin practicing your diagnosis skill, take your personal job description (whether it be a paid or volunteer job) and evaluate your development level on each important aspect of your job that is described there by writing D1, D2, D3, or D4 in front of each task. Remember, development level is a task specific concept. You are probably not at the same development level for all of the tasks that make up your job. Bring your work to the study group meeting.*

# Diagnosis: The First Skill of a Situational Leader

As a servant leader using *Situational Leadership II®*, you should always first determine the development level of the people you are leading. Yesterday we began looking at how leaders learn to diagnosis the development levels of the people they lead for assigned tasks and goals. *Situational Leadership II®* teaches that people can be at different development levels for each task or goal based on two variables: their *commitment* (confidence and enthusiasm) and their *competence* (knowledge, skills, and experience).

Look back at the Developmental Level graphic in yesterday's study. Note that there are four basic combinations of competence and commitment that can help determine a person's development level—low or high competence and low or high commitment. In the following illustrations of the four development levels, we will use Jesus as our leadership example.

When Jesus called the disciples, He was calling them to the task of becoming "fishers of men." For the next three years, He spent time "making them fishers of men."

In the following four illustrations, we will focus on the development level of the disciples as they moved over time toward becoming "fishers of men."

### D1–ENTHUSIASTIC BEGINNERS (Development Level 1)

Whenever people begin a new task or goal, commitment is usually high but competence is usually low. Why? Because they're excited about the opportunity although they have never done that task before.

✚ *Read the following account in Matthew 4:18-22 and then circle your diagnosis of the level of competence and commitment that the disciples had at this time in terms of being fishers of men.*

> *"As Jesus was walking beside the Sea of Galilee, He saw two brothers, Simon called Peter and his brother Andrew. They were casting a net into the lake, for they were fishermen. "Come, follow Me." Jesus said, " and I will make you fishers of men". At once they left their nets and followed Him. Going on from there, He said two other brothers, James son of Zebedee and his brother John. They were in a boat with their father, Zebedee, preparing their nets. Jesus called them, and immediately they left the boat and their father and followed Him."*

### C O M P E T E N C E (knowledge, skills and experience)  H I G H  I  L O W

### C O M M I T M E N T (confidence and enthusiasm)  H I G H  I  L O W

Jesus saw in these hardworking fishermen the raw material for the future leaders of His mission that He would leave in their care when His earthly ministry was completed. In their enthusiasm, they literally dropped what they were doing when He called them to the higher purpose of being fishers of men. Although they were highly committed, they had little or no idea of how to accomplish their new task. Remember, the task was to be fishers *of men*—not fishermen. Their level of development was that of enthusiastic beginners.

As a servant leader you must remember as you assign new tasks and goals to those you lead, they may be like the disciples were when they started their ministry. The people you lead may have high commitment and enthusiasm for the new task, yet their competence level may be very low. We believe that leaders in churches and in business many times set people up for failure because they do not accept the responsibility of recognizing their development level. Jesus knew the disciples were just starting out in their new role, and as we will see tomorrow, He was flexible in His leadership style in order to meet their needs as Enthusiastic Beginners.

✝ *Can you think of a time when you were an Enthusiastic Beginner? Explain how you felt and why.*

_____

_____

_____

_____

✝ *Can you think of someone you are leading who might be an Enthusiastic Beginner for a particular task, goal, or responsibility?*

_____

### D2–Disillusioned Learners (Development Level 2)

After you have begun to do a task your competence level will increase some, but often your commitment level will drop due to a failure or realization that the task is harder than you thought. The disciples quite possibly experienced this on one occasion as we see in Matthew 17:15–16 when they were unable to cast a demon out of a boy that a father had brought to Jesus. Casting out demons was one of the tasks that Jesus had assigned to them in Matthew 10 when He sent them out. Now it was obvious they could not cast out *this* demon.

✝ *Read the following account in Matthew 17:15-19 and then circle the appropriate level of competence and commitment that the disciples had at this time in terms of being fishers of men.*

> "Lord, have mercy on my son," he said. "He has seizures and is suffering greatly.
> He often falls into the fire or into the water. I brought him to your disciples,
> but they could not heal him." . . . Jesus rebuked the demon, and it came out of the boy,
> and he was healed from that moment. The disciples came to Jesus in private and asked,
> "Why couldn't we drive it out?"

COMPETENCE (knowledge, skills and experience) HIGH ⎮ LOW

COMMITMENT (confidence and enthusiasm) HIGH ⎮ LOW

When the disciples were new to the task of being fishers of men they experienced a setback to their confidence when they discovered they were not competent to handle every situation. It is easy to imagine their disillusionment as they sought an explanation from Jesus in private. Think how the disciples must have felt when they were not able to succeed at casting out the demon. They must have been frustrated, uncertain, and embarrassed.

Your people experience the same feelings when confronted with a task or goal they cannot do or in which they experienced a failure or a problem. Often the people you lead are disillusioned about a specific task while you as the leader are completely unaware of their disillusionment. It is at this stage, if people become disillusioned and no one reaches out to them, they can become so discouraged that they give up and quit.

Several years ago, Ken Blanchard's children encouraged him to learn how to use a computer. You might think with all the books he has written that he would know something about computers. However, he had a bad experience with computer operators while working on his doctorate, so he decided he would stay as far away from computers as possible. As a result, he has written more than twenty books using a yellow pad of paper, scissors, a stapler, and a mechanical pencil! But his kids encouraged him to learn the computer because everybody in the company was on e–mail and he was not able to communicate with them. They hired someone to work with computer–challenged people like Ken. As he began his first lessons he was very excited about learning. He had seen people on airplanes and at the airports working on their computers and he could hardly wait to begin the process himself. He was particularly excited about learning Solitaire. Ken was a classic Enthusiastic Beginner! However, after his first lesson, his teacher warned him not to touch the computer until his next lesson. Not following instructions, Ken began to erase things and soon found himself frustrated and unable to do the simplest tasks on the computer. After only a short while away from his computer teacher he was ready to go back to paper and pencil. What happened? As his wife, Margie, told him when he complained, "You just moved from a D1 to D2—a Disillusioned Learner." Ken had quickly found out that learning the computer was harder than he thought.

You probably have people who look to you for leadership who feel the same way about assigned goals and tasks because they are D2s in these areas. Their attitude and overall commitment to the job may be suffering.

✚ *Has there ever been a time in your life when you were a Disillusioned Learner? Explain how you felt and why.*

_____

_____

_____

_____

✚ *Can you think of someone you are leading who might be stuck in disillusionment for a particular task, goal or responsibility?*

_____

### D3–Capable but Cautious Performers (Development Level 3)

At the D3 level of development people have acquired a moderate to high level of competence but may have lost some of their enthusiasm or confidence, or they are cautious because they have never performed the task on their own. Ken felt that way the first time he took his computer on a trip away from his teacher after she had gotten him over disillusionment.

✚ *Read the following account in Matthew 14:26-30 and then circle your diag-*
*nosis of the level of competence and commitment that Peter showed here in*
*terms of walking on water.*

*When the disciples saw Him walking on the lake, they were terrified. "It's a ghost," they said, and cried out in fear.*
*But Jesus immediately said to them: "Take courage! It is I. Don't be afraid." "Lord, if it's You," Peter replied, "tell me to*
*come to You on the water." "Come," He said. Then Peter got down out of the boat, walked on the water and came*
*toward Jesus. But when he saw the wind, he was afraid and, beginning to sink, cried out, "Lord, save me!"*

## COMPETENCE (knowledge, skills and experience) HIGH ׀ LOW

## COMMITMENT (confidence and enthusiasm) HIGH ׀ LOW

Peter is a great illustration of someone who exhibits a moderate to high level of competence as he
steps on the water and begins to walk! It took a tremendous amount of faith for Peter to step out of the
boat and onto the water. So often we forget that Peter actually did walk on water! In fact, he was the
only one besides Jesus who had it on his resume. Peter's problem, though, came when he took his eyes
off of Jesus and began to worry about the storm. Peter's confidence moved from high to low and when it
did, his demonstrated competence sank into the water with him.

As you progress through the development process, you and the people you lead, will experience
times when you know how to do the task or goal (moderate to high competence), but for whatever reason, your commitment level will drop. Just as with the Disillusioned Learner, people left in this Capable
but Cautious level of development without proper leadership actually can lose both competence and
commitment and quit trying.

✚ *Has there ever been a time in your life when you were a Capable but*
*Cautious Performer? Explain how you felt and why.*

_____

_____

_____

✚ *Can you think of someone you lead who might be a Capable but Cautious*
*Performer level (D3) for a particular task, goal or responsibility?*

_____

### D4–Peak Performers (Development Level 4)

The D4 Peak Performers are people who are highly competent and highly committed to perform a
particular task or goal. I believe it was Jesus' desire for His disciples to be both highly committed to the
task of being fishers of men and highly competent.

✛ *Read the following account in Acts 2:36-41 and then circle your diagnosis of the level of competence and commitment that Peter showed here in terms of becoming a fisher of men:*

*"Therefore let all Israel be assured of this: God has made this Jesus, whom you crucified, both Lord and Christ." When the people heard this, they were cut to the heart and said to Peter and the other apostles, "Brothers, what shall we do?" Peter replied, "Repent and be baptized, every one of you, in the name of Jesus Christ for the forgiveness of your sins. And you will receive the gift of the Holy Spirit. The promise is for you and your children and for all who are far off—for all whom the Lord our God will call." With many other words he warned them; and he pleaded with them, "Save yourselves from this corrupt generation." Those who accepted his message were baptized, and about three thousand were added to their number that day.*

**COMPETENCE** (knowledge, skills and experience) **HIGH | LOW**

**COMMITMENT** (confidence and enthusiasm) **HIGH | LOW**

Once again we can look at Peter and see how in Acts, under the annointing of the Holy Spirit, he shows high levels of both competence and commitment as he speaks to a crowd of thousands and three thousand are baptized that day. He has truly become a "fisher of men." Peter has both the knowledge to share the message of Christ, and he also exhibits a high level of commitment to share this message. Notice how Peter boldly shares the message of Christ. He speaks with authority. He is a real "fisher of men."

What is your desire for the people who look to you for leadership? Frustrated individuals who do not have the competence or commitment to accomplish the assigned task? Or people who are highly competent and highly committed? Can you imagine the benefits of having people around you who feel good about their jobs and are good at doing them? Take your local church for example. Just imagine if the leaders throughout your church were functioning as Peak Performers in their assigned tasks. The impact on the mission of the congregation would be tremendous!

You can see that diagnosing development level is vital if you as a leader are to help the people around you accomplish their assigned goals and tasks. How well are you doing at assessing the developmental needs of the people with whom you work?

✛ *Consider one person you are leading and answer the following questions as you diagnose his or her level of development.*

*Who is the person?*

_____

*What is the specific goal or task that you would like this person to perform?*

_____

*How strong or good are the individual's demonstrated knowledge and skills in this task area?*

_____

*How much experience does this person bring to this task?*

_____

*How motivated, interested, or enthusiastic is the individual about this task?*

_____

*How confident/self–assured is the individual about this task?*

_____

*What is this person's developmental level for this task?* **D1  D2  D3  D4**

Remember: Do not categorize *people* at the D1, D2, D3, or D4 level of development. Only categorize their *development levels* in regard to tasks or goals. Consider someone in sales who has four major areas of responsibility: sales, service, administration, and team contribution. It is conceivable that this person could be at a different level of development for each of these responsibilities. This person could be a D3 in sales, a D4 in service, a D2 in administration and D1 in team contribution. There is nothing bad about being at any one of the four development levels on a particular task, just like it is not bad to be an adolescent—both indicate where you are on your development journey.

# Flexibility: The Second Skill of a Situational Leader

Once again we want to remind you that leading like Jesus is not about you but about honoring God by investing your life into the lives of the people you are leading. As we look at the life of Jesus, we see a perfect example of a leader who first wanted to accomplish His father's will. One of the ways He did that was by molding His disciples into men who would change the world.

Today let's examine the second skill of a *Lead Like Jesus* situational leader—flexibility. As we have discussed over the last two days, it is imperative for you to diagnose the development level of a individual for a particular task or goal. It is equally important for you to be willing to vary your leadership style based upon the needs and the development level of the person in each task. In order to be flexible in your leadership style, you must first understand that there are two leadership behaviors that you can use as a situational leader to help people develop:

*1. Directive Behavior:* Telling people what to do, when to do it, where to do it, how to do it and then providing close supervision.

*2. Supportive Behavior:* Listening to people, involving them in decision making, encouraging them, praising their progress and facilitating their interactions with others.

As the styles portion of the *Situational Leadership II®* model illustrated below suggests, a leader can use four combinations of directive and supportive behavior in the four basic leadership styles. For example, if noise in the hall was bothering you and you wanted to use Style 1 (Directing), you would say to the person you were assigning the task of resolving the problem, "Go outside and ask those people to move their conversation down the hall and when you finish that report back to me." If you wanted to use Style 2 (Coaching) on the noise in the hall, you would say, "What I think you ought to do is go out there and tell those people to move their conversation down the hall, what do you think? Do you have any suggestions? Do you have any questions?" If you wanted to use a Style 3 (Supporting) on the problem, you would say, "There's noise in the hall that's bothering us, what do you think we should do?" Finally, if you want to use Style 4 (Delegating) on the noise in the hall, you would say, "There's noise in the hall that's bothering us. Take care of it." It is important to note that the goal in the example—to do something about the noise—stayed the same. But we demonstrated four different leadership styles to deal with the problem.

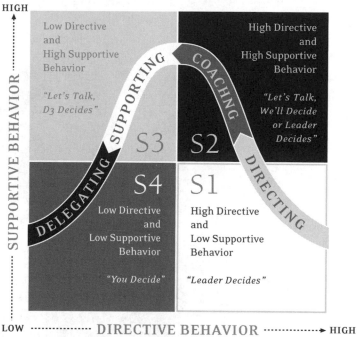

BASIC LEADERSHIP STYLES

✛ *The four styles of Leadership may be self-evident. Try to identify the descriptions below with one of the four leadership styles illustrated in the model by circling S1, S2, S3, or S4 in front of the proper description.*

S1 S2 S3 S4   In using this leadership style you would provide encouragement, praise, reassurance and involvement in decision making.

S1 S2 S3 S4   In using this leadership style you would not only provide clear direction and close supervision, but you would also provide encouragement, praise, feedback and someone to listen to concerning the problems encountered in working on a task.

**S1 S2 S3 S4** In using this leadership style you would tell people what to do, how to do it, where to do it, when to do it and provide close supervision.

**S1 S2 S3 S4** In using this leadership style you provide little direction or support. Now the ball is in the follower's court.

Were you able to identify the order of the descriptions as S3, S2, S1 and S4? We hope so. Great, read on.

## MATCHING LEADERSHIP STYLE TO DEVELOPMENT LEVEL

An important part of Partnering for Performance is working with people to match the appropriate leadership style with each of the development levels. Before the in–depth discussion of Partnering for Performance that will occur during Day Four, let us give you some practice on matching the appropriate leadership style to each development level.

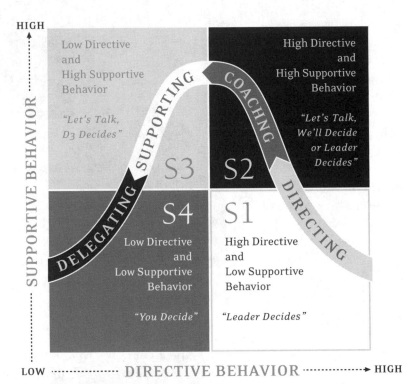

✠ *Above is depicted the Situational Leadership II® Model. You will notice that this model includes both the four Development Levels and the four basic Leadership Styles. In fact, as should become apparent, the S1, S2, S3, and S4 Leadership Styles correspond to the D1, D2, D3, and D4 Levels of Development. Study the diagram and write in the spaces after the diagram the appropriate behavior of a leader for each Development Level.*

An *Enthusiastic Beginner* (D1) needs a _____ Leadership Style.

A *Disillusioned Learner* (D2) needs a _____ Leadership Style.

A *Capable, but Cautious Performer* (D3) needs a _____ Leadership Style.

A *Peak Performer or Self Reliant Achiever* (D4) needs a _____ Leadership Style.

Did you match up Development Level D1–*Enthusiastic Beginner* with Leadership Style S1–*Directing*; Development Level D2–*Disillusioned Learner* with Leadership Style S2–*Coaching*; Development Level D3–*Capable But Cautious Performer* with Leadership Style S3–*Supporting*; and Development Level D4–*Peak Performer* with Leadership Style S4–*Delegating*?

### S1 Leadership Style (For D1 Development Level)

In the S1–Directing leadership style, you provide specific directions about roles and goals, and closely track performance in order to provide frequent feedback on results. This is a very "hands on" style of leadership. In the directing style of leadership, when working appropriately with a D1–Enthusiastic Beginner, your behavior includes acknowledging enthusiasm for the task, but also being very specific in defining goals, setting limits, developing action plans, and giving examples of what a good job looks like. One of the mistakes that you can make with an Enthusiastic Beginner is not giving adequate direction as the he or she begins the task, therefore unintentionally setting the person up to fail.

When Jesus called the disciples He knew that they did not understand what it meant to be fishers of men. They were, as we identified earlier, Enthusiastic Beginners. Therefore, Jesus needed to be very directive in the beginning and tell them exactly what to do and how to do it.

✠ *Read the Scripture below in Matthew 10:5-10 and circle the leadership style that Jesus used with the disciples when He sent out those enthusiastic beginners.*

*These twelve Jesus sent out with the following instructions: "Do not go among the Gentiles or enter any town of the Samaritans. Go rather to the lost sheep of Israel. As you go, preach this message: 'The kingdom of heaven is near.' Heal the sick, raise the dead, cleanse those who have leprosy, drive out demons. Freely you have received, freely give. Do not take along any gold or silver or copper in your belts; take no bag for the journey, or extra tunic, or sandals or a staff; for the worker is worth his keep."*

Leadership Style Jesus Used   S1   S2   S3   S4

In Matthew 10:5–10, Jesus used an appropriate directing leadership style with His disciples when He sent them out for the first time to be His ambassadors. He told them who they were to go to, what they were to say, and what they should take with them on their journey.

If you have an Enthusiastic Beginner on a task, that individual needs you to be as specific as possible about the "how to's" and the outcomes you are expecting. Remember the goal is for you to provide the leadership that the person needs in order for him or her to succeed.

✝ *Think of a time when someone you were leading was an Enthusiastic Beginner who needed a Directing leadership style. Describe the situation and the level of leadership you provided. Was it the appropriate style that the person needed at the Enthusiastic Beginner development level?*

_____

_____

_____

### S2–Coaching Leadership Style (For D2 Development Level)

The Coaching leadership style is a combination of both leadership behaviors—high directive behavior and high supportive behavior. Look at the diagram above. The most effective use for the Coaching style of leadership is when you discover a person in the D2 stage of development (Disillusioned Learner) on a specific task.

First, you provide clear direction as outlined in our discussion of S1. But you also add supportive behaviors because you recognize that as a disillusioned learner, the person is in need of encouragement, praise, feedback, and someone to listen to him or her concerning the problems encountered in this task. It is easy for you to focus only on the failure of the individual to accomplish the task and forget the developmental level of the person in that task instead of choosing the appropriate leadership style.

In our discussion of the disillusioned learner we looked at Matthew 17:15–19, when the disciples were not able to cast the demon out of the boy. We looked at these verses from the perspective of the disciples. Now we are examining the response of Jesus to the disciples.

✝ *Read the story below in Matthew 17:18-20 and circle the leadership style that Jesus used with the disciples in this situation.*

> *Jesus rebuked the demon, and it came out of the boy, and he was healed from that moment.*
> *Then the disciples came to Jesus in private and asked, "Why couldn't we drive it out?"*
> *He replied, "Because you have so little faith. I tell you the truth, if you have faith as small as a mustard seed, you can say to this mountain, 'Move from here to there' and it will move. Nothing will be impossible for you."*

Leadership Style Jesus Used   **S1  S2  S3  S4**

Notice that in addressing the cause for their failure, Jesus gave the disciples truthful information as to why they were unable to cast out the demon—"you have so little faith." In the account of the same incident as recorded in the gospel of John, Jesus tells them that casting out of these demons comes only by prayer and fasting. That is supportive behavior. They must have felt discouraged and embarrassed because they were unable to cast out the demon. We know that Jesus loved and cared for His disciples, and we know that He wanted His disciples to succeed (John 17:6–25). We also know that Jesus was without sin (Hebrews 4:25), which means He never lost control of His temper in a sinful manner. Even though the disciples had failed and He had to come behind them to "clean up their mess," He still loved them and, we believe, expressed that love to them by telling them the truth in love.

Now what does this say to you as a leader trying to *Lead Like Jesus* in a Coaching leadership style? It is vital that you provide clear direction and information, but that you do so in a loving manner. If you are to follow the example of Jesus as a leader never demean people or try to make them feel "small" because of a failure on their part. As Jesus did, you should let the love you have for those with whom you work come through and let your desire to Lead Like Jesus always direct your behavior.

✝ *Can you think of a time when you were in need of a Coaching style of leadership? What did you need from the person who was leading you?*

_____

_____

_____

### S3–Supporting Leadership Behavior (For D3 Development Level)

The Supporting style of leadership behavior is a combination of high supportive, low directive behavior from the leader. See the diagram above. In this style, if used appropriately, the leader is responding to a person who is in the D3 level of development (Capable, but Cautious Performer) for a specific task. Remember, the D3 has moderate to high competence for a task but is experiencing a variable level in commitment. There is a need at this level for the leader to provide encouragement, praise, and reassurance. The leader also should provide the opportunity for the individual to take the lead in solving the problem.

On Day Three of this week we saw how Peter, in Matthew 14:26–30, exhibited the behaviors of someone who has moderate to high competence but varies in his commitment. The passage tells us that Peter walked on the water, yet when he took his eyes off of Jesus he sank into the water.

✝ *Read the Scripture below in Matthew 14:28-31 and circle the leadership style that Jesus used with Peter in this situation.*

*"Lord, if it's You," Peter replied, "tell me to come to You on the water." "Come," He said. Then Peter got down out of the boat, walked on the water and came toward Jesus. But when he saw the wind, he was afraid and, beginning to sink, cried out, "Lord, save me!" Immediately Jesus reached out His hand and caught him. "You of little faith," He said, "why did you doubt?"*

Leadership Style Jesus Used   **S1  S2  S3  S4**

What can we learn from the response of Jesus as a Supporting leader when Peter sank into the water? Notice that Jesus acted immediately. He did not let Peter sink in the water and think about his mistake. It was Jesus' desire to let Peter know immediately that He was there—to give the support he needed. Next notice that Jesus *"reached out His hand and caught him."* He used a personal touch to save the drowning apostle! Jesus knew that Peter's primary need was support so He used His hand to save him. It is only after Jesus has caught Peter that He says to him, *"You of little faith . . . why did you doubt?"* In light of what Peter has just done, I would consider this a low directive response! I think it is also important to remember that after Jesus caught Peter, that he and Jesus were still outside the boat. The image we have of that scene is one where Jesus wraps His arm around Peter and walks him back into the boat.

Based on the actions of Jesus in Matthew 14:28–31, how should we respond to people whom we lead whose competence levels are moderate to high, yet their commitment level is variable?

✚ *Can you think of a time when you were in need of a Supporting style of leadership? What did you need from the person who was leading you?*

_____

_____

_____

### S4–Delegating Leadership Style (For Development Level 4)

The Delegating style of leadership behavior is a combination of low directive behavior and low supportive behavior. As a person progresses to the level of a D4–Peak Performer (high competence/high commitment), the leader needs to provide low levels of directive and supportive behaviors. Where then does the person get direction and support? From themselves! The role of the leader then becomes to encourage and expect the person to take responsibility for goal setting, action planning, and providing additional resources as needed.

When Jesus gave the Great Commission, He assumed they were ready to perform as Peak Performers for the task of being "fishers of men." While Jesus would not be directing them every day or be present physically to support them as He had for three years, He did not turn His back on them.

✚ *In Acts we showed Peter as a Peak Performer in his role of being a "fisher of men." Read below the final passages of Matthew (28:19-20) which record the time just before Jesus left them. Circle the leadership style that Jesus used.*

> *"Therefore go and make disciples of all nations, baptizing them in the name of the Father and of the Son and of the Holy Spirit, and teaching them to obey everything I have commanded you. And surely I am with you always, to the very end of the age."*

Leadership Style Jesus Used   **S1   S2   S3   S4**

It is important to note that Jesus said, *"I am with you always,"* Jesus' promise was not to leave the disciples alone to accomplish their task of being fishers of men. He would always be available for them. In the delegating leadership style, illustrated here, it is important for the leader to not confuse delegating with abdicating. In abdicating, leaders turn their backs on their people and do not gather information on their own. They only become involved again if they hear bad news. When delegating, leaders stay in the information loop and are ready to help if they are called. Jesus delegated but did not abdicate. Even Peak Performers need to be able to call on their leaders occasionally to discuss problems and new ideas. Jesus knew His disciples would need Him in the future, and He was ready when they called. As a leader, remember, don't confuse delegating with abdicating!

✝ *Can you remember a time when you were left to complete a job, which you could do well, yet your supervisor left you alone to figure our how to do the job and was unavailable for dialogue? How did it make you feel? What were you able to do?*

_____

_____

_____

✝ *List the types of needs a Peak Performer would have and how you should respond as his or her leader.*

_____

_____

_____

## Partnering for Performance:
## The Third Skill of a Situational Leader

**4 DAY**

### BARRIERS TO BECOMING A LEAD LIKE JESUS SITUATIONAL LEADER

One of the greatest barriers to becoming a *Lead Like Jesus* situational leader is the intimacy it requires. Being held accountable for providing leadership that recognizes and responds to the needs to others, rather than just as a means of getting things, presents a major EGO challenge. It can require conquering fears of failure, loss of control, rejection, and position–based pride. To be willing to admit to yourself and others that you might not have been providing the best leadership will take faith in "whose you are" and "who you are" in Christ. Until these two questions have been answered there is a danger that you as a leader will be threatened by someone who excels beyond your level of development. Jesus was never concerned about this; as a matter of fact He said in John 14:12, *"I tell you the truth, anyone who has faith in Me will do what I have been doing. He will do even greater things than these, because I am going to the Father."* Jesus wanted His disciples to succeed, and even do greater things through power of the Holy Spirit. Do you want the people you lead to succeed beyond what you have accomplished?

Another barrier that can keep you from becoming a *Lead Like Jesus* situational leader is failing to invest the time and intimacy needed to partner with the people you lead to help them be more effective. When it comes to effective leadership, this is where the "learning–doing gap" kicks in. A lot of people know what they should do as a leader, but it doesn't seem to translate into real servant leader behavior. This leads us to the third skill of a situational leader:

*Partnering for Performance*—*Help Others Along the Way to Lead Like Jesus*

Because He instinctively knew the hearts, minds and needs of His followers, Jesus always applied the appropriate style of leadership as He transformed His disciples into "Fishers of Men." In His loving kindness and with great patience, Jesus guided them from ignorance and ineptitude to knowledge and competence in accomplishing a new and completely unprecedented task. Many times during the process Jesus was confronted with alternative suggestions on how things should be accomplished and what the desired result should be like. As the only One knowledgeable about how and what was to be accomplished, Jesus was never in the position of needing to modify His approach based on the input of anyone other than His Father. We are not in the same position. As we seek to influence others with less than perfect confidence in our abilities to discern and deliver perfect leadership, it is appropriate that we engage others in the process. The concept of Partnering for Performance describes a way to do so that requires both humility and a heart for service.

There are five steps to partnering well. Once you know how to work the process with a few people it can become a comfortable and natural way to ensure that you are there for your people and that you will give them a way to grow.

## PARTNERING FOR PERFORMANCE

The skill of Partnering for Performance is a vital part of becoming a *Lead Like Jesus* leader. This is where your Head and your Hands are integrated with your Heart and Habits. It is a behavioral process that involves both leader and follower, and it focuses on both *people* and *results*. The word "partnering" signals the importance of people, and the word "performance" identifies results as important.

For many years when Ken Blanchard and his colleagues were teaching *Situational Leadership II®* they focused mainly on the Head, your assumptions and beliefs about leadership—and on the Hands, your leadership behaviors and methods. Ken realized when he began studying Jesus as a leadership role model that the beginning of effective leadership starts on the inside with the Heart—your motivations and your intentions to lead—and then it moves outward, where it is reinforced by your Habits—the daily recalibration of your commitment to serve and not be served. As the leader, your role in Partnering for Performance is to help people lead their lives, make decisions, and focus on goals at a higher level. Jesus was clear what that might mean when the Pharisees asked Him what the greatest commandment was. His answer revealed what our priorities should be in life in interacting with others.

Jesus replied: "'Love the Lord your God with all your heart and with all your soul and with all your mind.' This is the first and greatest commandment. And the second is like it: 'Love your neighbor as yourself.' All the Law and the Prophets hang on these two commandments." Matthew 22:37–40

Jesus' words set the priorities for life. First comes God and His agenda, and He constantly wants us to see leadership first as an act of service. He had no "Plan B." Next come your neighbors—the people you attempt to influence at home, in the community, and at work. Finally, then comes your own agenda. If in working with others you can help them integrate these three priorities into their daily lives, their effectiveness will soar. They will get the right things done for the right reasons, and they will do them in the right way.

## RECOGNIZING THAT PARTNERING FOR PERFORMANCE IS A PROCESS

This skill requires that you reach agreements on what you and the person you are leading will do to work together to increase their development level and to help them effectively accomplish their goals. You as a leader will need to commit to take time out of your calendar and have regular meetings with the people you lead. In meeting together you will discuss goals, tasks, development levels, and leadership styles. Although the meetings might be scheduled a month apart you will continue to give the person the appropriate leadership style as needed between meetings. The main purpose of Partnering for Performance is increasing the quality and quantity of conversations between you and the people you are attempting to serve. There are five steps to Partnering for Performance:

1. Teach your people *Situational Leadership II*®.
2. Agree on key goals and objectives and desired levels of performance on each.
3. Diagnose the individual's development level (D1, D2, D3, or D4) on each task or goal.
4. Agree on an appropriate leadership style for each goal—what the individual can expect from you in terms of direction and support based on his or her developmental level.
5. Continue to communicate as you follow through with the agreed–upon leadership style, adapting that style individual's development level changes.

## WHY PARTNERING FOR PERFORMANCE?

We have found over the years that *Situational Leadership II*® is not something you do *to* people; it is something you do *with* people. The way we found that out is observing what happened to managers who were trained in *Situational Leadership II*® and then began to apply it on the job. Suppose the manager diagnoses one of his team members as someone who has the competence and commitment to do his job, including all the different tasks involved (D4). As a result, the manager decides to use a Delegating style (low supportive and low directive behavior). Consequently, the leader leaves the person alone and seldom provides either direction or support. Because the person with whom the manager is working does not know *Situational Leadership II*®, how do you think this person will start to feel? Abandoned! The person might wonder, "What did I do wrong? Why don't I see my manager anymore?"

Take another person who also works with this leader. The leader sees this person as enthusiastic but inexperienced (D1). Applying the model, the leader decides this person needs a considerable amount of Directive behaviors (S1). Everyday the leader goes to see this person, gives directions and closely supervises performance. After a while, what do you think this person will feel, not knowing *Situational Leadership?* Mistrusted! The person might wonder, " Why is my manager always hovering over me?"

And what if these team members meet in the hall one day? The first person we described says, "I wonder what happened to my manager; I never see him anymore." The second person responds, " I know where he is, he's always in my office, on my case."

What has happened is that there is no partnership process. As a result, even if both of these diagnoses are correct, the corresponding leadership style has been misinterpreted because of a lack of communication.

It is amazing the response from the people you lead when you involve them in the partnering process and you agree on their current developmental level on tasks and the appropriate leadership style they need. Now instead of a supervisor demanding improved performance, you become a coach and mentor helping the person develop and become effective in his or her job.

Let's look more closely at each of the five steps of the Partnering for Performance process.

### Step #1—Teach the Situational Leadership II® Model

Over the last few days, you have learned the basic principles found in *Situational Leadership II®* and also discovered how Jesus used similar concepts as He led the disciples. Throughout the Gospels we read how Jesus took time to teach His disciples and the people who were following Him.

- Mark 4:2—"He *taught* them many things by parables . . ."
- Mark 10:1—"*Again crowds of people came to Him, and as was His custom, He* taught *them.*"
- Luke 5:3—"*Then He sat down and* taught *the people from the boat.*"

The first step in the partnering process is that you teach your people the basic principles of *Situational Leadership II®*. It is important for them to understand the basic terminology and concepts as you start this process.

If you lead more than one individual you might want to teach these concepts in a group setting and then schedule individual partnering meetings with your people. In Week Seven, we will give you an opportunity to do this step with someone as well as the other four steps of Partnering for Performance.

### Step #2—Agree on Key Goals and Objectives and Performance Standards for Each

Why are Key Goals and Objectives important? Because all good performance starts with clear goals. As we've said before, if you don't know where you're going, your leadership doesn't matter. Effective servant leadership involves clear vision and direction and implementation. One mistake that leaders often make, especially in volunteer organizations, is that they do not clearly define the goals and expectations for people. Consequently, this can cause frustration and conflict. When an individual who is being led and his or her leader independently develop a list of the person's five key goals, we have discovered that when we compare the list, fewer than two out of the five are in agreement. Based on this comparison, we see that sixty percent of what people do in their jobs, whether paid or volunteer, or with your kids at home, may not be doing what the leader or parent considers to be vital or relevant to the job.

Having clear goals is important for any leader. The Scriptures tell us that Jesus spoke of goals. In Luke 13, the Pharisees came to warn Jesus that Herod was trying to kill Him. Jesus replied, in verse 32, "*Go tell that fox, 'I will drive out demons and heal people today and tomorrow, and on the third day I will reach my goal'.*" Jesus says that He will reach His *goal*. Here Jesus asserts that on the third day His purpose will be accomplished, that is, He will have finished and brought to an end the goal His Father had set for Him. Jesus lived His life with one primary goal in mind, His death and resurrection for the salvation of all mankind. Jesus was a leader who lived His life based on the purpose and goals His Father had set for Him.

As leaders, it is important that you help your people set SMART goals. SMART is an acronym to help you write clear goals. It stands for goals that are:

**S** PECIFIC AND MEASURABLE

*A smart goal sets the parameters so that you will know when you have accomplished the goal. It not a general or vague statement.*

**M** OTIVATING

*A goal is smart when it is compelling. In other words, can you take the goal to heart? Does it contribute to your personal growth or the growth of the organization?*

**A** TTAINABLE

*A smart goal is a goal you know you can reach. At the same time though, the goal should stretch you. Remember what Paul said in Philippians 3:14 "I press on toward the goal . . ."*

**R** ELEVANT

*The goal needs to relate to the mission and values of the organization and be important. We believe in the 80/20 Rule: 80% of the performance you want from people will come from 20% of their activities. What you want to do is set goals in the 20% that will give you the 80%.*

**T** RACKABLE AND TIME—BOUND

*Can you break the goal into individual tasks that will enable you to check progress and make necessary assignments for completion? Every smart goal needs a beginning and an ending date. This helps prevent procrastination.*

### Step #3—Diagnose the Individual's Development Level (D1, D2,D3, or D4) on each task or goal

When you go to the Doctor you are not just looking for him to dispense a prescription so you can go buy the medicine. A pharmacist can do that. The best and most respected doctors are the ones who can diagnose the problem. No matter how long or short the time it takes to properly diagnose the illness, it is money well spent—especially in serious cases. Earlier this week you saw that Jesus diagnosed the needs of the disciples. As a leader, you need to follow the example Jesus set for you and learn to diagnose the development level of the people with whom you work. When the people you are working with also understand *Situational Leadership II®*, the diagnostic process is a mutual responsibility.

### Step #4—Agree on an Appropriate Leadership Style for Each Goal

Diagnosing the development level of people is vital for the leader. However, it is just as important that once you diagnose, you then are able to match the correct leadership style to the development level of the person with whom you are working. Leading like Jesus will require that you develop a willingness to vary your leadership style based on the needs of people. In the partnering process after you and the person with whom you are working have agreed on the development level for each of the goals that you are tracking, then it is fairly easy. Next you must make sure that you match the development level with the appropriate leadership style. Our experience in doing Partnering for Performance sessions suggests that the best way to do Steps 3 and 4 is this: Have the person you are working with take some quiet time and analyze his or her development level on each of the SMART goals that you have agreed upon. Then that person should consider what leadership style would be appropriate given that development level. You, as the leader, would be doing the same thing on your own. Then you would come back together and share each other's diagnoses and agree on both the appropriate development levels and leadership styles. If you and your partner disagree with on a development level and you cannot settle it, we suggest you go with that person's diagnosis, but put them on a short leash. That means, ask them what they will have accomplished in this goal area within a period of time in order to show that their diagnosis is right. You want your people to be right!

Once you have agreed on the development level and the appropriate leadership style to use for each goal area, then you and the person with whom you are working with must agree on what will that leadership style mean in terms of your interaction. For example, suppose you agree on an S3–Supporting leadership style for a goal area. Then you would say, "How would you like my supportive behavior delivered?" Your partner might say, "Why don't we have lunch once every two weeks so that I can show you what I am doing in this area and get your support?" If you negotiate an S2–Coaching style with someone, that might mean that you would both get out your calendars and schedule a couple of hours once a week over the next month to work closely with this person on that goal. Your people need to know what agreeing on a particular leadership style will mean in terms of your interaction.

### Step #5—Deliver on What You Promise

Once you and your partner have agreed on development level, appropriate leadership style, and what that leadership style will mean in terms of your behavior, the next step is to deliver what you promised. If you say you are going to meet with a person for lunch, you don't break the appointment. If you schedule coaching, you show up. If you agree to do things with your people and then don't follow through, it won't take long for them to realize that you are more "fluff than stuff" and you don't walk your talk. Partnering for Performance means that you really are a partner with your people and they can count on you as a partner they can trust and respect. Therefore, in light of our discussion on leading like Jesus, Partnering for Performance is all about working with others to accomplish the right goals in the right way, for the right reasons, so they can continue to develop as people.

Next week we will provide you some resources that will help you integrate the Heart, the Head, and the Hands by developing the Habits that enable you to keep your commitment to *Lead Like Jesus*.

# Becoming a Jesus-like Situational Leader Is About Change

## CHANGING THE WAY YOU THINK ABOUT LEADERSHIP

Becoming a *Lead Like Jesus* leader requires you to change both what you think about leadership and the way you act as a leader. Let's go back to the time when Jesus called His disciples. In Matthew 4:19 Jesus said, *"Come, follow Me, and I will make you fishers of men."* Note that Jesus did not say, *"Come, follow Me, I am <u>expecting you to</u> be fishers of men,"* or *"I am <u>expecting you to already be trained</u> to be fishers of men."* No, what Jesus said to the disciples was, *"I will make you . . ."* Jesus was promising the disciples "to build them up or equip them" to be fishers of men. Jesus took the responsibility to help His disciples become fishers of men. For leaders this is a very important lesson. Too often we think leadership is about how many people are following us, or what our titles are, or what we can accomplish ourselves. But Jesus demonstrated that leadership is about the development of people. It is about investing your life into the lives of the people you lead. As Rick Warren said in *The Purpose Driven Life*, "It is not about you!" Too many leaders think that leadership is about them!

Last week we examined Jesus' prayer in John 17:6–19 in light of Jesus' example as a role model for leadership. Let's read it one more time in relationship to Jesus' focus of leadership.

✝ *Read John 17: 1-17 in your Bible and take note of Jesus' view of leadership focus. Then answer the following question: Who was the focus of Jesus' prayer? Rank the three possibilities from 1 to 3.*

_____ *The Disciples*      _____ *Himself*      _____ *The Father*

In this passage, Jesus focused on all three of the possibilities listed above. The order of priority above is 2, 3, and 1. I believe Jesus' focus was *not* on Himself; instead, it was first on His Father and then on His disciples. In verse 9 Jesus says the disciples were *"given to Him"* and that they *"belong to (the Father)."* Of course, Jesus clearly understood that His primary focus was always to be accomplishing His Father's will for His life. He also understood the other primary focus in His ministry was the development of the disciples. It is also obvious that He was recounting how He had been faithful to the Father and to the disciples as He fulfilled His mandate.

✝ *On whom should you focus?*

_____

## CHANGING THE WAY YOU ACT

As we talk about changing the way you think and act as a leader, you must apply basic principles that relate to change. Over the years you have developed certain habits and actions as a leader. As you have already begun to experience, incorporating the concepts of servant leadership into your life is not always easy. Similarly, changing the attitudes or behaviors of those you lead will not be easy.

## CHANGING THE PEOPLE YOU LEAD

Do you remember how you felt when you experienced the effects of change in last week's group activity when you had to change your appearance for another person? The exercise was to help you experience how change feels so that you can identify with the people you lead when you make changes like implementing a Partnering for Performance process. Leading like Jesus will have ramifications that will change the way you work with everyone around you.

✛ *Why is change so difficult? Look again at the seven reasons why changing your leadership behavior and the behavior of those you lead may not be as easy as you think. Think back to the solutions that we gave for helping your people face change. Write the solution that best reflects what you think you should do in each situation.*

**1. The Problem:** *You feel awkward, ill at ease and self–conscious.* Any time you try to change accustomed behaviors, the change will make you feel uneasy. Remember, you are changing many behaviors that have been engrained in you over time. **How can you overcome this awkward feeling in yourself or others?**

*Your Solution:*

_____

_____

_____

The solution for this problem is for you to know what to expect and help the people you lead to know that they may feel awkward as you begin leading like Jesus. Help them expect change and to realize that in time they will adjust to the changes. If you *Lead Like Jesus* it will be more natural than if you try to make the changes based on your authority, personality, or inducements.

**2. The Problem:** *You may feel alone.* Leading like Jesus may require that you lead the people around you differently than other leaders might lead. It also may mean that you make choices based upon the example Jesus has set for us as leaders, rather than those choices that traditional leadership experts would direct you to make. **What do you do when you feel alone in making changes?**

*Your Solution:*

_____

_____

_____

One of the ways you can overcome this problem is to become involved in a *Lead Like Jesus* accountability/support group, where you can share with other leaders who may be experiencing the same type of problem. Another is to recognize that to be a leader you have to make changes. It goes with the territory. The price of being a leader is having a target on your back. But if you are following Jesus you can depend on Him to work in your life and in the lives of those you are leading.

**3. The Problem:** *You may have to give up certain habits and behaviors. You are also faced with the difficult task of helping those who follow you to change ingrained habits and behaviors of their own.* Leading like Jesus will require that you take a hard look at how you act as a leader and how you treat those you lead. As you look at your leadership behaviors you will find actions that are not consistent with those of a *Lead Like Jesus* leader, and you will have to work at changing those habits. **What do you do when you or those who lead face difficulties when you try to change?**

*Your Solution:*

_____

_____

_____

The key to this problem is for you to ask for God's help as you make these changes. You may also talk about the difficulties of making these changes in your life with your accountability group or truth–tellers. You should warn those you lead of the changes and identify with the difficulties they will face as you try to Partner for Performance and *Lead Like Jesus*. You can point out the options and show them the benefits of the changes. You can support them as they make the changes.

**4. The Problem:** *You realize that you and they can only change so much at any given time.* As you work through this study you will encounter a number of actions and behaviors you need to change. If you are not careful you may become overwhelmed and frustrated. **How do you handle the situation personally or with those you lead when the changes are so many or so great that you or they feel overwhelmed?**

*Your Solution:*

_____

_____

We would recommend that you remember the question, "How do you eat an elephant?" The answer is "one bite at a time." You can only handle so much change at once. Take the lessons you are learning and begin to set priorities for changes you need to make. The three skills of a situational leader that you have learned will help you *Lead Like Jesus* as you lead others to change. The directive and supportive behaviors that we are going to teach you will help you as you lead others to change. Remember, you are in this for the long run! Becoming a leader who leads like Jesus is a lifelong process!

**5. The Problem:** *You or those you lead may also be concerned that you don't have enough resources to become a leader who leads like Jesus.* **Where do you get the resources you need to make the changes and how can you help your people find the resources they need?**

*Your Solution:*

_____

_____

It is very easy, if you are not careful, to try to make the necessary changes in your behavior on your own—by your own strength. Remember that Jesus did not lead alone. The Scriptures remind us over and over again how He spent time alone with His Father. We have all the resources we will ever need through Christ. The solution for this problem is for you to spend time each day with your Heavenly Father, just as Jesus did. God has all the resources you need. You just need to involve Him in the problem.

**6. The Problem:** *You will find that some behaviors will be easier to change than others.* As we said earlier, you have established leadership habits and behaviors which will need to be changed. In some areas of your leadership life you will be ready for change, but in others, change will not be as easy. **How do you deal with the difficult long–range changes you need to make?**

*Your Solution:*

_____

_____

The key to this problem is for you to recognize those areas that you do find difficult to change and ask God to give you the strength and fortitude to change that behavior. If your boss is a *Lead Like Jesus* leader, he or she will be an excellent long–term resource. This also may be an area where you will need the support of an accountability group—asking for their help and prayer. An accountability partner who is not in line leadership is another resource for working through difficult changes.

**7. The Problem:** *If you take the pressure off, you will revert to your old behaviors.* As we said before, leading like Jesus is a lifelong process. If you do not keep the pressure on yourself to continue to live the principles of *Lead Like Jesus*, then you most likely will revert to your old leadership behaviors.

**How do you keep your focus and the focus of those you lead on the changes that need to be made, then stick with it until they are made?**

*Your Solution:*

_____

_____

The key to this challenge is for you to find ways to "keep the pressure on." Daily revisit your life purpose/mission statement, keep the EGO diagram taped to your mirror or as a screen saver on your computer so you see it and utilize accountability relationships you have all day long. There are many ways you can "keep the pressure on." Find the one that works for you—and stick with it!

Next week, we will study the Habits of a *Lead Like Jesus* leader. They will build on what we have talked about in this section on change.

# LEAD LIKE JESUS

## BEGINNING THE JOURNEY

# WEEK SIX

### THE HABITS —

*A Daily Recalibration of Leading Like Jesus*

*"But his delight is in the law of the Lord, and on his law*
*he meditates day and night. He is like a tree planted by streams of water,*
*which yields its fruit in season and whose leaf does not wither.*
*Whatever he does prospers" (Psalm 1:2-3).*

No matter how good the tools are, if you don't use them they will not work. Thousands of people have learned the skills of Situational Leadership, but many fail to implement them. We have discovered that the problem is the Heart. If you don't have the heart of a servant leader who wants to develop his or her people then you won't spend the time necessary to partner with them. That is why we began this study with the Heart. Now we come back to it because simply studying the principles of the Heart for those two weeks will not transform you into a servant leader. You need more than an interactive study; you need a daily transfusion! If you continue to practice all the Habits after this *Lead Like Jesus* study, then the Master will continue to lead you to be a servant leader. So our goal this week is to brief you of the five habits that will be your daily communication links with the Lord.

## THE RECALIBRATION TOOLS FOR LEADING LIKE JESUS

The daily pressures and concentration on various duties can isolate and distort a leader's perspective and ability to focus. In this week's study we will explore some of the key habits Jesus modeled for staying on track with His mission. The five habits Jesus modeled that are essential components of leading like Him are:

1. Solitude
2. Prayer
3. Study and application of Scripture
4. Accepting and responding to God's unconditional love
5. Involvement in supporting relationships

These habits reflect the central theme of all that Jesus sought to do—to know the will of God and to do the work that had been given Him to do. The habits were simple expressions of who He was and His intimacy with the Father. In your case they must first take on the form of disciplines before they can become habits. They require experiencing all the dynamics of change and levels of development that we studied in the Hands section. Depending on your experience and current habits, it will take time to integrate all of them into your efforts to Lead Like Jesus. All of them are powerful and transforming. All of them will feed and nourish your soul and your relationships.

The biggest temptation you face in making the journey from discipline to habit will be impatience for measurable and sustainable results. The immediate price to be paid for acquiring the habits of Jesus is time, effort, and trust in the process and in the One who beckons, "Follow Me." If you develop the relationship with Jesus through the Habits, they truly will become a lifestyle that serves you in all seasons of life.

# The Habit of Solitude

*"Be still, and know that I am God" (Psalm 46:10).*

Jesus spent significant time alone throughout His season of leadership. In solitude He found what was essential to deal successfully with the trials and challenges He faced. We can be very sure that what Jesus found useful for the conduct of His life in the Father will also be useful for us. In fact, He gave us many commands about the Habits.

What do we mean by solitude? Solitude is being completely alone with God away from all human contact. It is stepping outside the back door of your noisy, demanding world of agendas and interactions to breathe in some fresh air. Solitude is being refreshed and restored by the rhythms of life going on all around you, but being challenged and comforted by the fact that the world doesn't depend upon you to rotate on its axis. It's remembering that you don't depend on your work in the world to provide meaning and value. It is resting in God's presence and pleasure. It is being alone without being lonely.

You can make better sense of the world, of yourself and of others after time alone with God. Without it you are playing a frantic game of hide and seek that can turn your goals in life and your leadership from "being more than conquerors" (Romans 8:37) to just trying to make it through the day, the week, the month, and the year. Jesus is our example. Long ago Matthew Arnold said: "He was alone with God; He went out into a mountain, to pray, where He might have no disturbance or interruption given Him; we are never less alone than when we are thus alone. He was long alone with God: He continued all night in prayer. We think one half hour a great deal to spend in the duties of our faith; but Christ continued a whole night in meditation and secret prayer. We have a great deal of business at the throne of grace, and we should take a great delight in communion with God and by both these we may be kept sometimes long at prayer." How difficult we find it in our modern day to spend significant time with our Significant Other—God.

✚ *How much do you practice the Habit of Solitude—completely away from all human contact—just communing with God? Evaluate your experience by answering the following questions:*

How long has it been since you spent an hour in solitude? _____

How long has it been since you spent a day with God? _____

How much time have you spent in solitude with God in the past week? _____

## SOLITUDE IN TIMES OF TESTING

Let's look at Jesus, our example and our Lord. Even Jesus engaged in external solitude as a means of fortifying His inner peace and purpose.

✝ *Read Matthew 4:1-11 below when Jesus was preparing for the tests of leadership and public ministry. He spent forty days alone in the desert. As you read compare Jesus' experience with any times of solitude you have spent before facing a new ministry or a critical crossroads in your life.*

*Then Jesus was led by the Spirit into the desert to be tempted by the devil. After fasting forty days and forty nights, He was hungry. The tempter came to Him and said, "If You are the Son of God, tell these stones to become bread. Jesus answered, "It is written: 'Man does not live on bread alone, but on every word that comes from the mouth of God.'" Then the devil took Him to the holy city and had Him stand on the highest point of the temple. "If you are the Son of God," he said, "throw yourself down. For it is written: He will command His angels concerning You, and they will lift You up in their hands, so that You will not strike Your foot against a stone.'" Jesus answered him, "It is also written: 'Do not put the Lord your God to the test. Again, the devil took Him to a very high mountain and showed Him all the kingdoms of the world and their splendor. "All this I will give You," he said, "if You will bow down and worship me." Jesus said to him, "Away from Me, Satan! For it is written: 'Worship the Lord your God, and serve Him only.'" Then the devil left Him, and angels came and attended Him.*

✝ *Describe a time when you spent significant time in solitude as you faced a ministry opportunity or a crossroads experience in life. Note the challenge you faced, how you spent your time in solitude, and what the results were.*

_____

_____

_____

_____

Immediately after humbling Himself by being baptized to "fulfill all righteousness" (Matthew 3:15), Jesus was led by the Holy Spirit into a time of prolonged solitude where He was tempted by the devil. In our humanness it is easy to focus on what Jesus gave up during that time and miss what He received. In His time alone with God, He received the spiritual nurture and perspective that allowed Him to overcome the powerful and subtle temptations of the enemy for that time. This gave Him a perspective for all His ministry. Although physically hungry after His prolonged fast, Jesus was spiritually at "the top of His game." Though sorely tempted in the three areas most devastating to a leader—instant gratification, recognition and power—Jesus used the power of God's Word against His adversary and won.

### SOLITUDE WHEN SELECTING LEADERS

To encourage you in the Habit of Solitude, let's look at other times that Jesus spent in solitude. They will give you other reasons to spend time in solitude this week. Before choosing the Twelve, Jesus spent the entire night alone in the desert hills.

✝ *Are you facing the challenge of selecting new leadership? Whenever you do, whether it is now or later, how will you go about it? Will you just look at resumes and interview people to select the right one(s)? Will you go by your gut feeling? Jesus gives us the right example. Read Luke 6:12-16 and think about what you will do when you need to choose leaders.*

*One of those days Jesus went out to a mountainside to pray, and spent the night praying to God. When morning came, He called His disciples to Him and chose twelve of them, whom He also designated apostles: Simon (whom he named Peter), his brother Andrew, James, John, Philip, Bartholomew, Matthew, Thomas, James son of Alphaeus, Simon who was called the Zealot, Judas son of James, and Judas Iscariot, who became a traitor.*

One of the key aspects of good leadership is selecting the right team. There are always EGO challenges involved. Do you select only people who think like you? Do you only pick people based on past performance? Do you pick only safe people? Do you pick people who are all the same, or do you take the chance to capture the enrichment of diversity? Do you use only your own judgment, or do you seek wisdom from others you trust? There certainly were other candidates for the role of apostles—some more accomplished, some more articulate, many more knowledgeable, some more powerful, some more personable, some wiser in the ways of world, some more trustworthy than the twelve who were chosen. But in solitude, God in His sovereignty and Jesus in His obedience selected the exact ones to carry out the Kingdom plan. In John 17:6 Jesus prays: *"I have revealed You to those whom You gave Me out of the world. They were Yours; You gave them to Me and they have obeyed Your Word."*

✝ *Make a plan now for how you will choose leaders the next opportunity you have. Write some guidelines that you will want to follow.*

_____

_____

_____

### Solitude When You Face Challenges and Doubts

No doubt you will face doubts when crises come in your season of leadership. Jesus faced many. What will you do? Look what He did. When Jesus received the news of John the Baptist's death, He withdrew from there in a boat to a lonely place apart.

✝ *Read Matthew 14:12-14, 22-23 and think about what you will do when you have to face the next crisis.*

*John's disciples came and took his body and buried it. Then they went and told Jesus. When Jesus heard what had happened, He withdrew by boat to a solitary place. Hearing this, the crowds followed Him on foot from the towns. When Jesus landed and saw a large crowd He had compassion on them and healed their sick . . . Immediately Jesus made the disciples get into the boat and go on ahead of Him to the other side, while He dismissed the crowd. After He had dismissed them, He went up on a mountainside by Himself to pray. When evening came, He was there alone.*

The implications of the death of John the Baptist were significant for Jesus. He had lost His cousin, who had jumped in his mother's womb when Jesus' mother Mary came to visit John's mother. John was Elijah—Jesus' forerunner. His death turned even more attention on Jesus, whom some later claimed was John the Baptist risen from the dead. Many of John's followers now attached themselves to Jesus. It was the latest martyrdom of a prophet sent to turn God's people back to Him. It was a prelude to Jesus' own journey to the cross.

When storms are on the horizon, a key aspect of leadership is learning how to interpret the warning signs, check the navigation instruments, and prepare the crew for what lies ahead. Taking time alone with God to recalibrate your spiritual compass in times of bad news is the first service a leader can provide to those who follow.

✚ *Think about what will you do first when you face your next leadership crisis.*

_____

✚ *Devote 30 to 60 minutes for solitude this week. Be prepared to report back to the group in the next session.*

# Solitude & Prayer

*"Do not be anxious about anything, but in everything, by prayer and petition, with thanksgiving, present your requests to God. And the peace of God, which transcends all understanding, will guard your hearts and your minds in Christ Jesus"* (Philippians 4:6–7).

Today we want to continue examining Jesus' use of solitude as we emphasize the second Habit—prayer.

### Solitude When You Achieve Success and Receive Recognition

After the miraculous feeding of the five thousand, Jesus used solitude as an antidote to the EGO temptations of success and popularity:

✚ *Read John 6:15 and consider how you handle people rushing to you for the answers to their problems.*

*"After the people saw the miraculous sign that Jesus did, they began to say, "Surely this is the Prophet who is to come into the world." Jesus, knowing that they intended to come and make Him king by force, withdrew again to a mountain by Himself."*

Success and the roar of the crowd can be intoxicating to a leader, especially to one who has bought into the idea that "self worth is equal to performance plus the opinion of others." Taking time alone with God as "the audience of One" will continue to be an important habit to keep EGO from compromising your leadership. "The crucible for silver, the furnace for gold, but man is tested by the praise he receives" (Proverbs 27:21).

✚ *One of the most difficult challenges a leader faces is to not pay too much attention to either criticism or praise. We tend to agree with this advice concerning criticism, but we often ignore the advice about praise and recognition. As a leader you face both. Jot down your responses to these two questions: How are you doing with each? How will you handle them in the future?*

Criticism _____

Praise _____

## SOLITUDE WHEN YOU HAVE TO MAKE DIFFICULT CHOICES

Now we come to the heart of the Habit of Solitude—daily time with God that enables you to make the difficult choices of leadership. As you read Mark 1:32–38 below, note that Jesus used the early morning hour to find solitude so that He could make the tough choices between *good* use of His time and the *best* use of His time.

*That evening after sunset the people brought to Jesus all the sick and demon–possessed. The whole town gathered at the door, and Jesus healed many who had various diseases. He also drove out many demons, but He would not let the demons speak because they knew who He was. Very early in the morning, while it was still dark, Jesus got up, left the house and went off to a solitary place, where He prayed. Simon and his companions went to look for Him, and when they found Him, they exclaimed: "Everyone is looking for you!" Jesus replied, "Let us go somewhere else—to the nearby villages—so I can preach there also. That is why I have come."*

The words *"Very early in the morning, while it was still dark, Jesus got up, left the house and went to a solitary place and prayed"* stand between Jesus and the temptation to spend His precious time doing the good and popular things instead of doing the primary work for which He had come. Imagine Jesus' intense compassion for the sick and demon–possessed people He would have to leave. Imagine how strong the temptation would have been for Him to stay and use His healing powers to the delight of all. His disciples came expecting Him to seize this wonderful opportunity because He was the Messiah who would call Israel to God. But they thought like men, and Jesus had just heard from His Father. What allowed Him to resist doing this good work and pick the best? We believe that in solitude, in prayer, away from the hopes and hurts of those who looked to Him with high and compelling expectations, that He again received the answers of the best use of the next day from the Father.

The single most important Habit to help you grow as a leader is time alone with God each day. Unless you punctuate all your busyness with times of quiet reflection and rest from human communication, you will never be able to transact your business with God or enjoy the gift of resting in His presence. Many call this time a *Quiet Time* that they have each morning with God.

✛ *Do you have a daily Quiet Time with God?* ____ *Yes* ____ *No* ____ *Sometimes*

**How many days in a row have you had your Quiet Time?** _____

✛ *Do It! If you are not in the habit of a Quiet Time, begin with ten to fifteen minutes each morning. Here are some practical guidelines to help you. Underline the ones important to you.*

## HOW TO DEVELOP A QUIET TIME[8]

**1.** If you are not already doing so, find **a regular time each day** to spend time with God that fits your schedule. Having that time in the morning begins the day with recognition of your dependence on God and His all–sufficiency. A Quiet Time should be the first priority of the day. Spending time with God gives you an opportunity to yield your will to Him and consciously dedicate the day to His glory. However, you might find that another time suits your schedule better.

**2. Prepare the night before.**

If your Quiet Time is in the morning, set your alarm. If it is difficult for you to wake up, plan to exercise, bathe, dress, and eat before your quiet time.

Select a place where you can be alone. *"But when you pray, go into your room, close the door and pray to your Father, who is unseen. Then your Father, who sees what is done in secret, will reward you"* (Matthew 6:6). You will find that you can concentrate best when you have an established place away from noise, distractions, and other people. Wherever you choose, make sure it is a place where you can focus on the One to whom you are praying.

Gather materials, such as your Bible, notebook, and a pen or pencil, and put them in the place you selected the night before so that you will not waste time in the morning.

**3. Develop a plan.** Unless you consciously follow a pattern for your Quiet Time, you might get off–track or your mind may wander.

Pray for guidance. During your time with the Lord, you may want to include any number of these elements: prayer, Bible reading or study, memorizing Scripture, quietly waiting on Him, worship, and intercession.

Follow a systematic plan for your Scripture reading. For example, you may read from one of the gospels as well as another book of the Bible so that you can see Christ live out what the Scripture is teaching. You may choose to read through the Bible a chapter a day or choose one psalm, one proverb, and one chapter of the Old or New Testament each day.

Allow enough time to read His word reflectively. Do not try to read so much Scripture at one time that you cannot meditate on its meaning and let God speak directly to you and your situation.

[8]MasterLife Discipleship Training for Leaders, Avery T. Willis, Jr LifeWay, 1996,

Make notes of what God says to you through His Word. Your journal will become a living testimony to your relationship. I suggest you use two headings. The first is, "What God Said to Me." Make notes of what God said to you through the Scriptures. You may write it in a personal letter form or make an outline or summary.

The second heading in your personal journal is "What I Said to God." Pray in response to the Scriptures you have read. As you pray, use various components of prayer. We will show you later how to use the acronym ACTS—adoration, confession, thanksgiving, supplication—as a guideline for your prayers.

Develop your own procedure. Choose what is helpful and manageable within the time you have. The important thing is to have a plan so you do not waste this precious time with the Lord wondering what to do or wasting time "getting started".

**4. Be persistent until you are consistent.**

Strive for consistency rather than length of time spent. Try to have a few minutes of Quiet Time every day rather than long devotional periods every other day.

Expect interruptions. Satan tries to prevent you from spending time with God. He fears even the weakest Christians who are on their knees. Plan around interruptions rather than being frustrated by them.

**5. Focus on the Person** you are meeting rather than on the habit of having the Quiet Time. If the president of the United States were scheduled at your house at 6:00 A.M. tomorrow, would you be ready? Of course! Meeting God is even more important. He created you with a capacity for fellowship with Him, and He calls you to fellowship with Him.

✝ *Write out a plan you will follow for your Quiet Time, and commit to God to begin the discipline today (if it is not already a habit with you).*

When? _____

Where? _____

What? (Your Plan) _____

_____

✝ *Talk to a friend about your Quiet Time plan and ask him or her to be your accountability partner. Give the person the right to ask you at any time how you are doing or what God has said to you lately. If the person is in your study group, you could set that time or another time for regular checkups. Maybe your friend will begin a Quiet Time also if you share how.*

Name of friend _____ Phone _____

Regular time for checkup _____

## TO LEAD LIKE JESUS, YOU NEED TO PRAY LIKE JESUS

The one thing that is most instructive about knowing how and where a leader might take their followers is found in their prayer life. A *Lead Like Jesus* leader develops the instinctive habit of actively and constantly seeking to follow His model and His instructions on prayer and obedience. In the Heart section we spoke about Inviting God In as the only way to put ourselves in position for the heart transplant required to move from Edging God out to Exalting God Only. Prayer is an essential act of our "free will" that demonstrates whether we are really serious about living and leading like Jesus. Without it we will never open the way for the Holy Spirit to do His work in us and through us. Seeking God's will through prayer, waiting in faith for an answer, acting in accordance with that answer, and being at peace with the outcome, calls for a level of spiritual maturity that will keep anyone seeking to Lead Like Jesus in lifelong training. The nature and object of our prayers will determine whether we're fortifying an EGO–driven end or glorifying God.

## THE ACTS OF PRAYER

A simple acrostic—ACTS—can help you remember four basic parts of prayer. ACTS has helped many beginners in prayer and served as a compass for weather–beaten veterans. Try it for a few days.

**A** DORATION:  All prayer should begin here. Tell the Lord that you love Him and appreciate Him for who He is. *"Yours, O LORD, is the greatness and power and the glory and the majesty and the splendor, for everything in heaven and earth is yours. Yours, O LORD, is the kingdom; you are exalted as head over all"* (1 Chronicles 29:11).

**C** ONFESSION.  Immediately when we come into the presence of a Holy God we sense our inadequacies and are convicted that we fall short of God's glory. Therefore our first response to meeting and adoring God is confession. Sometimes we have to confess even before we express our adoration and love. *"If we confess our sins He is faithful and just and will forgive us our sins and purify us from all unrighteousness."* (1 John 1:9).

**T** HANKSGIVING.  Thanksgiving is the heartfelt expression of gratitude to God for all He has done in creation, in redemption, and in our lives. During this part of your prayer, thank God specifically for all that He has done for you since the last time you talked. As the old hymn says, "Count your blessings, name them one by one. Count your many blessings; see what God has done." What if tomorrow you only had the things that you thanked God for today? Toothpaste, air, water, clothes, family, job . . . you name it. Heed the Scripture: *"Sing and make music in your heart to the Lord, always giving thanks to God the Father for everything, in the name of our Lord Jesus Christ"* (Ephesians 5:19–20).

**S** UPPLICATION.  Finally we get to the part of prayer where most of us start—asking. "Supplication" is just a big word for asking for what you need. Start by praying about others' needs and then ask for your own needs to be met. It's okay to have a big "wish list." According to God's Word, we can ask with confidence. *"Ask and it will be given to you; seek and you will find; knock and the door will be opened to you"* (Matthew 7:7)

✛ *Stop now and spend a few minutes in prayer using ACTS.*

As you embark on this journey to become a *Lead Like Jesus* leader you will face some leadership challenges. Let us examine Jesus' example as a model to follow. Nowhere in the Bible are the elements of what it means to pray like Jesus more powerfully provided for us than in the dark hours of the night before He was betrayed and when the temptation to abandon His mission were at an almost unbearable level.

✛ *Read the prayer of Jesus and answer the questions of where He prayed, why He prayed, His posture in prayer, His request, and the answer to His prayer.*

*Then Jesus went with His disciples to a place called Gethsemane, and He said to them, "Sit here while I go over there and pray." He took Peter and the two sons of Zebedee along with Him and He began to be sorrowful and troubled. Then He said to them, "My soul is overwhelmed with sorrow to the point of death. Stay here and keep watch with Me." Going a little farther, He fell with His face to the ground and prayed, "My Father, if it is possible, may this cup be taken from Me. Yet not as I will, but as You will."*
Matthew 26:36–39

**1. Where did Jesus pray and why?** _____

He went off by himself for prayer. A troubled soul finds the most ease when it is alone with God, who understands the broken language of sighs and groans. While alone with God, Jesus could freely pour His heart out to the Father without restraint. Christ has taught and modeled for us that secret prayer is to be done secretly.

**2. What was His posture in prayer?** _____

He fell on His face before His Father, indicating the agony He was in, the extremity of His sorrow, and His humility in prayer. At other times Jesus prayed looking up to heaven, with His eyes open, or kneeling. The posture of the heart is more important than the posture of the body, but prostrating our physical selves before God helps our heart posture.

**3. What did He ask in prayer?** _____

Jesus asked; *"If it is possible, let this cup be taken from Me."* He was asking if He could avoid the sufferings ahead. But notice the way Jesus couched His request: "If it is possible." He knew the Father would only allow what was for His glory and Jesus' good. Jesus trusted the Father and left the answer to Him when He said, *"Yet not as I will, but as You will."* Although Jesus keenly sensed the bitter sufferings He was to undergo, He freely subjugated His desire to the Father. He based His own willingness upon the Father's will.

**4. What was the answer to His prayer?** _____

His answer was that the will of the Father would be done. The cup did not pass from Him, for He withdrew the petition in deference to His Father's will. But He got an answer to His prayer. He was strengthened for the mission He had come to fulfill: *"An angel from heaven appeared to Him and strengthened Him"* (Luke 22:43).

As leaders, doing the right thing for the right reasons might require you to drink the bitter cup in form of ridicule, rejection, and anger. Your human tendency will be to try to avoid the pain. Leading like Jesus will call you to proceed in faith and to trust in God's grace to provide you with the courage to do the right thing and finish the task.

## THE POWER OF PREEMPTIVE PRAYER

In leading like Jesus, prayer should never be restricted or relegated to our last resort in times of deep distress. It is our most powerful, most immediately accessible, most useful pre–emptive resource for responding to the moment to moment challenges of both good and bad times. Phil Hodges has written a poem that shows the possibilities of prayer.

### JUST SUPPOSE

*Just suppose, when I pray, there really is someone listening who cares about me and wants to know what's on my mind*

*Just suppose, when I pray, it changes me and my view of how the universe operates and who is involved*

*Just suppose, I put my doubts aside for a minute and consider the possibility that someone who knew me before I was born loves me, warts and all, without condition or reservation, no matter how badly I have behaved in the past.*

*Just suppose, a prayer was my first response instead of my last resort when facing a new challenge or an old temptation.*

*Just suppose, I lived each day, knowing that there is an inexhaustible supply of love for me to pass along to others*

*Just suppose.*

✚ *You don't have to just suppose. Sometime this week before the group session, get away from all human contact to spend time with God. Find someplace where you can be totally out of contact with all kinds of human noise (TV, cell phone, fax, voicemail, that secret pile of paperwork, magazines, even this book) for a minimum of an hour. Don't talk to anyone. The ideal place is out in nature, in a quiet place where you won't be disturbed, or even on an extended "prayer walk" while you talk with God and listen without interruption. Or anywhere you can be alone. You might want to take a Bible and notepad with you but nothing else. Once you are seated in a comfortable position, place your hands on your knees in a "down" position. If walking, visualize yourself in this position. In harmony with the position of your hands, mentally set down at the foot of the Cross everything you are concerned about or trying to manage or control. Be specific—name each burden as you put it down. When you have exhausted your list, take a couple of deep breaths and turn your hands, physically and mentally, into an "up" position and quietly receive what God reveals to you. Have no expectations or agenda for this time with God. Let it be His to fill. Talk to God and listen to Him through the Spirit and His Word. Ask the Spirit to tell you what to pray for. Write what you learned out of the experience so that you can share with the group.*

_____

_____

_____

_____

# Study of Scripture

Each day this week we are building the Habits and showing their relationships. Today we continue with Habit #1, Solitude, and we see how it links to Habit #2, Prayer, and Habit #3, Study of Scripture. When God calls you to Himself it is a call to solitude. You need the habits of prayer and Scripture as God's cell phone to help you talk to Him and hear from Him during your times of solitude. Solitude plus prayer will be incomplete if you do not hear from God through the Scripture. All of us know the value of Scripture. If not, just begin studying it, and you soon will experience the benefits of knowing and doing the Word of God.

## STUDY GOD'S WORD

If you only used the Bible to study and apply the practical wisdom it contains about dealing with people and overcoming your own internal challenges, it still would stand absolutely alone as the greatest book ever written. But it is so much more than a people manual—it is an intimate love letter written to you from your Father. Through it He invites you daily to experience new and exciting dimensions of His love. The Scriptures are God's holy Word from the holy God, delivered by holy men, to teach holy truths, and to make people holy.

> ✝ *Read 2 Timothy 3:16-17 and answer the questions about God's Word.*

> *All Scripture is God–breathed and is useful for teaching, rebuking, correcting and training in righteousness, so that the man of God may be thoroughly equipped for every good work.*

**What is the origin of all Scripture?** _____

Scripture is given by inspiration of God and therefore is His word. It is a divine revelation, which you may depend upon as infallibly true. The same Spirit who breathed reason into you also breathes revelation to you through the Word.

**What is it useful for?** _____

The study of Scripture is profitable for all the purposes of the Christian life. It teaches you the truth. It rebukes you when you are wrong. It corrects you when you stray. It trains you in righteous living.

**What is the ultimate result?** _____

By Scripture you are thoroughly equipped for every good work. Whatever duty you have to do, or whatever service is required from you, you find help in the Scriptures to equip you to do it.

It is all well and good to know that the Bible is useful, reliable, and valuable. It is another thing to make it your own in a practical way. It is only profitable if you read it. How can you make the Word of God more effective in your life as a leader?

## APPLY THE WORD TO YOUR LIFE

The most effective way to get the Word into your life is to apply it. Delving into the Word and getting the Word into you are essential, but the only way to abide fully in the Word is to apply it to your life. Jesus told this story: *"Why do you call Me 'Lord, Lord' and do not do what I say? I will show you what he is like who comes to Me and hears My words and puts them into practice. He is like a man building a house, who dug down deep and laid the foundation on rock. When a flood came, the torrent struck that house but could not shake it, because it was well built. But the one who hears My words and does not put them into practice is like a man who built a house on the ground without a foundation. The moment the torrent struck that house, it collapsed and its destruction was complete."* (Luke 6:46–49) What was the difference between the two men who built the house? Both of them heard, but only one acted. Only one was able to stand firm.

Here are five practical ways you can cultivate Habit #3, the Study of Scripture. You probably already know these steps, but the question is, "Are you practicing them?" If you are not, it will take some time for all of them to become habits. After each explanation, evaluate where you are with your own practical application, what you plan to do to make it a habit, and when you will set as a target deadline for each one to be a habit. Give yourself time to add one discipline to another until all are part of your life. You are in the process of becoming a *Lead Like Jesus* servant leader for life, and it will be better for you to master one discipline at a time, beginning with the one that most appeals to you. Then you can add another on your own schedule. We are not trying to teach you these skills but rather give you a manual to use in your development. (If you want to master them, participate in a small group discipling process such as *MasterLife*.) You might want to imagine each finger on your hand representing one of the following ways to cultivate Scripture:

1. Hear the Word     2. Read the Word     3. Study the Word
4. Memorize the Word     5. Meditate on the Word

## 1. HEAR THE WORD

The simplest way to receive the Word is to hear it. Even a child or a person who cannot read can hear the Bible. *"If anyone has ears to hear, let him hear"* (Mark 4:23). *"Faith comes from hearing the message, and the message is heard through the word of Christ"* (Romans 10:17). The Parable of the Sower, found in Matthew 13:3–23, lists four kinds of hearers of the Word: the apathetic hearer who hears the Word but is not prepared to receive and understand it (v.19); the superficial hearer who receives the Word temporarily but does not let it take root in the heart (v. 20–21); the preoccupied hearer who receives the Word but lets the worries of this world and the desire for other things choke it out (v.22); and the reproducing hearer who receives the Word, understands it, bears fruit, and brings forth results (v.23). Which kind of hearer are you?

*Here are four examples of resources for hearing the Word:*
1. Sermons in church, on the radio, CDs, or tapes
2. *The Audio Bible* that dramatizes the reading of God's Word.
3. *The Visual Bible* that dramatizes the NIV version of selected books
4. *Following Jesus: Making Disciples of Oral Learners*—over 400 Bible stories told orally.

However you choose to hear the Word, if you don't find a way to capture it you will soon forget. For example, can you remember what was said the last time you heard the Word or a sermon! One way to apply what you hear is to ask yourself the following questions and jot down the answers. You might want to record them in your personal journal or make a form to help you remember.

What did God say to me through this message?

How does my life measure up to this Word?

What actions will I take to line up my life with this Word?

What truth do I need to study further?

What truth can I share with another person?

✚ *My evaluation of how much hearing of the Word is a Habit of my life:*
  *1 / 2 / 3 / 4 / 5*

✚ *My plan to make this a Habit of my life:* _____

_____

✚ *My schedule for improving on this discipline:* _____

## 2. READ THE WORD

The second way you learn God's Word is to read it. *"Blessed is the one who reads the words of this prophecy, and blessed are those who hear it and take to heart what is written in it, because the time is near"* (Revelation 1:3). Here are a few suggestions on how to read the Word so that you hear everything God says to you in your Quiet Time.

**Allow enough time to read His Word reflectively.** God told Joshua, *". . . meditate on it day and night, so that you may be careful to do everything written in it. Then you will be prosperous and successful"* (Joshua 1:8). Do not try to read so much Scripture at one time that you cannot meditate on its meaning and let God speak directly to you and your situation. Our memory verse for this week is, *"But his delight is in the law of the LORD, and on His law he meditates day and night. He is like a tree planted by streams of water, which yields its fruit in season and whose leaf does not wither"* (Psalm 1:2–3).

**Balance your reading of the Word.** Jesus said, *"Everything must be fulfilled that is written about Me in the Law of Moses, the Prophets, and the Psalms. Then He opened their minds so they could understand the Scriptures"* (Luke 24:44–45). These three designations of Scripture cover all the Old Testament, which was the Bible Jesus used. Be sure to vary your reading so that all the counsel of God will be available to you. You may read the Bible from Genesis to Revelation over a year's time by reading three chapters a day and five on Sunday. Another plan is to read a chapter from the Old Testament and a chapter from the New Testament each day. Or you might prefer to read through a book of the Bible one chapter a day before moving to another book.

**Apply the Word to your life each day.** Revelation 1:3 says, *"Blessed is the one who reads the words of this prophecy, and blessed are those who hear it and take to heart what is written in it, because the time is near."* To take it to heart, ask God to show you what His Word means to you and for your life. Jesus promised, *"If you obey My commands, you will remain in My love, just as I have obeyed My Father's commands and remain in His love"* (John 15:10). Every time you apply the Word of God to your life you grow closer to Him. Every time you fail to apply it, you leave the Word, like scattered seed, beside the road where the Satan can steal it. Once you have heard His Word you are prepared to respond to it in prayer and obedience. Jesus said, *"If anyone loves Me, he will obey My teaching. My Father will love him, and we will come to him and make our home with him"* (John 14:23).

✝ *My evaluation of how much hearing of the Word is a Habit of my life:*
    1 / 2 / 3 / 4 / 5

✝ *My plan to make this a Habit of my life:* _____

_____

✝ *My schedule for improving on this discipline:* _____

## 3.  STUDY THE WORD

When you study the Word, you go deeper into it. *"The Bereans were of more noble character than the Thessalonians; for they received the message with great eagerness and examined the Scriptures every day to see if what Paul said was true"* (Acts 17:11). With study you begin to have more power in your handling of the Word. Bible study is an in–depth look into the Scripture, to learn and discover more than you would see during a simple overview or in a devotional reading. Study involves comparing what the Bible says in one passage to other passages throughout the Bible. It might begin with a question that you search the Bible for its answer. It often includes gaining additional information through commentaries and study helps. Time will not allow us to go into detail on how to study the Word, but there are many books on the subject.

✝ *My evaluation of how much hearing of the Word is a Habit of my life:*
    1 / 2 / 3 / 4 / 5

✝ *My plan to make this a Habit of my life:* _____

_____

✝ *My schedule for improving on this discipline:* _____

## 4.  MEMORIZE THE WORD

A deeper way to get the Word into your heart is to memorize it. When you remember the Word, it really lives in you, you live in it, and God's promises become your possessions. *"How can a young man keep his way pure? By living according to Your word . . . I have hidden Your word in my heart that I might not sin against You"* (Psalm 119:9, 11).

There are several reasons to memorize Scripture. In the account of Christ's temptation in the wilderness (Matthew 4:1–11) Jesus set the example. He used Scripture as the sword of the Spirit against Satan, even when Satan tried to misuse Scripture as a part of the temptation. Memorizing Scripture helps you gain victory over sin. It also helps you answer when people have questions about your faith. *"Always be prepared to give an answer to everyone who asks you to give the reason for the hope that you have"* (1 Peter 3:15). Being able to recite Scripture by heart helps you to meditate on it and gives you direction for your daily life at any moment. Most of all, the greatest benefit of memorizing Scripture comes from obedience to doing what God commands. *"These commandments that I give you today are to be upon your hearts"* (Deuteronomy 6:6).

✞ *Here are a dozen ways to memorize Scripture. Circle the numbers of the methods you already use; draw a triangle around the numbers of the ones you want to improve on; and put a box around the numbers of those you want to try.*

## H O W   T O   M E M O R I Z E   S C R I P T U R E [9]

1. Choose a verse that speaks to your need or that the Lord points out to you.

2. Understand the verse. Read it in context and in different translations.

3. Commit the verse to memory in your favorite translation. Divide it into natural, meaningful phrases and learn it word by word. If you learn it word–perfect in the beginning, it will be set in your memory, will be easier to review, will give you boldness when you are tempted, and will convince the person with whom you are sharing that he or she can trust your word. Memorize the verse reference and say it before and after the verse to fix it in your memory. Be ready if someone asks where it is in the Bible.

4. Develop some memory aids to help you remember the verse. For example, you might record it on a cassette tape, MP3, or CD so you can listen to it. Leave a long pause after each verse so you can practice quoting it. Then record the verse a second time so you can hear it again after you have quoted it without having to rewind it. Include the reference before and after.

5. Locate and underline the verse in your Bible so you can visualize it on the page.

6. Write the verse on a card or put it in your electronic organizer, including the Scripture reference and the topic it addresses. This allows you to relate the verse to a particular subject and enables you to find it when a need arises.

7. Place the written verse in prominent places so you can review it while you do other tasks. Put it over the kitchen sink, on the bathroom mirror, on your desk, on the dashboard of your car for reviewing at stoplights, or any place you will see it often.

8. Meditate on the verse, savoring each word. Say it over and over emphasizing a different word each time. Turn the meaning around by adding a "not" to the verse. This will help you see the positive truth in context.

9 .Use these activities to set a verse in your mind: see it in pictorial form; sing it making up your own tune; pray it back to God; practice it by making it a part of your life; and use it as often as possible.

10. Review, review, review. This is the most important secret of Scripture memorization. Review a new verse at least once a day for six weeks. Review the verse weekly for the next six weeks and then monthly for the rest of your life.

11. Have someone check your ability to quote the verse, or write the verse from memory and check it yourself.

12. Make Scripture memorization fun. Make a game of it. Get people to ask you any verse you have memorized at any time. This can be fun if a partner is also memorizing verses.

[9]Adopted from The Disciples Cross: MasterLife Discipleship Training for Leaders, pp.110–113

✝ *My evaluation of how much hearing of the Word is a Habit of my life:*
    *1 / 2 / 3 / 4 / 5*

✝ *My plan to make this a Habit of my life:* _____

_____

✝ *My schedule for improving on this discipline:* _____

## 5. MEDITATE ON THE WORD

Another way you live in the Word and the Word lives in you is to think about it or meditate on it. *"His delight is in the law of the LORD, and on His law he meditates day and night"* (Psalm 1:2–3). Memorization puts God's Word in your head. Meditation puts it in your heart.

You meditate on God's Word when you focus on a specific verse of Scripture, such as Philippians 4:13, and chew on it and digest it until have fully understood it. You might meditate a few minutes each day, concentrating on one verse a week. Select a verse you want to memorize or that has been a key verse in a passage you have just read. Ask the Holy Spirit for His revelation as you meditate. You might use some or all of these ideas:

✝ *Here are some practical way to meditate on God's Word. Circle those you will try.*

1. Read the verses before and after to establish the theme and setting. These will aid you in interpretation. Then you may write a summary of the passage.

2. Write the verse(s) in your own words. Say your paraphrase aloud.

3. Read the verse over and over again, emphasizing a different word each time you repeat it. For example, in the verse *"I can do all things through Christ who strengthens me"* (Philippians 4:13, KJV), first emphasize the word "I", then the word "can" and so on so that each word yields its full impact.

4. State the opposite meaning of the verse. For instance: "I cannot do anything if Christ does not strengthen me." What impact does the verse have now?

5. Write at least two important words from those you have emphasized in the verse. Ask these questions about the two words to relate the Scripture to your needs: What? Why? When? Where? Who? How?

6. Personalize the verse: Let the Holy Spirit apply the verse to a need, a challenge, an opportunity, or a failure in your life. What will you do about this verse as it relates to your life? Be specific.

7. Pray the verse back to God. Put your own name or situation in the verse.

8. Refer to other passages that emphasize the truth of the verse. List thoughts or ideas you might not understand or might have difficulty applying in your life. Seek out instruction or help in these areas.

9. Write a way you can use the verse to help another person.

✝ *My evaluation of how much hearing of the Word is a Habit of my life:*
    *1 / 2 / 3 / 4 / 5*

✝ *My plan to make this a Habit of my life:* _____

_____

✝ *My schedule for improving on this discipline:* _____

Do not be overwhelmed by all the ways you can apply Scripture to your daily life. Begin systematically to master one skill at a time. As you grow in your application of the Word, the other ways to use it will be more meaningful for you. If you need to go back and adjust your schedule to give yourself more time, please do. The direction you are going is more important than when you get there.

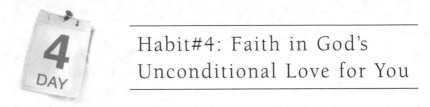

# Habit#4: Faith in God's Unconditional Love for You

*"For God so loved the world that He gave His one and only Son, that whoever believes in Him shall not perish but have eternal life" (John 3:16).*

## EMBRACING THE REALITY THAT GOD LOVES YOU

Your great challenge in becoming a *Lead Like Jesus* leader is that your human ego causes you to seek the worthiness of the unconditional love that is already yours. It hurts your pride to accept that you cannot increase God's love for you by anything you do. He loves you totally and unconditionally as much today as He ever has or ever will. He cannot love you more; His love for you is perfect. It is breathtaking even to glimpse how much He loves you and what it cost Him.

The implications of God's personal, unchanging, unrestrained, love for you are enormous—so enormous that it might seem easier to consider that love as so far beyond comprehension that you don't even try to understand it. If you do, you leave the dearly purchased gift unopened and the joy of the Giver unrealized.

### Experiencing Unconditional Love

✝ *In this week's group session you'll experience an activity that focuses on affirmation and unconditional love. In preparation for the experience, answer the following questions:*

1. **How do you feel when someone affirms you and your actions?**

_____

2. **Why should leaders unconditionally love the people they lead?**

_____

The power of unconditional love is lived out in your relationships. For example, whenever we ask parents to raise their hands if they love their kids, all their hands go up. When we ask parents if they love their kids only if they're successful, all the hands eventually go down. You love your kids unconditionally, right? If God's love for you was based on your performance to the standards that His righteousness requires, you would never have another moment free from anxiety. But what if you accept God's unconditional love for you? What if you admit that you can't earn enough, achieve enough, or control enough to get any more love? You already have all the love there is through Jesus! That is so powerful! Once you believe that you're perfectly, unconditionally loved, you won't get misled by earthly things. A teenager once said to Avery Willis, "I am afraid that if I really surrender to God that He will send me to Africa as a missionary." Avery I replied, "If someone says that they will do anything you ask, would you punish them by making them do what they did not want to do? God loves you and He will only ask you to do what is for His glory and your good. Now He might have to change your heart so you are willing. Ask any missionary in Africa and he or she will tell you they are happier in the middle of God's love in Africa than they would be anywhere else in the world."

✝ *Do you have enough faith in God's character and His promises to surrender to His love for you? Will you give up control? Will you open your leadership to the influence of the love you have received? Check one of the following responses:*

_____ Yes, I totally accept God's unconditional love for me, and will live in that reality.

_____ Yes, I accept as true God's love for me, but I still think I must be worthy of it.

_____ I want to accept the reality that God loves me unconditionally, but I'm having a hard time believing it.

_____ No, God's love is incomprehensible to me.

## TO LEAD LIKE JESUS YOU MUST LOVE HIM

Everything that you attempt in trying to *Lead Like Jesus* hangs in the balance of your response to the question that Jesus asked Peter, "Do you love Me?" Your answer should not be given lightly because Jesus will take it seriously. Your answer will reveal your true motivations for all you have done. Like Peter, all of us have given Jesus good reason to doubt our sincerity. We all fall short—sometimes in soul-shaming ways that we can hardly admit to ourselves, let alone to the One we have failed.

✝ *Read John 21:15-19 in your Bible and answer the question, how did Jesus expect Peter to prove that He loved Him more than anything?*

_____

Do you love God enough to love His sheep—His lost sheep? Jesus had a right to suspect Peter's love after his denial at His trial. Jesus always has the right to ask the question, "Do you love Me?" He did not ask Peter if he feared Him, respected Him, or admired Him, but He asked, "Do you *love* Me?" Jesus wants to see evidence that you love Him. Jesus said, "In as much as you have done it to one of the least of these, you have done it unto Me." Jesus says that how you treat other people is how you treat Him.

## TO LEAD LIKE JESUS YOU MUST LOVE LIKE JESUS

If you do not really love Jesus, then you will not truly love the people you lead. Nothing but the love of Christ will compel you to go cheerfully through the difficulties and discouragements you experience as a leader. However, Christ's kind of love will make your work easier, and it will encourage those you lead to serve wholeheartedly. Margie Blanchard says, "The antidote for fear and pride is faith in God's unconditional love for us." The true servant leader is one who clearly understands unconditional love and puts it into practice every day. All individuals need to be heard; they need to be praised; they need to be encouraged; they need to be accepted. As a leader, you need to practice these expressions of love. Why? Because you express your love of Jesus by loving those He puts in your path. Jesus said, *"But I tell you who hear Me: Love your enemies, do good to those who hate you, bless those who curse you, pray for those who mistreat you"* (Luke 6:27–28). At times, we're sure you have said, "Lord, I just can't love that person." But over time you may have learned to change your response to, "Although I can't make myself love that person, I will give You full right to love that person through me. Do anything You want to do through me, and I will do it as if to You." We have discovered that if we let Jesus love others through us and do good things for them, we learn to love them, too.

✝ *What do you want to tell Jesus now about His unconditional love? What commitment will you make about loving Him unconditionally? Will you let Him love others unconditionally through you? Stop now and tell Him what is on your heart.*

# Habit#5: Support & Accountability Relationships

*"As iron sharpens iron, so one man sharpens another"* (Proverbs 27:17).

Leadership is a lonely business. When we rely on our own perspective of how we are doing, we are bound to slip into convenient rationalizations and blind spots that can quickly undermine our integrity and the trust of those who look to us for leadership.

## TRUTH—TELLERS

We all need trusted truth–tellers, preferably those not directly impacted by what we do, who can help us keep on course. If you can't name any active truth–tellers in your life, or if you have avoided or undervalued the ones you have, it's time to change. Having truth–tellers is probably the greatest resource for growth that you can have. Ken's father used to tell him, "I learned in the Navy if you don't hear about any problems watch out, because you are about to go over the side. You have mutiny on your hands because the people around you have cut you off from the truth."

Too often in organizations, self–serving leaders cut off feedback by killing the messenger. Eventually the leader is fired, and although people had been available who could have given him or her helpful information, these leaders cut off the opportunity to grow. Feedback is a gift. If somebody gives you a gift, what do you say to them? "Thank you." Then you ask more questions to understand what is being said and why such as, "Where did you get it? Are there any special instructions to help me use it? Can you tell me more about it? Who else do I need to ask about it?"

Bring truth–tellers into your life, and they will tell you the truth if they know you'll listen. It doesn't mean you have to do everything that they say, but they want to be heard. And in the process if you'll share some of your vulnerability, then the give–and–take is fabulous. *"Two are better than one, because they have a good return for their work: if one falls down, his friend can help him up. But pity the man who falls and has no one to help him up. . . . Though one may be overpowered two can defend themselves. A cord of three strands is not quickly broken"* (Ecclesiastes 4:9–10, 12).

✚ *Name some truth-tellers in your personal life and in your leadership role:*

_____

_____

✚ *Whom would you like to choose to be a truth-teller in your life?* _____

_____

*Let us encourage you to contact that person and work out an accountability relationship with regular times of truth–telling*

Being open to feedback from other people is not the only way to grow. Being willing to disclose vulnerabilities to other people is another. We're all vulnerable. We all fall short. Don't be afraid to share your vulnerability. It's one of the most powerful things you can do to build a team and to build relationships with people you're leading. They know you're not perfect, so don't act as if you are. More times than not they know your imperfections long before you reveal them.

Disclosing your vulnerabilities doesn't mean expressing all your inner thoughts. Rather, you want to share task–relevant information, struggles you're working on as a leader. If a truth–teller says you're not a good listener, then what a wonderful thing to come in front of the team and share that. "Bill was kind enough to share feedback with me about my listening. I didn't realize that when you say things to me, I jump right on to my own agenda. But now I know and I would like to improve it, and the only way I can improve it is if you will help me." *"Wounds from a friend can be trusted, but an enemy multiplies kisses"* (Proverbs 27:6).

✚ *Name some times when you have been vulnerable as a leader and willing to share this with others. What was the result of your disclosure?*

_____

_____

_____

## SMALL GROUP ACCOUNTABILITY FELLOWSHIP

In *Leadership by the Book*, Michael, one of the central characters, explains how he got into trouble after a successful start at becoming a servant leader. Michael observes, "When I boil it down, it was a combination of ego and self–imposed isolation."

Throughout His earthly ministry, Jesus had all kinds of relationships with all kinds of people, but He maintained a special, intimate relationship with a small group of His disciples. To put things in perspective, Jesus had hundreds, or even thousands, of people flocking to Him everywhere He went. Dozens of men and women followed Him consistently from town to town. And yet He had twelve specially chosen disciples to whom He entrusted His mission, and three inner–circle confidants—Peter, James and John—to lean on in crucial times. All of us need someone, or several someones, who love us enough to still be our friend no matter what they learn about us.

In Mark 9:2–12 we are told that Jesus took Peter, James, and John with Him to a high mountain and revealed to them the full reality of His God nature on the Mount of Transfiguration. There He instructed them to keep what they had observed in confidence. In Mark 14:33 Jesus again gathered the same three men to Himself as He approached the crucifixion. Jesus demonstrated how much He valued the fellowship of those who knew Him best by taking them into the inner circle of His suffering in Gethsemane. As we commit to becoming more like Jesus in our leadership service, it is vital that we don't miss the important example Christ provided on how to combat the loneliness and isolation that can often be a part of being a leader.

If you are to maintain and grow in your daily walk as Jesus–like leaders you need similar relationships. The temptations and challenges to be an ego–driven and fear–motivated leader are going to continue and probably intensify. The value of having a safe harbor relationship of support and accountability cannot be overemphasized. *"Let us consider how we may spur one another on toward love and good deeds. Let us not give up meeting together . . . but let us encourage one another"* (Hebrews 10:24–25).

✜ *If you are not already in an accountability group, make plans to form one. Your Lead Like Jesus group could serve in this capacity after you have completed this study, Or you might want to select a smaller group of confidants. Follow the guidelines given below.*

## AN ACCOUNTABILITY GROUP MODEL

**Purpose**: To provide mutual support and accountability for continued growth and maturity in leadership as disciples of Jesus.

**Group Size**: Two to seven people, preferably all of the same sex.

**Commitment:** Six months of regular participation. The group will assess its effectiveness after six months and determine whether it should continue to meet.

**Meeting Schedule**: Weekly

**Meeting Time Frame**: 60–90 minutes

**Agenda:**

Opening prayer—5 minutes

Devotional prepared on a rotating basis by group members—20 minutes

Accountability questions processed—45 minutes

The group will mutually determine a maximum of **six** of the questions to be answered by each member at each meeting. These questions should reflect areas of importance to the individual efforts of the group to walk the faith on a daily basis as they *Lead Like Jesus*.

Prayer and worship—20 minutes (This may be interspersed as members answer the questions.)

## Ground Rules

All discussions are strictly confidential and are not to be shared with anyone outside the group.

Advice is given only when requested.

Members should not be pressed to be more specific about personal struggles than they feel comfortable in sharing with the group. No "open heart surgery" is to be performed by the group.

## Sample Questions

Since our last meeting have you maintained a daily habit of prayer and time in God's Word?

Have you treated your peers, co-workers, supervisors, and employees as objects of God's love?

Have you allowed your pride or fear to drive your leadership decisions?

Have you maintained a healthy balance between work, family, church, and personal time?

Have you compromised your integrity in any way?

Have you been anywhere this week that could be seen as a compromise?

Have you exposed yourself to any sexually explicit material?

Have you trusted God's timing for your life?

Have you missed an opportunity to teach and grow others?

Have you fulfilled the demands of your calling this week?

Have you missed an opportunity to give an apology or forgive someone?

What sin has plagued you in your efforts to Lead Like Jesus since we last met?

Have you just lied in answering any of the above questions?

### Practicing the Habits Gives You Peace

Peace may sound like a strange characteristic in a leader. However Jesus, the Prince of Peace, exhibited it throughout His ministry. Peace is an attractive trait in a leader, and many leaders rise to power on promises of peace. Jesus demonstrated peace most when everything around Him seemed to be in conflict. People sense when a leader is in control of himself and has explicit faith in what he is doing.

✚ *Look at the following examples and match Jesus' response to a difficult situation by writing the number of the event next to the response.*

| | |
|---|---|
| 1. When there was a storm at sea | _____ Jesus withdrew to a mountain alone. |
| 2. When Jesus was on trial | _____ Jesus told disciples to put up their swords. |
| 3. When the Pharisees accused Him of being demon possessed | _____ Jesus calmly walked through the crowd. |
| 4. When Judas betrayed Him | _____ Jesus taught calmly. |
| 5. When the people of Nazareth tried to throw Him over a cliff | _____ Jesus called him friend. |
| 6. When the soldiers came to arrest Him | _____ Jesus was silent. |
| 7. When the people wanted to make Him King by force | _____ Jesus was asleep. |

No wonder the *"People were overwhelmed with amazement. 'He has done everything well,' they said"* (Mark 7:37). Did you match the events in this order to which Jesus responded? 7, 6, 5, 3, 4, 2, 1. Even if you did not match them all correctly you can see that Jesus demonstrated the quality of peace in all kinds of situations with different kinds of people.

Where did Jesus get this peace? He totally depended on the Father. *"Jesus gave them this answer: 'I tell you the truth, the Son can do nothing by Himself; He can do only what He sees His Father doing, because whatever the Father does the Son also does. For the Father loves the Son and shows Him all He does. Yes, to your amazement He will show Him even greater things than these'"* (John 5:19–20). When the soldiers arrested Him in the garden He told the disciples to put away their swords because, Jesus said, *"Do you think I cannot call on My Father, and He will at once put at My disposal more than twelve legions of angels?"* (Matthew 26:53).

Where do you get such a peace as a leader? From Jesus. He said, *"Peace I leave with you; My peace I give you. I do not give to you as the world gives. Do not let your hearts be troubled and do not be afraid"* (John 14:27). The world thinks peace is absence of conflict. Jesus said He gives peace that passes understanding, because it endures even in the midst of all kinds of conflict. Peace is a gift from God. *"I have told you these things, so that in Me you may have peace. In this world you will have trouble. But take heart! I have overcome the world"*(John 16:33).

Doesn't it make you want to follow a Leader like that? The same will be true with those who follow you. When everyone else is losing their head they will look to see how the leader is reacting. This characteristic of Jesus fits this week's study, because if you practice what we have been teaching you about the Habits, you will develop a relationship with Jesus that will give you the fruit of the Spirit: *"But the fruit of the Spirit is love, joy, **peace**, patience, kindness, goodness, faithfulness, gentleness and self–control. Against such things there is no law"* (Galatians 5:22–23).

✚ *Whenever you realize you don't have peace, review the Habits to see if you are in tune with the Prince of Peace.*

Continue to work on these Habits through the rest of this study and make special plans to devote at least as much time to them as you have been spending each week leading like Jesus.

# LEAD LIKE JESUS

# WEEK SEVEN

## LIVING AS A
### Lead Like Jesus Leader

*"Do not merely listen to the word,*

*and so deceive yourselves.*

*Do what it says." (James 1:22)*

OVER THE PAST SIX WEEKS we have introduced you to key leadership principles and behaviors modeled by Jesus. This week we want to take you to the next level of Servant Leadership. It is important for you to make a commitment to *Lead Like Jesus*, yet it is just as important that you turn your initial commitment into action. In our memory verse this week, James reminds us that we are not just to "listen to the word" we must be willing to do what it says. As we have said before, "The gap between knowing and doing is greater than the gap between ignorance and knowledge." As a result this week, rather than giving you a lot of new content, we are going to encourage you to take what you know and apply it in a way that can make what we've taught you come alive. Over the next five days, we will prepare you to practice the principles of *Lead Like Jesus* in a partnering relationship in your daily life as a leader.

## Living Every Day With Jesus

We mentioned that Partnering for Performance is where your Head (what you know and believe) and your Hands (what you do) integrate with your Heart (your character) and your Habits (how you keep your commitments). If you are really going to partner with someone and help them do the right things in the right way, not only must you have a Heart for being a servant leader, but the Habits to recalibrate your good intentions on a day to day basis. John Ortberg , author of *If You Want to Walk on Water, You've Got to Get Out of the Boat* and teaching pastor at Menlo Park Presbyterian in California, motivated us to take a hard look at how we can live every day with Jesus. That will be our emphasis today.

### GOING TO SLEEP WITH JESUS

Most people think the day begins either when the alarm clock goes off or when Starbucks opens. Actually the Biblical day begins with sunset. How you go to sleep at night is important because it sets the tone for how you will live the next day. If you go to sleep with God, then God can go to work. As John Ortberg suggests, going to sleep with God is an act of trust—a gift from God—for God really grants sleep for those He loves. It's hard to live like Jesus if you are sleep–deprived. So sleep is a spiritually important step. Because how you go to sleep is so important to set you up for the next day, we want you to try something every day this week.

Before you lie down to go to sleep, decide what shoes you are going to wear the next day and then get down on your knees and push those shoes under your bed far enough that you'll have to get on your knees the next day to get them out. Now while you're down on your knees you're set to spend some good time with God. Remember our first three Habits: Solitude, Prayer, and Study of Scripture. If you have your Bible beside your bed you can do all three on your knees. If you try it, it is very, very special. Ken Blanchard says as he's getting older, being on his knees for a period of time is also a wonderful flexibility exercise for him.

We suggest that while you are down on your knees, in addition to spending time with the first three habits, you do three more things. First of all, review your day with God. If sin comes to mind, confess and ask forgiveness. God knows you goofed, so 'fess up! Admit it! If you had some blessings during the day, give thanks. Give all the credit to God. And finally if you have any problems or concerns give those over to God because He'll be up all night.

Bill Bright and his wife, Vonette, when they started the Campus Crusade for Christ Ministry decided that they would do two things. First of all, any good that came out of their ministry, they would give God all the credit. Secondly because they were giving God all the credit, it only made sense to turn over all the problems to Him, too. After all He's the greatest problem–solver of all time.

These two suggestions have had a powerful impact on Ken and Margie Blanchard with the Center for FaithWalk Leadership as well as their training and Development Company. Ken confesses, "We are doing pretty well at giving God all the credit, but we have difficulty giving Him all the problems. When we turn our problems over to God, a half hour later we say, 'Step aside, God, and watch an expert work,' as we take them back from Him."

When Ken told Bill Bright that one time, Bill laughed and said, "That's the real tough one for people. We hate to give up control." What you do at night with your concerns or problems has a lot to do with control.

One final thing before you get up from your knees. Tell God, " I want to spend tomorrow with You."

✚ *What is your strategy for going to sleep with God? Do you have one?*

_____

_____

If you have a better strategy than we are suggesting with putting your shoes under the bed, by all means keep on using it. But if you don't, then every night this week, place your shoes under your bed and while you are on your knees see if you can spend some quality time with God.

## WAKING UP WITH GOD

Ken Blanchard and Norman Vincent Peale, when they wrote their book *The Power of Ethical Management,* argued that we all have two selves. We have an external task–oriented self that is used to getting jobs done, and we have an internal, more reflective self that's very thoughtful. Which of those two selves wakes up quicker in the morning—our external task–oriented self or our inner reflective self? Of course, it's our external task–oriented self. What happens? The alarm goes off! Have you ever thought about that phrase—alarm clock? What an awful concept. Why isn't it the "opportunity" clock? Or "it's going to be a great day" clock? The "alarm" immediately ignites your task-oriented self and you jump out of bed. Pretty soon you're trying to eat breakfast while you're washing. You race to the car and immediately pick up the car phone and rush off to meetings all morning, followed by a lunch meeting, afternoon meetings, and a dinner meeting. Finally, you get home at 9 or 10 P.M. and fall into bed without any energy to say goodnight to anybody who might be lying next to you. What happens the next day? The "alarm" goes off and you're at it again. Pretty soon your life becomes a rat race. As the great philosopher Lily Tomlin once said, "The problem with a rat race is even if you win it, you're still a rat."

So the next important step in living with Jesus is to enter your day slowly. Our first order of business should be to arrange to have a few minutes with God. So get on your knees, drag your shoes from under the bed, and while you're down there give God your first word, your first thought.

Secondly, you should acknowledge your dependence on Him. Say something like, "God, I am not going to live through this day banking on my own strength and power. I acknowledge my dependence on You."

Thirdly, tell Him about your concerns for the day—this meeting, that challenge. Say to Him, "Lord, identify and remove any fears from me. I know You are with me." One of the great Bible verses that can give you real strength to overcome any problem is: *"I can do all things through Christ who gives me strength"* (Philippians 4:13).

Fourth, lay your requests before God:

*"In the morning, O LORD, You hear my voice. In the morning, O LORD, I lay down my requests before You and wait in expectation"* (Psalm 3:15).

Finally, ask Jesus to spend the day with you. "Lord, I want You to spend the day with me—knowing that You will I enter the day with tremendous confidence." *"In Him we live, and move, and have our being"* (Acts 17:28).

One of our favorite sayings is, "Every morning I rest my arms awhile on the window sill of heaven and gaze upon the Lord. Then with that vision in mind, I turn strong." *"Therefore do not worry about tomorrow. For tomorrow will worry about itself. Each day has enough trouble of its own"* (Matthew 6:34).

✠ *Do you have any strategies for entering your day slowly? How do you keep your task-oriented self from taking over?*

---

---

## STRATEGIES FOR DEALING WITH YOUR EGO

In Week Two you had a chance to work on your own vision—mission statement, picture of the future, and values. After you have spent some time with God it would be a good idea for you to review those three and recommit yourself for this day to be the kind of person that your vision suggests. When you wrote your own personal vision your EGO probably was well under control. In reviewing these three things it helps you identify what kind of person you want to be do today and sets a standard for how you want to live.

If false pride is your biggest EGO issue and your problem is thinking more of yourself than you should, a good idea would be to read "One Solitary Life" by James A. Francis.

*He was born in an obscure village, the child of a peasant woman. He grew up in still another village, where He worked in a carpenter's shop until He was thirty. Then for three years He was an itinerant preacher. He never wrote a book, never held an office, never had a family or owned a house. He didn't go to college. He never visited a big city. He never traveled two hundred miles from the place where He was born. He did none of the things one usually associates with greatness. He had no credentials but Himself.*

*He was only thirty–three when the tide of public opinion turned against Him. His friends ran away. He was turned over to his enemies and went through the mockery of a trial. He was nailed to a cross between two thieves. While He was dying His executioners gambled for His clothing, the only property He had on earth. When He was dead He was laid in a borrowed grave through the pity of a friend.*

*Twenty centuries have come and gone, and today He is the central figure of the human race and the leader of mankind's progress. All the armies that ever marched, all the navies that ever sailed, all the parliaments that ever sat, all the kings that ever reigned have not affected the life of man on this earth as much as that ONE SOLITARY LIFE.*

If you wake up in the morning and think you're a big deal, reading "One Solitary Life" really puts things into perspective. Look at all that Jesus accomplished without the trappings of wealth, recognition, power and status—the things that we push and shove for in life.

If fear is your biggest EGO issue and your problem is thinking less of yourself than you should, a wonderful daily affirmation from Norman Vincent Peale might help.

*I affirm that God's power is now arising in me. He is renewing and healing my body, giving power to my mind and giving me success in my work. I affirm health, energy, enthusiasm, and the joy of life. All this I owe to Jesus Christ, my Lord and Savior. He has given me the victory principle for which I thank Him every day.*

## LETTING GOD SPEND THE REST OF THE DAY WITH YOU

Most people, if they spend time with God, have a special time during the day when they do it, and then the rest of the day they don't involve God much in their daily life. John Ortberg suggests that you invite God into your everyday activities, whatever they may be.

Orberg suggests that an activity as common as eating should be seen as an opportunity to spend time with God. Most believers are pretty good about giving a blessing at meal time because food is a gift from God—*"Give us this day our daily bread . . ."* Eating with God, however, also should affect what you eat. Can you say, "Bless this food to the nourishment of my body?" The human body is a creation of God and a temple of the Holy Spirit. We need to be serious about what we eat, because we are stewards of our bodies.

*Reading God's Word* is another important aspect of living every day with God. As we said it is a good idea to memorize verses and have a small pocket Bible with you during the day from which you can get inspiration. The words should fill your day.

Can you *go to work with God*? Sure you can. The big question to ask is how would your work go differently if Jesus did your work? Stopping for a moment to think throughout the day will make a real difference.

✝ *What are your strategies for bringing God into your daily life? Even your recreation—would God be pleased with how you are spending your free time? What new plans do you want to make to spend more time every day with Jesus?*

_____

_____

_____

Now that you have some strategies for living every day with Jesus and putting God in the center of your life, you are ready to Partner for Performance with people around you, using a mindset of: *"Love your neighbor as yourself."* That means that those folks come first, ahead of you. Your role is both to help them get the appropriate results in their life and work as well as to provide opportunities for them to grow and develop as individuals.

Before we begin the partnering process, tomorrow we will review the Lead Like Jesus situational leadership characteristics that Jesus used. Then over the next three days we will examine how you can begin to practice in your daily life as a leader the principles of Lead Like Jesus in a partnering relationship.

In Week Five of our study we introduced you to the principles of *Situational Leadership II®*. During that week you discovered that there are three skills of a situational leader.

## Teaching Others to *Lead Like Jesus*

✝ *Can you match the skill with the description? Write the number of the skill in front of the correct description of that skill.*

**1. Diagnosis**          ____ Working with people to reach agreements on what the leader and the individual need from each other

**2. Flexibility**         ____ The ability of the leader to diagnosis development level for task or goal

**3. Partnering For Performance**   ____ The willingness of a leader to help others accomplish the right goals in the right way so they continue to develop themselves as people

Today I want us to begin to examine the principles and practices found in the concept of Partnering for Performance. Did you get the order as 3, 1, 2?

In Matthew 4:19 Jesus said to His disciples *"Come, follow Me and I will make you fishers of men."* As I mentioned in Week Five, the phrase *"I will make"* literally means "to construct or to build up." Jesus' promise is to work with the disciples and help them become *"fishers of men."* In much the same way, we as leaders must be willing to work and spend time with people in order for them to accomplish their goals and task. What will it mean for you to follow the example of Jesus to "construct and build up" people?

*Are you willing to take the time necessary to work with people to help them accomplish their goals and task assignments?*

One aspect of "building people" is that you take time with them. This means you will have to organize your calendar so that you have time to meet with the people you lead. For the leader who takes a hands–off approach for leadership, this may not be easy. The people you lead need to spend time with you, and you need to spend time with them. This is a vital step in practicing the principles of leading like Jesus. Jesus always made time for His disciples; we must follow His example as we make time for the people we lead. Although you may not be with them 24/7 you do need to be with them in all kinds of situations, not only at work. As you make this commitment to meet regularly with people, we want to introduce you to five steps that will help guide you through your first *Lead Like Jesus* Partnering for Performance meeting.

## TEACHING OTHERS

The first step in Partnering for Performance is to teach others what you've learned about being a Lead Like Jesus situational leader.

### Step #1—Teach the *Situational Leadership II®* model.[10]

In Week Five you learned the basic principles found in the *Situational Leadership II®* model, and also discovered how Jesus used similar concepts as He led the disciples. The best way to learn something is to teach it. What we'd like for you to do today is to find someone who is important in your life at work, at home or in the community who looks to you for leadership and share what you've learned about being a Lead Like Jesus situational leader. It is important for people you influence to understand the basic terminology and the concepts as you start this process. If you want to work with more than one person you might want to teach them together and then schedule individual Partnering for Performance meetings if it's appropriate. Decide now who will be the first person with whom you will begin the partnering process.

✝ *Write his or her name here:* _____

---

10 *Please note that in this study we are only able to give you a few of the basic principles and tools of Situational Leadership II. For a more complete understanding of the principles of SL II and to do the best job of teaching situational leadership, you can order the kit An Introduction to Situational Leadership II, from The Ken Blanchard Companies. If you are interested in training for your faith–based organization you can call the Center For FaithWalk Leadership at 800–383–6890 or visit www.leadlikejesus.com. If you are a leader in a non–faith–based organization and want more information on training or if you want to order supplemental Situational Leadership II materials, please call The Ken Blanchard Companies at 800–728–6000 or visit www.kenblanchard.com.

## ✚ Prepare to teach SLII principles.

You need to remember several things about the *Situational Leadership II®* model. There is no one best leadership style. It all depends on the situation and the development level of the person or persons you are trying to influence.

The first skill of an effective situational leader is Diagnosis. As you can see from the *Situational Leadership II®* Model, four Development Levels describe a person's competence and commitment on a particular task or goal:

**D1–Enthusiastic Beginner**—High Commitment/Low Competence

**D2–Disillusioned Learner**—Low Commitment/Some Competence

**D3–Capable but Cautious Performer**—Variable Commitment/Moderate to High Competence

**D4–Peak Performer**—High Commitment/Low Competence

The second skill of an effective situational leader is Flexibility, the willingness and ability of leaders to vary their leadership styles based on the development levels of the people they lead. There are four basic Leadership Styles:

**S1–Directing**—High Directive Behavior/Low Supportive Behavior

**S2–Coaching**—High Directive Behavior/High Supportive Behavior

**S3–Supporting**—Low Directive Behavior/High Supportive Behavior

**S4–Delegating**—Low Directive Behavior/Low Supportive Behavior

Partnering for Performance is the third skill of a situational leader. One of the key aspects of this process is matching the appropriate leadership style to development level:

*D1–Enthusiastic Beginner needs an S1–Directing leadership style.*

*D2–Disillusioned Learner needs an S2 (Coaching) leadership style.*

*D3–Capable, but Cautions Performer needs an S3–Supporting leadership style.*

*D4–Peak Performer needs an S4–Delegating leadership style.*

✛ *What other things do you want to remember about Situational Leadership II® to share with your partnering teammate?*

_____

_____

✛ *After sharing the basic concepts of Situational Leadership II® with your partnering teammate you might want to practice diagnosis with them using the following case study of the bright, skilled youth pastor. Diagnose Jack's development level in each of the five scenarios:*

As a bright, energetic, youth volunteer for a dynamic, midsize church (350–500 attendees), Jack has worked hard and given his best. He has good project–planning skills and interpersonal skills. He is known as a hard worker. People like Jack, and he likes situations that require teamwork. He has a knack for getting people to cooperate even though they may not want to do so initially. Jack now is being asked to take on some new tasks to prepare him for his new full–time position as youth pastor.

**SCENARIO 1:** Jack has been asked to develop a budget for a very complicated mission project that is important to the church. He will need to put in a lot of time on weekends just to get it done, which will cut into his weekend youth activities, and he doesn't see enough of his wife or kids as it is. It is overwhelming. His executive pastor has told him to tackle this project on his own. Jack is concerned that he may not have a good enough grasp of the entire project. He wishes he could get more direction from others, but there is no time, which is frustrating.

✛ *Circle Jack's developmental level in regard to the complicated mission trip.*
**Development Level**     D1     D2     D3     D4

**SCENARIO 2:** Jack has been asked to put together a multinational missionary team. This is a fabulous opportunity for him, he has led several local mission projects, and he is excited about this new opportunity; however, he doesn't have any contacts in several of the mission contact points and hasn't worked internationally. He isn't sure where to start.

✛ *Circle Jack's developmental level in regard to the multinational mission trip.*
**Development Level**     D1     D2     D3     D4

**SCENARIO 3:** Jack's executive pastor wants an assessment of each of his volunteers' strengths, weaknesses, spiritual gifts, and personalities. One of them will be selected to take Jack's place as the leader of the volunteer ministry when he assumes other responsibilities. The volunteers have always perceived Jack's discernment and assessments as fair and comprehensive. The church leadership respects his opinion and knows he has done a great job of developing each of the volunteers. Jack wants the opportunity to influence the choice of his replacement.

✝ *Circle Jack's developmental level in regard to evaluating his volunteers.*

Development Level      D1      D2      D3      D4

**SCENARIO 4:** Jack appreciates the opportunity the church has given him to attend a Leadership Conference. He has completed a number of different assessment instruments in regard to his leadership skills and had his colleagues and team members do the same. He is interested in getting feedback from his volunteers. Jack has used assessments in other positions, both at the church and in his former career, and knows how valuable they can be in improving performance. He is excited about participating in the training, but is a little nervous, too. He hopes the feedback he gets will not be surprising. He is a little worried because his pastor will probably want to see his results when he gets back. He is concerned the feedback results might affect his new ministry position.

✝ *Circle Jack's developmental level in regard to the assessment of his leadership skills.*

Development Level      D1      D2      D3      D4

**SCENARIO 5:** Jack has been asked to cut expenses in his area of work by ten percent. He is concerned that the cuts, like last year, will have an impact on their ability to finish several ministry projects already in the works. He believes that if he delays making the cuts, he can streamline some other areas over the next two months and show a savings. Jack is convinced that this is the best approach and has his executive pastor's support. His executive pastor has asked him to present his case to the Budget and Finance Team. He is nervous. What if his presentation isn't persuasive?

✝ *Circle Jack's developmental level in regard to making the budget cuts and the financial presentation.*

Development Level      D1      D2      D3      D4

How did you do? Was the person you were teaching able to diagnose which level the bright, skilled youth pastor was in each case? Were you able to coach them? In real life the answers aren't as easy as they might seem.

In the first scenario Jack is D2 because he is a Disillusioned Learner. Notice that Jack was frustrated because he did not have the knowledge and skills necessary to complete the task. Also, he was upset that he was not able to spend enough time with his family. He had low competence/low commitment.

In the second scenario, you might think that Jack is at a D3 or D4 stage of development, instead, Jack in this illustration is D1–Enthusiastic Beginner. Notice that although Jack has some experience in putting together missionary teams and leading mission projects, he has not worked internationally. Therefore, Jack is starting a new task, with transferable skills from previous experiences. By definition, every time you start a new task, you begin at the D1 level of development.

In the third scenario Jack is D4–Peak Performer, because he has both high competence and commitment in the task of knowing the strengths and weaknesses of his volunteer staff.

In scenario four Jack is highly competent in the use of assessments; however he is nervous about the training and also the feedback he will receive from his pastor. Jack in this scenario is D3–Capable But Cautious Performer because his competence is high, but his commitment is variable.

In scenario 5 Jack is D4–Peak Performer on making the cuts in the budget and D3–Capable But Cautious Performer on making the presentation. Sorry if we confused you on the last scenario, because there are really two tasks in that one.

Don't worry if you did not get them all. We will have many more opportunities to practice diagnosis before we are finished. Besides, in real life you also would ask Jack what his level was. Doctors don't learn to diagnose with only one case!

## MATCHING DEVELOPMENT LEVEL WITH LEADERSHIP STYLE

Now that you have worked with your partner on diagnosis, it would be a good experience to help that person learn to match the correct Leadership Style with the Development Level of the person with whom the leader is working. Leading like Jesus will require that you develop a willingness to vary your leadership style, based on the needs of people. Review the SLII model above with your teammate and then complete the activity below together.

## THE CASE OF THE BRIGHT SKILLED PASTOR

The following activity will help you learn to match the appropriate Leadership Style with Development Level. From the scenarios above and using the *Situational Leadership II® Leader Model*, choose the appropriate response for Jack's pastor.

*As Jack's supervisor, the pastor is excited to have Jack serve on the full–time staff. Throughout his time as a layman in the congregation, Jack showed his love and excitement to for youth ministry. The pastor believes that as a leader he has the responsibility to help his staff achieve personal and organizational goals. He wants to help them be successful in their ministry areas. Now as Jack's supervisor and pastor, he has the opportunity to provide Jack with the leadership he needs as he approaches a variety of assignments.*

### Scenario One: Jack as a D2–Disillusioned Learner

As Jack's pastor you should:

A. Give Jack a deadline for the completion of the budget. Explain what the budget project should entail and outline steps that Jack can take to become more savvy regarding the budget process. Plan weekly meetings to track his progress.

B. Ask Jack to prepare the budget and explain the importance of doing the job correctly. Ask Jack to set a deadline for completion. Give Jack the resources he needs. Ask him to provide periodic progress reports.

C. Ask Jack to produce the budget and discuss the importance of an accurate and complete report. Explore the barriers that he foresees and strategies for removing them. Ask him to set a deadline for completion of the budget and periodically check with him to track his progress.

D. Tell Jack when he needs the budget and explain the importance of an accurate and complete report. Outline the steps he should take to learn more about the budget process. Listen to his concerns and use his ideas when possible. Reassure Jack. Set weekly meetings and track his progress.

### Scenario Two: Jack as a D1–Enthusiastic Beginner.

As Jack's pastor you should:

A. Tell Jack exactly what is needed as he begins the task. Specify the requirements for establishing the multinational team of workers. Check with him frequently to monitor progress and to specify corrections.

B. Ask him if there is anything you can do to help. Explore his ideas for putting together the missionary team. Check with him during the week to see how he is doing.

C. Specify the team format and solicit his ideas. Check with him frequently to see how the recruiting of the team is progressing and to help with any problems he may encounter.

D. Let him know you have confidence in his ability to put together the team. Ask him to check back if he has any problems.

### Scenario Three: Jack as a D4–Peak Performer

As Jack's pastor you should:

A. Help Jack explore alternative assignment possibilities. Be available to help him with the assessment of volunteers. Support the work he does. Check to see how he implements the assessment.

B. Design the assessment process of volunteers yourself. Explain the rationale behind your design. Listen to Jack's reaction, ask for his ideas and use his recommendations when possible. Check to see that the assessment is on schedule.

C. Allow Jack to set his own work schedule. Let him implement the plan after you approve it. Check back at a later date to make sure the assessment process is working.

D. Design the assessment process yourself. Explain how the assessment process will work and answer any questions. Frequently check to see if the process you outlined is being followed.

### Scenario Four: Jack as a D3–A Capable But Cautious Performer (the task of making the presentation)

As Jack's pastor you should:

A. Reassure Jack. Outline the steps he should use to make the presentation. Ask for his ideas and incorporate them when possible, but make sure he follows your general approach. Frequently check to see how things are going.

B. Reassure Jack. Ask him to handle the presentation as he sees fit. Be patient and available to help. As for frequent updates.

C. Reassure Jack. Ask him to determine the best way to approach making the presentation. Help him develop options and encourage him to use his own ideas. Agree on frequent checkpoints.

D. Reassure Jack. Outline the overall presentation and specify the steps you want him to follow. Frequently check to see how the steps are being implemented.

How did your teammate do? How did you do? Let's check and see how well you were able to match the correct response of the pastor with Jack's development need.

In the first scenario Jack is a D2–Disillusioned Learner, therefore Jack will need an S2–Coaching style of leadership. The correct match for this scenario is letter "D." Jack needs his pastor to reassure him and listen to him. He also needs for his pastor to outline the specific steps needed for the task. Remember that disillusioned learners need advice, ideas, and involvement in problem–solving. They also need for their leaders to listen to their concerns and frustrations.

In scenario two Jack is an Enthusiastic Beginner–D1. He needs from his pastor an S1–Directing style of leadership. The correct match for this scenario is letter "A." Jack's pastor needs to tell Jack exactly what is needed for the task, detail what is needed to put the team together, and stay in touch with Jack to check on his progress. When a person begins a new task it is important that the leader defines goals and roles. The leader should also give an example of what a good job looks like.

Scenario three places Jack as a D4–Peak Performer. He is highly competent and committed to accomplish the task. Jack as a D4 is in need of an S4–Delegation style of leadership from his pastor. The correct answer for scenario three is letter "C." He needs to be able to set his own schedule for putting together the assessment and the freedom to implement the plan after it is approved. The D4 needs for the leader to allow them to use their own skills in the accomplishment of the assigned task.

In scenario four—the task of making the presentation, Jack is a D3–Capable But Cautious Performer. Jack needs for his pastor to give him an S3–Supporting style of leadership. The correct answer is letter "C." Because Jack's commitment is low, he needs to be reassured. Then his pastor needs to ask him how he would make the presentation. Remember, the Capable but Cautious Performer has moderate to high competence for the task, so the leader needs to let the person practice problem solving.

After you have taught your teammate the basic concepts of *Situational Leadership II®* and practiced diagnosing both Development Level and appropriate Leadership Style, it's worth talking with your partnering teammate about what happens when you mismatch Leadership Styles and Development Levels.

## MIS—MATCHING LEADERSHIP STYLES WITH DEVELOPMENT LEVELS

The concept of matching your leadership behavior to the development needs of people is vital if you are going to practice leading like Jesus every day. It is also an essential element in the partnering meeting you will have with people. You are surrounded with people in your personal life, church life, and professional life who have been assigned a task and yet have never been given clear direction as to how to complete the task. You need to match your leadership style on each task that you are helping them complete successfully.

In Week Five we mentioned the process Ken went through to learn how to use a computer. You will remember that he knew nothing about computers when he first began his training. He was excited about learning how to use a computer, but had no idea what to do, or even how to turn it on! He was a classic D1–Enthusiastic Beginner (low competence/high commitment). His teacher began by telling him very specific details about what each piece of equipment was, what its function was, and yes, how to turn the machine on. She explained step by step everything he needed to know about getting started. What this instructor really did was to use an S1–Directing style of leadership. She knew that he was excited about learning the computer, so she did not need to give him much encouragement. What he did need though, was specific direction on the first steps for using a computer. She was able to "match" her leadership style with his development needs. This is what we want you as a leader to learn to do with those with whom you work.

✝ *Now let's look at some scenarios where the leader mis-matched the leader-ship style with the person's development level. In these scenarios tell how it feels when someone mis-matches your development level with his or her leadership style.*

**SCENARIO 1:** Think for a moment how you would feel if you had been assigned a new task for your job. You are excited about the prospects of doing and completing the new task. You are a D1–Enthusiastic Beginner (low competence/high commitment). You set up a meeting with your leader, and he simply tells you that he knows you will do a great job. He says that he is expecting great things from you and if you encounter a problem to call them. He gives no directions at all, just support.

*Ask your partnering teammate how he or she would feel.*

_____

_____

**SCENARIO 2:** Now imagine you have a task that you have mastered and feel very confident in doing. You have all the skills and motivation needed to continue. You are functioning as a D4–Peak Performer (high competence/high commitment)! Your leader asks to meet with you. As the meeting begins your leader starts to spell out exactly what is needed to accomplish the task. The leader sets goals for you, gives you a timeline for completion and wants to meet with you each week to check on your progress. All direction; no support.

*Ask your partnering teammate how he or she would feel.*

_____

_____

Both of these scenarios illustrate how failing to match the appropriate leadership behavior to the development needs of people can have devastating effects. Matching is a major part of the partnering process. As a leader you have three choices:

*1. Match      2. Oversupervise      3. Undersupervise*

It will be up to you as a leader to decide when you will vary your leadership style to meet the needs of the people you are leading. The choice is yours. Just remember that Jesus has set the example for us as we lead. If you want to *Lead Like Jesus*, then you will be ready and willing to do what it takes to help the people you lead to succeed!

Have fun sharing *Situational Leadership II®* with an important person in your life—someone who you can help accomplish goals and develop them to their fullest potential. Tomorrow we will move to the next step of the Partnering for Performance process—agreeing on key goals and objectives.

# Writing SMART Goals:

As a leader it is imperative that you help people with whom you work set important goals for their professional lives and their personal lives, depending on where you interact with them. We have found that goals are important because they help guide and give direction to the tasks people are trying to accomplish. Goals also clarify people's intentions. Whether you work in a faith–based or non faith–based organization, goals are an important part of the day–to–day application of leading like Jesus. Today what we want you to do is meet with your Partnering for Performance teammate and first share what a SMART goal looks like. Explain that whenever you are writing goals you need to ask is the goal . . .

S | PECIFIC AND MEASURABLE?

M | OTIVATING?

A | TTAINABLE?

R | ELEVANT?

T | RACKABLE AND TIME–BOUND?

*After explaining what a SMART goal looks like, work with your partnering teammate to establish one or two goals either in their personal life or professional life and make sure those goals are SMART goals!*

Have fun with this goal–setting process. Some people back off from goal–setting because they think it is too tedious and it is not exciting. And yet, without clear goals, your leadership really doesn't matter. Even Alice learned that in *Alice in Wonderland* when she came to the fork in the road. Confused about which direction to go, she asked the Cheshire Cat, "Which road should I choose?" His response was, "Where are you going?" She said, "I don't know." His response was quick, "Then it really doesn't matter." Unless people are clear on goals, any help that you give them as a leader really doesn't matter. Without clear goals they can't get started on being the best that they can be and get the kind of results that are desired. In having these conversations with your teammate now you're focused on doing things the right way. Keep your ego out of the game, focus your energy on that person, and see if you really can help him or her develop. If that person is a believer, goal–setting takes on a higher meaning. With believers, how can you get them to understand what God's agenda would be for them? What goals, if that person accomplished them, would make Jesus smile? If in your discussions you find out that they are not happy with what they are doing then obviously that is not God's agenda for them. God doesn't want us to grind our teeth through life. He puts us in places where we can use the talents He has given us. So have a great discussion. Make sure that you share what comes out of this discussion with your study group.

# Diagnosing Development Levels & Matching Leadership

✠ *Let's review the steps you have already done in your Partnering for Performance meeting. Complete the verbs in the first two steps.*

Step 1: _____ *people the Situational Leadership II® model.*

Step 2: _____ *on key goals and objectives.*

Today we will experience steps three, four, and five for your Partnering for Performance meeting.

**Step 3: Diagnose Development Level for each goal.**

✠ *After you have taught your teammate about Situational Leadership II®—and the four Development Levels and the four Situational Leadership Styles— then work with your partner to diagnose that person's development on each of the goals they have set up.*

The best way to do this is to have your partnering teammate sit quietly and analyze his or her own Development Level for each of the goals you agreed on yesterday. While that is going on, you should be doing the same thing. What do you think is this person's Development Level on each of the goals? Before you start this process it would be a good idea to pray together so that both of you can get your egos out of the way and recognize that God is first. Just as you are not afraid to give a blessing at meals with other believers present, don't back off bringing God into the partnering process. God is your ultimate Partner and He wants to be involved.

After separately doing some developmental analysis, share with each other what you discovered. Try this process: Decide who will share first. The person who is listening to the diagnosis should sit quietly and only say, "Tell me more." At the end of the presentation the listener should repeat back what he or she heard the speaker say until the speaker agrees that's what he or she said. Then it's the other person's turn to share what he or she thinks the Development Level is on the goal and to make sure that the perception is heard. Once both of you have shared your diagnosis, now a dialogue is important. If there is any disagreement over Development Level seek common ground. Remember, with the Development Level, if you can't resolve the difference, the leader should go with the other person's diagnosis and create a situation where that person can prove that he or she is right.

If you are going to do Partnering for Performance in a way that helps another person, this process of diagnosing that person's Development Level is key. Remember this is not a win/lose conversation. This is a "How can I help you?" meeting. If someone overestimates his development in your opinion give him a chance to prove that he is better than you thought. But put him on a "short leash." In other words say to him, "What will happen in the next week or two that will suggest to both of us that you really are at that Development Level?" Then don't turn your back on that person during that period of time but continually ask, "Is there any way I can help?" because you want the person to succeed.

If people underestimate their Development Level in your mind, tell them you will give them the Leadership Style that they are suggesting, but as soon as possible, you want to prove to them that they are better than they think they are.

This is good time to share with people that the curve going through the four basic Leadership Styles of *Situational Leadership II®* is like a railroad track. If you start at Station 1 (Directing) and you want to get to Station 4 (Delegating) you have to go through stations 2 (Coaching) and 3 (Supporting) before you can get to Station 4 (Delegating). If at any point you move too quickly from one Station to another you can always move back to provide the person what he or she needs. Even if you have gotten to a Delegating Leadership Style appropriately with someone and he feels confident that he can handle the task or goal himself, share with him that you are always there if he needs help. That's essentially what Jesus was saying in the end of Matthew after He delegated to His disciples. His final comment was "I am with you always, to the very end of the age" (Matthew 28:20). What He was saying was that even though He was delegating, He would be there if they needed Him.

When a D4 calls for help, your first move is one Station back to S3–Supporting where you say to your partner, "What's happening? How can I help?" After you have listened to their thoughts, together you can decide whether you need to go back one more station to an S2–Coaching style or if you need to return to an S4–Delegating Style.

Jesus wants us to call Him constantly if we need Him. Unfortunately the human ego suggests that we need Him less than reality would dictate. The fact that He is there waiting is a tremendous comfort.

## STEP 4: LEARN TO MATCH DEVELOPMENT LEVEL TO THE APPROPRIATE LEADERSHIP STYLE

Once you have agreed on the Development Level of your partnering teammate on the specified goals or objectives, you have to determine the appropriate Leadership Style. Theoretically that is very easy because all you do is match up the Leadership Style number with the Development Level number. D1–Enthusiastic Beginners get S1–Directing; D2–Disillusioned Learners get S2–Coaching; D3–Capable, but Cautious Performers get S3–Supporting; and finally D4–Peak Performers get S4–Delegating. What you need to do here, though, is make sure that you know what using each of the Leadership Styles means in relation to your communication with this person. It is also important to reiterate at this time that Development Level is not a global concept, but a task specific concept, so if you are working on several goals with a person they might be at different Development Levels for each of the goals.

The question that has to be asked with each Leadership Style is, "What does that mean in terms of your behavior with someone?" For example suppose the person is taking on a new task area and he has enthusiasm but needs your Directing. What does that mean? Are you going to spend significant time directing him? Would it be better to send him to a training program or could you refer him to an expert in that area? What does it mean to provide him with direction? The same questions have to be asked about Coaching, Supporting, and Delegating. What does it mean to engage in any one of those styles? A Coaching style might mean looking at your calendar and scheduling some meetings over the next few weeks so that you can actually work with this person on the particular task. The difference here is that in using a Directing style they have to learn the basics, where with a Coaching style you are helping them begin to use what they have learned. What does a Style 3 mean? It might mean having lunch every two weeks so that person can share with you how she is doing in that area and so that you can provide the support and encouragement that she needs. What about Delegating? Does that just mean that you leave the person alone? No. You want to be kept in the information loop so that you are not abdicating. You want to know enough about what is going on so that if a change to an S3–Supporting is needed you are ready to intervene. The more specific you can be in terms of how you are going to deliver a particular Leadership Style for a particular Development Level with someone the more helpful it will be.

## STEP 5: DELIVER ON WHAT YOU PROMISE.

As a leader, it is very important that you deliver on what you promise to the people you are leading. They will be depending on you to follow through with the behaviors and promises the two of you have agreed upon. The principle here is commitment. You as the leader must determine to commit to adjust your leadership behavior based on the needs of the person you are leading. Once again we look to Jesus as our example. He was and still is today always faithful—we know that He always delivers on what He promises!

This "How May I Help You?" meeting where you are analyzing Development Level and Matching Style is vital to the Partnering for Performance process.

✚ *After your meeting, review the process above and write how you could improve your performance for each point.*

**Step 1:** *Teach the Situational Leadership II® model.*

_____

_____

_____

**Step 2:** *Agree on key goals and objectives.*

_____

_____

_____

*Step 3:* *Diagnose Development Level for each goal.*

_____

_____

_____

*Step 4:* *Learn to match Development Level to the appropriate Leadership Style.*

_____

_____

_____

*Step 5:* *Deliver on what you promise.*

_____

_____

_____

✚ *How did you feel about the "How May I Help You?" meeting you had with a colleague, a family member, or volunteer? Do you think you really were helpful?*

_____

_____

_____

✚ *Would Jesus have run your meeting differently?*

_____

_____

_____

✚ *Prepare to share the results of your Partnering for Performance meeting in the group session. Make notes below.*

_____

_____

_____

_____

_____

# Getting Help for Yourself

What we have been doing the first four days of this week is giving you a chance to experience a Partnering for Performance meeting or what we are calling a "How May I Help You?" meeting. What we would like you to do today is to consider whether you might need some meetings like this yourself. Think about the tasks or goals that you are working on in your various responsibilities and determine whether you could use a Partnering for Performance session with someone who could help you.

✚ *In what areas of responsibilities or goals do you think you could use some help?*

_____

_____

_____

✚ *Who do you think could help you in these areas? It doesn't have to be your manager. It could be a co-worker, friend, family member—somebody who you think could really help you. Write their names here.*

_____

_____

_____

Did you write down God as one of your choices to help you? If so, great! Henry Blackaby, author of *Experiencing God*, would suggest that God should be your first choice and we agree. God certainly can shore up any shortcoming you have if you trust him. As Henry Blackaby shared with Ken Blanchard in a session they did together at a leadership conference, "Name one person who God called in the Bible who was qualified. Most of them complained that they could not do what He wanted them to do. God doesn't call the qualified; He qualifies the called." What does it mean to be called? We think it means you are humble, willing to admit you don't have all the answers, and are willing to surrender yourself to God's agenda. So remember, you have the greatest Partner waiting to help you.

## SETTING UP A "HOW YOU CAN HELP ME" MEETING
One of the ways God helps us all is He sends people into our lives who can teach and support us. So having a "How You Can Help Me" meeting with someone else can be very beneficial.

Setting up a "How You Can Help Me" Meeting may be difficult for you because you will have to share your vulnerability or concerns with someone else. Yet without help you may not succeed in the way you want. Once you decide you need help you can go through the same steps that we have outlined for you to do with someone you are attempting to help with your designated mentor. If you don't want to explain all the theories, though, you can lead the discussion in such a way that you can pinpoint the areas that you want to work on and do your own diagnosis so that you can ask the person for what you need. One of the most powerful phrases that you can put into your repertoire is, "I need." If you go to someone and say, "I need fifteen minutes with you" or "I need you to read over this report" or "I need your advice" few people will refuse. "I need" is a powerful statement. It shows that you are in touch with your own vulnerabilities and willing to reach out for help from someone else.

✛ *Pick goals or tasks in which you need help. Write them below:*

_____

_____

_____


✛ *Identify potential mentors and write their names beside the goals or tasks you listed above.*

✛ *Write your plan to contact each person and the approach you will make as you ask them to help you.*

_____

_____

_____

_____

_____

_____

_____

_____

_____

_____

_____

We hope that this week has been a powerful opportunity for you to have some "How May I Help You?" meetings with people who are important to the functioning of your family, volunteer organization or your work setting. We hope it has been useful. When consulting partners with the Ken Blanchard Companies teach the partnering process, they have people fill out several forms. We decided not to do that here. Your ultimate Partner is Jesus and He will guide your way if you ask Him to help. Don't exclude Him. As we suggested in Day One of this week, we need to live every day with Jesus. If that's true, He certainly wants to be part of your working life, particularly if you are trying to help others.

We also hope that you will try some "How You Can Help Me" meetings. Sometimes the most important leadership assignment you have is leading yourself. Again, don't leave your Partner, Jesus out of the process.

Next week we will try to pull together all the things we have been sharing with you over the last seven weeks and give you some very specific strategies for utilizing what you've learned in your life. What we want to do is make sure we don't delegate to you at the end of the program without giving you the direction and support that you will need to carry on and close the "knowing–doing gap."

# LEAD LIKE JESUS

## BEGINNING THE JOURNEY

# WEEK EIGHT

## MY NEXT STEPS FOR
### *Leading Like Jesus*

*"Now that you know these things, you will be blessed*

*if you do them."* —John 13:17

## Whom Are You Following?

This is our last week in this study of *Lead Like Jesus*. Our hope is that like the disciples' time with Jesus on earth this is only a beginning of a lifelong process of your learning to *Lead Like Jesus*. Our study this week is not so much to add new information as to review and apply what you need to take on your journey.

### THE CHALLENGE OF A LEADER

Throughout this study we have discussed key principles of what it means to be a servant leader and how to *Lead Like Jesus*. Today we want you to look at a case study from the life of Abraham Lincoln, a person whom most people would identify as a servant leader. In studying this case we hope to embed in your deepest heart the differences between a servant leader and a self-serving leader and the challenges we have every day to behave on our good intentions.

### THE SITUATION[11]

*During the Civil War, President Abraham Lincoln was visited by Colonel Scott, one of the commanders of the troops guarding the Capital from attack by the Confederate forces in Northern Virginia. Scott's wife had drowned in a steamship collision in Chesapeake Bay when returning home after a journey to Washington to nurse her sick husband. Scott had appealed to regimental command for leave to attend her burial and comfort his children. His request had been denied; a battle seemed imminent and every officer was essential. But Scott, as was his right, had pressed his request up the chain of command until it reached the secretary of war, Edwin Stanton. Since Stanton had also denied the request, the colonel had taken his appeal all the way to the top.*

*Scott got to his commander in chief in the presidential office late on a Saturday night, the last visitor allowed in. Lincoln listened to the story and as Scott recalled his response, the president exploded, "Am I to have no rest? Is there no hour or spot when or where I may escape these constant calls? Why do you follow me here with such business as this? Why do you not go to the War Office where they have charge of all matters of papers and transportation?"*

*Scott told Lincoln of Stanton's refusal, and the president replied, "Then you probably ought not to go down the river, Mr. Stanton knows all about the necessities of the hour; he knows what rules are necessary, and the rules are made to be enforced. It would be wrong of me to override his rules and decisions of this kind: it might work disaster to important movements. And then, you ought to remember that I have other duties to attend to heaven knows, enough for one man and I can give no thought to questions of this kind. Why do you come here to appeal to my humanity? Don't you know we are in the midst of a war? That suffering and death press upon all of us? That works of humanity and affection, which we cheerfully perform in days of peace, are all trampled upon and outlawed by war? That there is no room left for them? There is but one duty now, to fight! Every family in the land is crushed with sorrow; but they must not each come to me for help. I have all the burdens I can carry. Go to the War Department. Your business belongs there. If they cannot help you, then bear your burden, as we all must, until this war is over. Everything must yield to the paramount duty of finishing this war." Colonel Scott returned to his barrack, brooding.*

✚ *Answer the following questions:*

**Was Lincoln's behavior like:**

_____ *a self–serving leader?*        _____ *a servant leader?*

2. *What were the internal and external forces that caused Lincoln to respond as he did?*

_____

_____

_____

3. *Describe a time when you faced a somewhat similar leadership decision.*

_____

_____

_____

4. *Did you respond as a servant leader or self–serving leader? Explain.*

_____

_____

_____

**Complete your answers to the questions before reading ahead.**

Did you react better than Lincoln? Was your situation as desperate as his? How do you think a Lead Like Jesus leader should react in that situation? The Lincoln case is particularly interesting in that you could argue that Lincoln was serving a higher good—the welfare of the nation. As a result some people argue that he was behaving as a servant leader. Although Lincoln was focused on the greatest good for the greatest number, the way he treated Scott was self–serving. His language was "I oriented." He was more focused on his concerns than on Scott's. It was at the end of the day, Lincoln was tired, emotionally drained, and unable to take any more requests. So when Scott came in, he lost it. Lincoln did what we all do at times, and responded in a self–serving way.

✚ *Could Lincoln have denied Scott's request and still be seen as a servant leader? If yes how? If not, why not?*

_____

_____

As we said in the beginning of this study, servant leadership is not about pleasing everybody. If Lincoln had focused his energy not on his own plight, but on Scott's tragedy and listened empathetically to Scott's situation he may have then been able to lift up Scott's focus to a higher level. But responding with "I" statements left Colonel Scott with no choice but to brood.

NOW, HERE'S THE REST OF THE STORY.

*Early the next morning, Colonel Scott heard a rap at the door. He opened it and there stood the president. He took Scott's hands, held them, and broke out: "My dear Colonel, I was a brute last night. I have no excuse to offer. I was weary to the last extent, but I had no right to treat a man with rudeness who has offered his life to his country, much more a man in great affliction. I have had a regretful night and now come to beg your forgiveness." He said he had arranged with Stanton for Scott to go to his wife's funeral. In his own carriage the commander–in–chief took the colonel to the steamer wharf on the Potomac and wished him Godspeed.*

✚ *Having read the rest of the story do you feel differently about Lincoln's response? If you were Colonel Scott how would Lincoln's actions and apology affect your loyalty and future service? You might want to share your thoughts in your study group time this week.*

_____

_____

THE ONE MINUTE APOLOGY

Jesus said *"Be perfect, therefore, as your heavenly Father is perfect"* (Matthew 5:48). This is a high standard that Jesus has set for us, and we need to remember that we all fall short of it! You may have answered each question in this book, attended every weekly meeting of your study group, and memorized every memory verse, yet, when you finish this class, you still will not always act like a *Lead Like Jesus* leader! You will make mistakes. Jesus never lost His temper, never spoke an unkind word, never responded in a self–serving way, and never gave into the problem of the EGO. However, we will.

Several years ago after writing *The One Minute Manager* Ken Blanchard got a letter from a manager that who said, "I loved the book, but it suggests that managers are always right. That's not true! Managers make mistakes all the time. I think the fourth secret of the one minute manager should be the one minute apology." That thought made sense to Ken. His mother always told him that there are two phrases that people should use more often. They could change the world: "Thank you" and "I'm sorry." *The One Minute Manager* had "thank you" covered, but nothing handled "I'm sorry." That motivated Ken and Margaret McBride to write *The One Minute Apology*.[12] The foundation of the one minute apology is a solid self–esteem—in other words, knowing "whose you are" and "who you are." Although Jesus never had to apologize for a mistake He made, He clearly knew whose He was and who He was. He was confident that He was the person His Father had called Him to be!

Abraham Lincoln must have been a man who knew "whose" he was and "who" he was because after some rest and time to reflect, the next day he came to Scott and offered a sincere apology for how he had treated "a man who has offered his life to his country, much more a man in affliction." This does not show weakness, but humility and a solid self–esteem.

Let's take a look at what an effective one minute apology involves.

### The One Minute Apology . . . Starts With Surrender

The first part of a one minute apology always starts with recognition that you did something wrong. Many leaders never apologize, because they are not able to admit their mistakes. A part of overcoming the problem of the EGO involves a willingness to be vulnerable. When servant leaders make mistakes, they are willing to be vulnerable and admit it to themselves. Surrender also means that you take the next step and go immediately and admit your wrongdoing to anyone you may have harmed. Don't procrastinate; that just makes it worse. Also be specific about what you did wrong and share with anyone you harmed how you feel about your behavior.

> ✚ *Reflect on what Lincoln did and read the following quote. Then write an example of it, "The longer you wait to admit a wrongdoing, the quicker a weakness will be perceived as a wickedness."*

_____

_____

### The One Minute Apology . . . Ends with Integrity

In this part of the apology you recognize and admit to yourself that what you did is inconsistent with who you want to be, and you take action to realign your behavior with that image. That involves attempting to make amends for your actions and committing to change your behavior in the future. Without a change in behavior your apology will be hollow. So often leaders think they do not have to say they are sorry for a mistake or wrongdoing. That is so wrong! A popular movie ended with the oft–repeated saying, "Love means never having to say you are sorry." We think that is the worst statement we ever heard! Real love means "being able to say you're sorry." Be ready, because as you *Lead Like Jesus*, you will make mistakes. Don't forget the importance of saying "I'm sorry" or "I was wrong."

---

[12]*The One Minute Apology*, by Ken Blanchard and Margaret McBride

✚ *What did Lincoln do to show his integrity to Scott?*

_____

_____

✚ *Remember Steps 9 and 10 of our 12-Step Program:*

**Step 9.** I've made direct amends to people I may have harmed by my EGO–driven leadership, unless doing so would injure them or others.

**Step 10.** I will continue to take personal inventory regarding my leadership role; and when I am wrong I will promptly admit it and apologize.

✚ *Stop and pray and ask Him to reveal any person you need to apologize to and make things right. List their names here. Go to each person and attempt to make things right.*

_____

_____

# The Final Exam

When Ken Blanchard was a professor at Cornell University, he would always hand out the final exam the first day of class. Needless to say this got him in trouble with the faculty! However, his philosophy was that he would spend the rest of the semester teaching his students the answers. His hope was that each of his students would get an "A" in his class. It was his desire for them to learn as much as they possibly could during the months they had together. In much the same way, a leader should always be teaching the people he or she leads. Jesus said in John 17:14, *"I have given them Your Word and the world has hated them, for they are not of the world any more than I am of the world."* Jesus spent His time on earth teaching His disciples what His Father had taught Him. What a great legacy! Jesus at the end of His ministry could say that He had taught and trained His disciples to be fishers of men and prepared them for a time when He would be gone. When He returned to heaven He told His disciples to *"make disciples of all nations . . . teaching them to obey everything I have commanded you"* (Matthew 28:20). How many people are you training and teaching today in preparation for a time when you are gone?

✚ *In Week Seven you had the opportunity to teach someone who looks to you for leadership about Situational Leadership II® and have a Partnering for Performance session. What we'd like you to do this week is teach several people who are important to you either at home, at the office, or in the community what leading like Jesus means to you. Think about this as an opportunity to share key principles of leading like Jesus that you have learned from this group study process and to enlist a group to study Lead Like Jesus with you... Imagine that you had an opportunity to make a thirty-minute presentation to these folks on Lead Like Jesus. What would be your key points? Plan your presentation and we will help you using the points below.*

Any good speech has the following elements. Apply them to your preparation for your presentation.

**Introduction:** In your introduction you will want to get their attention. One way to do this is to tell how the *Lead Like Jesus* study has affected you personally and why you want to share your experience with them. Then tell them what you hope they will learn from this session.

**Body:** Most speeches have a few key points. Don't overload people with information. In teaching people about *Lead Like Jesus,* organize your thinking around the four domains of servant leadership as modeled by Jesus: The Heart, The Head, The Hands and The Habits. As you teach, first explain any concept you want them to know. Keep it simple. Next illustrate the concept with a personal story. You want to make the concept come alive for them. Finally help the people you are teaching to apply the concept in their own lives.

**Conclusion:** Summarize the key ideas you hoped the folks you are teaching would learn and then challenge them to *Lead Like Jesus* in their own lives.

## "MY LEADING LIKE JESUS PRESENTATION"
### Introduction
- Give your personal experience of what *Lead Like Jesus* has meant to you.
- Share the primary learnings you would like to convey to those attending your presentation. You may want to choose from the following:

  *1. Jesus is the greatest leadership role model for all time.*

  *2. Jesus calls us to a new and different approach to leadership—the role of servant leader.*

  *3. Effective leadership starts on the inside of the leader.*

  *4. Leaders need to incorporate into their lives the concepts of the Heart, the Head, the Hands, and the Habits of a leader, as modeled by Jesus.*

✚ *What has learning to Lead Like Jesus meant to you? You might want to review Week One and then write down some notes.*

---

 

---

 

---

 

---

 

---

## I. THE HEART (WEEKS TWO AND THREE)

**A. Explanation** (*Choose from the following or prepare your own explanation.*)
- You may want to explain the Edging God Out and Exalting God Only diagrams.
- Servant leaders welcome feedback and develop the leadership potential of their people.
- Edging God Out is the biggest barrier to Leading like Jesus.
- Self is at the heart of Edging God Out.
- Leading like Jesus will mean Exalting God Only through humility and God–grounded confidence.
- Humility is not thinking less of yourself, just thinking of yourself less.

**B. Illustrations** (*What stories could you share from your life that relate to the lessons on the Heart or what stories could you repeat from Weeks Two and Three?*)

---

 

---

 

---

 

---

 

---

 

---

 

---

**C. Application** (*You may want to ask them what they think of these concepts or what difference it would make if we all led like Jesus.*)

---

 

---

 

---

_____

_____

_____

## II. THE HEAD (WEEK FOUR)

### A. *Jesus clearly exemplified two parts of leadership:*

- A *visionary* role—doing the right thing.
- An *implementation* role—doing things right.
- The responsibility for making sure that a clear vision is established rests with the leadership hierarchy.
- The responsibility for implementing the vision rests with the people who the leader is attempting to influence.
- Leaders who *Lead Like Jesus* have a clear personal mission.
- Values should define personal and organizational behavior.
- Servant leaders serve the people they lead by knowing them, not just knowing about them.

### B. *Illustrations* (What stories could you share from your life that relate to the lessons in Week Four?)

_____

_____

_____

_____

_____

### C. *Application* (You may want to ask the folks you are teaching whether they have a clear vision for their lives: a mission statement, a picture of the future, and a set of personal values. Does their organization or family have a clear vision?)

_____

_____

_____

_____

_____

_____

III. THE HANDS (WEEK FIVE)

A. *Explanation* (Choose from the following or make your own explanation.)

- Leading like Jesus means that the leader is concerned about both results and the development of the people he or she leads.
- A leader first must diagnose the development level of the people he or she leads.
- Leaders who *Lead Like Jesus* will vary their leadership styles based upon the needs of the people they are leading.
- In Partnering for Performance it is critical for the leader to reach agreements with others about which leadership style would be most helpful.
- Leaders who *Lead Like Jesus* will be honest with those they lead, but will always speak the truth in love.

B. *Illustrations* (From your own life or the study.)

_____

_____

_____

_____

_____

_____

C. *Application* (You may want to ask them how they could use these concepts.)

_____

_____

_____

_____

_____

_____

_____

IV. The HABITS (Week Six)

A. *Explanation* (Choose from the following or make your own explanation of the Habits.)

- Leaders must follow the example of Jesus and find time for solitude with God.
- The *Lead Like Jesus* leader will instinctively and constantly seek the face of God through prayer.

- Scripture is the first manual every leader should turn to when faced with any leadership decision before consulting other textbooks.
- Leaders must accept the unconditional love of God for their lives and then must be willing to share that love with the people they lead.
- Leaders who want to *Lead Like Jesus* must bring "truth–tellers" into their lives who will give honest and open feedback to the leader.

**B. Illustrations** (From your own life or the study for each of the Habits.)

_____

_____

_____

_____

_____

_____

_____

_____

**C. Application** (You may want to ask them what they think they should do about the Habits.)

_____

_____

_____

_____

_____

_____

_____

_____

Now that you have your outline, why not pull together a group of people who are important to your life and look to you for leadership and teach these key concepts of leading like Jesus? This could be a group at work, at church, or at home. One of the best ways to continue the learning you have received from this study is to teach these principles. Make a commitment today to teach what you have learned to the people you lead! Be ready to lead a *Lead Like Jesus* group if they are interested.

Leading like Jesus is not a destination but a journey. Are you ready for the journey? Like any good traveler embarking on a journey, you will need to make sure you have the proper equipment. The following list should help you determine how ready you are to begin this new journey.

✚ *Check the appropriate box to indicate if you have the item in your backpack. If not then you will want to review that part of the study to be sure you are ready. Write your plans for securing these items in the blank space beside the item*

## WHAT TO PACK FOR YOUR LEAD LIKE JESUS JOURNEY

| # | Item | Yes | No |
|---|------|-----|-----|
| 1 | Personal mission statement that is understandable by a 12–year–old and that you can repeat on demand. | ____ | ____ |
| 1 | Personal definition of success that keeps God in mind. | ____ | ____ |
| 1 | Set of rank–ordered personal operating values to help you decide which road to travel when temptation or opportunity knocks. | ____ | ____ |
| 2–3 | Truth–tellers who will keep you headed in the right direction. | ____ | ____ |
| 1 | Journal to record the triumphs, challenges, and lessons learned that you will want to remember and pass along to others. | | |
| 1 | Well–used instruction manual for daily living (The Bible). | ____ | ____ |
| 1 | Set of positive addictions to solitude, prayer, study of Scripture, rest, and exercise. | ____ | ____ |
| 1 | Memorized set of emergency numbers to call when you are in trouble.[13] | ____ | ____ |
| 1 | Set of recalibration tools to help keep your path straight (from the EGO's Anonymous 12–Step Process). | ____ | ____ |

---

[13] Some Emergency Numbers you may choose to call are:

### Fear — Philippians 4:6–7
[6]Be anxious for nothing, but in everything by prayer and supplication, with thanksgiving, let your requests be made known to God; [7]and the peace of God, which surpasses all understanding, will guard your hearts and minds through Christ Jesus.

### Fear — Psalm 23
[1]The LORD is my shepherd;
    I shall not want.
[2]He makes me to lie down in green pastures;
    He leads me beside the still waters.
[3]He restores my soul;

He leads me in the paths of righteousness
    For His name's sake.
[4]Yea, though I walk through the valley
    of the shadow of death,
I will fear no evil;
    For You are with me;
    Your rod and Your staff, they comfort me.
[5]You prepare a table before me in the
    presence of my enemies;
You anoint my head with oil;
    My cup runs over.
[6]Surely goodness and mercy shall follow me
    All the days of my life;
And I will dwell in the house of the LORD
Forever.

If you are missing any of the recommended items for obtaining help for what you need, please see the resource list in the Group Leader's Guide or go to www.leadlikejesus.com.

You have taken the first step of an exciting new journey to *Lead Like Jesus* by completing this interactive study. In the initial stages as you begin to apply what you have learned at work, at home, or in the community the landscape will look familiar. The people you are interacting with and working with are more than likely be the same people you interacted with and worked with before you started. Expect them to behave just as they have in the past and respond to your leadership as they always have. Even as they sense a change in how you are treating them, they will, at times, continue to question your motivations, misinterpret what you are trying to accomplish, and test your commitment. Some will embrace the change you seek to create, some will be skeptical, some will feel threatened by you and some will oppose change for their own purposes. It is important to realize that they have been conditioned to respond to you in a particular way and will continue to do so until they sense your commitment is for the long haul and begin to trust in their own ability to be and do what is required to succeed. The longer you demonstrate a *Lead Like Jesus* servant leadership, the more they will begin to change. As they endorse these things themselves your workgroup, your family, or your community organization will change as well.

---

*Anxiety — Psalm 55:22*
[22]Cast your burden on the LORD,
    And He shall sustain you;
    He shall never permit the righteous to be moved.

*Worry — Matthew 6:25*
[25]"Therefore I say to you, do not worry about your life, what
    you will eat or what you will drink; nor about your body,
    what you will put on. Is not life more than food and the
    body more than clothing?

*Temptation — 1 Corinthians 10:13*
No temptation has seized you except what is common to man.
    And God is faithful; he will not let you be tempted beyond
    what you can bear. But when you are tempted, he will also
    provide a way out so that you can stand up under it.

Don't make the mistake of first trying to change other leaders with whom you work. Focus on yourself. Be the change you want in others.

The roles and responsibilities in your life and the problems you face probably have not changed since you started this study. What has changed is how you approach them. Hard choices between self–serving and servant leadership decisions are bound to occur at as rapid a pace as before. People will continue to tempt you to use your time in good ways, but not best ways.

Praise progress as you stand for your own operating values and resist the temptations to edge God out of His rightful place as the Audience of One in your life. You will find that it becomes easier to stand up for what is right after you do it the first time and feel the joy of giving honor to the One you follow.

If your organizational culture does not easily let you talk about Jesus, don't worry. Just behave like Him and become a great servant leader. Then when people are attracted to the way you lead and they ask you about it, you are free to share who you follow. When people look at you, let them see Jesus. If they like what they see then they will want to know where that came from and want some of it themselves.

# Your *Lead Like Jesus* Readiness Exam

Imagine you are sitting down with Jesus and you are going over key aspects of leading like Jesus just before He sends you off to represent His Kingdom with the people where you work and in all your personal relationships. What might that session look like?

✝ *You are sitting at your kitchen table and Jesus has just finished eating breakfast with you. You are in dialogue with Him. He asks questions and you answer. Take the time to write a brief answer for each question. This is not quick and easy, but it is true and loving and will help you clarify your readiness to be a servant leader. Don't skip any questions. Remember it is Jesus asking you the questions. You may want to take more than one day to answer all of them.*

I. HEART QUESTIONS

JESUS: *How much do you love Me?*

My Response: _____

JESUS: *How will you demonstrate that you trust Me?*

My Response: _____

JESUS: *How do you show you love Me by serving others?*

My Response: _____

JESUS: *How confident are you that I love you regardless of your performance or the opinion of others?*

My Response: _____

JESUS: *To what extent are you willing to set aside instant gratification, recognition, and power to do the right thing and honor Me?*

My Response: _____

II. HEAD QUESTIONS

JESUS: *Who do you say I am?*

My Response: _____

JESUS: *What is our relationship to one another?*

My Response: _____

JESUS: *How will others know we are related?*

My Response: _____

JESUS: *What is the purpose of the leadership work that I have set before you to do?*

My Response: _____

JESUS: *What is the vision of the future for your leadership work that we can agree upon?*

My Response: _____

JESUS: *What operating values flow from our mutual purpose and vision of the future?*

My Response: _____

JESUS: *Is there any symbolic way that you can use like My washing the feet of My disciples that can express your desire to serve others?*

My Response: _____

JESUS: *What do you see as your leadership role in this season of service and stewardship?*

My Response: _____

## III. HANDS QUESTIONS

JESUS : *How can you listen with a focus on others rather than a focus on yourself?*

My Response: _____

JESUS : *How can you lead and learn from people who are different from you, think differently, look
differently, are older or younger than you, and don't honor all work honestly performed as sacred?*

My Response: _____

JESUS : *How will you provide different styles of leadership as I did to meet the growth and development
levels of those who look to you for leadership?*

My Response: _____

JESUS : *How can you consistently get feedback as a way to improve your leadership service?*

My Response: _____

JESUS : *How much time and energy are you willing to invest in your possible successors through training
and development?*

My Response: _____

JESUS : *How much time, effort, and coaching are you ready to provide day to day to help others
grow as leaders?*

My Response: _____

JESUS : *What will you do to break down barriers between you and those you are leading so you can
provide for their needs?*

My Response: _____

JESUS : *To what extent are you willing to share your leadership point of view and your own vulnerabilties
with those who are trying to follow where you are leading?*

My Response: _____

## IV. HABITS QUESTIONS

JESUS: *How much time and how often are you willing to be with Me alone in solitude on a regular basis?*

My Response: _____

JESUS: *How should your prayer life be different to allow Me to communicate regularly with you in the areas where you need to grow?*

My Response: _____

JESUS: *How often are you actively seeking instruction and inspiration from My Holy Word?*

My Response: _____

JESUS: *With whom else do you have an active intimate truth–telling relationship?*

My Response: _____

# My *Lead Like Jesus* Leadership Legacy

Lee Ross relates the following story: "A young pastor friend named Dan shared that his father had been very ill and had recently died. Dan's father had been a strong Christian who modeled a Jesus–like attitude and behaviors in all areas of his life. He shared the story that his father had contracted a fast–moving form of melanoma and was told that he only had about one month to live. Just a few days before his death, Dan's father asked to see Bob, his best friend for over twenty–five years. Although Dan's father had repeatedly shared Christ with his friend, Bob had never accepted Jesus as Savior. When Bob arrived at the hospital, Dan's dad asked to speak with him alone. Dan's father once again shared how much God loved him and how Jesus had died on the Cross for his sins. There in that hospital room, Bob bowed his head and asked Jesus to forgive him and take control of his life. The next day, Dan's father passed away, but that is not the end of the story. Before he died, Dan's father had made one last request. He wanted Bob to be baptized as a part of his funeral service. What a legacy! Even at his funeral, this wonderful Christian man demonstrated his faith and his desire to lead others to know Jesus. He didn't care about the spotlight shining on his life or his accomplishments. He wanted everyone to see what God had done in Bob's life!"

We share that story with you so that you will seriously examine the leadership legacy you might be leaving behind. How do you want to be remembered as a leader by the people at work, at home, in your church, and in the community? Leading like Jesus is not a course, it is a lifestyle. Making the development of people an equal partner with performance is a decision you make. It is following the example of Jesus as a servant leader and pouring your life into the lives of other people. It is about leaving a leadership legacy of service!

✚ *Only two things on earth are eternal. Can you check the correct two?*

| ____ Diamonds | ____ Taxes | ____ Bible |
|---|---|---|
| ____ People | ____ Mountains | ____ Art |

Did you mark people and the Bible? Nothing else is eternal. If you want to leave a lasting legacy it must be done in people and through the Bible. As a leader of people you have the best opportunity to leave a lasting legacy that will be a passed down through the generations and also last through eternity. That's why President Lincoln wanted to apologize to Scott. After some solitude, prayer, and rest, we're convinced that Lincoln realized how he treated this brave but afflicted man was not the kind of legacy that he wanted to leave.

Look once more at the story of the Last Supper—the last time Jesus was with His disciples before His crucifixion. From this story we want give you four challenges for leaving a *Lead Like Jesus* Leadership Legacy.

## FOUR CHALLENGES FOR LEAVING A LEAD LIKE JESUS LEGACY:

*1. Remember: "It is not about you!"* *"When the hour came, Jesus and His apostles reclined at the table . . . Also a dispute arose among them as to which of them was considered to be greatest"* (Luke 22:14, 24). Seating arrangements at Jewish feast were very important. The host would always take the middle seat at the table. On the right side of the host would sit the first guest of honor, on the left side the second guest of honor; and on the second right–side would sit the third guest of honor, and so forth. It seems that the disciples spent much time worrying about their position at dinner and in the kingdom of God. Scripture tells us that this dispute had been going on among the disciples for some time. Apparently the disciples had a hard time hearing Jesus' message about leadership being first an act of service—*"the greatest among you should be like the youngest, and the one who rules like the one who serves"* (Luke 22:26). Jesus wanted the disciples to understand that following Him was not about position, it was about service. The disciples did not fully understand this until Pentecost.

The first challenge for the *Lead Like Jesus* leader is to recognize that "it is not about you." It is not about your position or your title or the amount of money you make; it is about following the servant leadership example of Jesus. The disciples were slow to understand this and many leaders today do not understand this either! As you decide to *Lead Like Jesus* remember "it is not about you," "it is about what God wants" that really matters.

✚ *What is the heart of the issue of leading like Jesus?*

_____

_____

_____

_____

_____

**2. Live your life with God–Grounded Confidence.** In John 13:3 we read, *"Jesus knew that . . . He had come from God and was returning to God."* It is interesting that John makes this statement just before Jesus washes the feet of His disciples. Jesus "knew that He had come from God". What does this tell us? We believe it reminds us of the two key questions any *Lead Like Jesus* leader must ask themselves—"Whose you are" and "Who you are." At the very beginning of His ministry Jesus clearly answered these two questions in the wilderness. There was no doubt in the mind of Jesus that he belonged to His Father and that His Father had sent Him to accomplish a very clear purpose. Because Jesus had settled these critical questions, He was able without any hesitation, to take on the role of the servant and wash the feet of the disciples. He was confident in the unconditional love that His Father had for Him and in the role He had been given.

The second challenge for the *Lead Like Jesus* leader is for you to develop a "God–grounded confidence" as we discussed in Week Three. Many leaders we know today are some of the most insecure people we have ever met. Out of a sense of insecurity and fear, they have never addressed these key issues in their lives and try to lead at home, at work, and at church. This will only lead to disaster for the leader. As one author has said, "all insecurity is rooted in an inadequate sense of belonging to God." [14] Jesus clearly knew who He "belonged to"! Just as Jesus "knew where He had come from," and therefore could wash the feet of the disciples, you also must determine "whose you are" and "who you are" if you are going to confidently serve the people you are leading. John says Jesus knew he was "returning to God." In other words, Jesus knew His destination. He knew that after the crucifixion and resurrection He would be with His Father in heaven.

✝ *Describe your confidence in your Leader, your destination, and your role as a Lead Like Jesus leader.*

_____

_____

_____

_____

_____

_____

**3. Live a life full of integrity.** *"So He got up from the meal, took off His outer clothing, and wrapped a towel around His waist. After that, He poured water into a basin and began to wash His disciples' feet, drying them with the towel that was wrapped around Him"* (John 13:4–5). Integrity means not only talking about being a *Lead Like Jesus* leader, but actually living it! Jesus had taught the disciples many times that leadership was about serving and not about position. In this Scripture we see that not only did Jesus talk about serving, but He actually did it! He got down on His hands and knees and washed the dirty feet of His disciples!

---

[14]Ogilvie, Lloyd John, The Bush is Still Burning, 1980 Word Incorporated

One of the problems we see in the lives of leaders today is that they love to tell everyone else how they should serve and act, and yet when it comes to their lives they do not practice what they are preaching! They "stumble the mumble!" Too often there is a real disconnect between what the leader says and what the leader does. We believe that the next great movement in Christianity will be demonstration. If we want people to be interested in our faith in the future, we as Christians must practice what we preach. In other words, people need to not only hear Christian leaders talking about the message of Christ, they need to see us living out this message in the way we lead and serve others.

**4. Submit to the will of God for your life.** *"When He had finished washing their feet, He put on His clothes and returned to His place. "Do you understand what I have done for you?" He asked them. "You call me 'Teacher' and 'Lord,' and rightly so, for that is what I am. Now that I, your Lord and Teacher, have washed your feet, you also should wash one another's feet. I have set you an example that you should do as I have done for you. I tell you the truth, no servant is greater than his master, nor is a messenger greater than the one who sent him. Now that you know these things, you will be blessed if you do them"* (John 13:12–17). After washing the feet of the disciples Jesus asks them a question: "do you understand what I have done for you?" This is a very important question as we come to the close of our study. Do you understand what Jesus has done for you? He has set the example of how you should live, and of how you should invest your life into the lives of the people you lead!

And in verse 17 Jesus is challenging the disciples that now that they understand, are they ready to do what He says? Are they ready to submit to His way of leading?

You have a variety of resources available if you have a leadership question or concern, but what we believe Jesus is challenging us to do, is first to submit to His will for our lives as leaders. Jesus should be the first resource we go to if we have a leadership question. Remember, "What's the problem?" Jesus is the answer. Why? Because we have made a decision to submit our will to the will of God for our lives. The issue is not just about commitment, but about submission. Henry Blackaby, in his book *Spiritual Leadership*, says "Some spiritual leaders try to be more committed. What they need is to be more submitted."[15] In your spiritual life you must first be willing to submit your life to God. This is the first and most important decision you will ever make. Have you submitted your entire life to God? Have you asked Jesus to forgive you of your sins? If not, you can do it right now! This is the first decision you must make if you are going to *Lead Like Jesus*. The next part of this decision is submitting your life to God and letting Him control every aspect of your life, including your leadership responsibilities! When Jesus said "You will be blessed if you do them" He meant it. This is a promise He gives to those who choose to follow His example of servant leadership. Submission to the will of God for our lives as leaders will mean the blessing of eternal life with Him, and it will mean blessing the lives of the people whom we have the privilege of leading!

✝ *In light of these challenges and the study over the past eight weeks, complete the following Next Steps Game Plan for becoming a Lead Like Jesus leader.*

---

[15] Henry and Richard Blackaby, Spiritual Leadership, 2001 Broadman & Holman.

## MY NEXT STEPS GAME PLAN FOR
## BECOMING A LEAD LIKE JESUS LEADER:

I, _____ , *submit to God, myself, and an accountability partner to accomplishing the following next steps in becoming more of a Lead Like Jesus servant leader during the next thirty days:*

*In seeking a closer discipleship relationship with Jesus as my leadership role model through practicing the spiritual disciplines of solitude, prayer, study of God's Word, unconditional love, and support and accountability relationships, I will:*

_____

_____

_____

_____

**In each of the following relationships in which I serve a leadership role, I will demonstrate my complete submission to Lead Like Jesus.**

*With those who report to me I will:* _____

_____

*With my peers I will:* _____

_____

*With those to whom I report I will:* _____

_____

*Within my family and with friends I will:* _____

_____

*In being held accountable for my ongoing steps to Lead Like Jesus I will seek the support of the following people:*

_____

_____

*In the next thirty days I will teach what I have learned about being a Lead Like Jesus servant leader to the following people who are important to me:*

_____

_____

_____    _____
                    *Signed*                                               *Date*

# LEAD LIKE JESUS: *Continuing the Journey*

It is our prayer that this study has been both meaningful and life–changing for you as a leader. These eight weeks have given you the foundational principles for leading like Jesus. As you incorporate these concepts into your life we pray and believe that God will bless your sincere efforts to follow the example that Jesus set for all of us.

Prayerfully consider your commitment to *Lead Like Jesus* as you surrender to His plan for your life as a leader.

---

If you have never made a commitment to receive Jesus as your Savior and Lord, please consider this most important decision first. You simply need to ask God to make up the difference between you and 100 and make Jesus Lord of your life. This simple act of faith is all that God requires. It is His gift of grace to you. When you ask Jesus to come into your life, you can be assured that He is trustworthy and will keep His promises. Receiving Jesus as your Savior is not about "religion"—it is about having a relationship with Him. We are praying that this study has brought you to the place where you are truly ready to choose Jesus. Will you make the following commitment?

I confess that I have sinned and ask God for forgiveness. I accept Jesus as my Savior and surrender to Him as Lord of my life.

_____     _____
*Signed*                                                                      *Date*

---

As a Christian leader, affirming my belief that Jesus was and is the greatest leadership role model of all time, I surrender to His mandate —"not so with you"—as I begin to *Lead Like Jesus* at home, in my work and in my community.

_____     _____
*Signed*                                                                      *Date*